D1625330

The Private Diaries of Sir H. Rider Haggard 1914-1925

The Private Diaries
of
Sir H. Rider Haggard
1914-1925

edited by
D. S. Higgins

STEIN AND DAY/*Publishers*/New York

First published in the United States of America in 1980

Copyright © 1980 by The Trustees of the Estate of the late Sir Henry Rider Haggard
Selection and editorial matter copyright © 1980 by D.S. Higgins
All rights reserved
Printed in the United States of America
STEIN AND DAY/*Publishers*/Scarborough House
Briarcliff Manor, New York 10510

Library of Congress Cataloging in Publication Data

Haggard, Henry Rider, Sir, 1856-1925.
   The private diaries of Sir H. Rider Haggard, 1914-
1925.

   Includes index.
   1. Haggard, Henry Rider, Sir, 1856-1925—Diaries.
2. Novelists, English—20th century—Biography.
I. Higgins, D.S.   II. Title.
PR4732.A36 1980   828'.803 [B]   80-5496
ISBN 0-8128-2738-4

Dedicated to
Nicholas, Duncan, and Julian

Contents

Introduction

On 25th July, 1914, Sir Henry Rider Haggard made the first entry in a diary that he was to keep regularly until 1925, the year in which he died. At the time he was sailing up the St Lawrence River, prior to landing in Canada where, with his fellow Royal Commissioners, he was to survey the country's natural resources and trade. The Dominions Royal Commission had already visited Australia and New Zealand in 1913 and South Africa earlier in 1914. Throughout both these visits Rider Haggard had kept a detailed diary to which he had referred when writing the confidential reports he sent to Lewis Harcourt, the Secretary of State for the Colonies. Clearly it was his intention to prepare a similar report during his visit to Canada, but events changed his plan. On 5th August, Rider Haggard heard that Great Britain had declared war on Germany and a few days later the Royal Commission was recalled. Despite this he continued to make daily entries in his diary. At first he did this because he wanted to have his own record of events so that later he could write a history of the War, so each day he summarized what he had read or heard about battles on land and at sea. Press censorship and his own lack of access to accurate news soon convinced him that such a project was not worthwhile.

He continued with his diary, however, certain that, following his work as a Royal Commissioner, he would be called upon by the Government to perform some important service for his country. As the months passed without any job being offered, Rider Haggard's growing impatience and frustration became increasingly apparent. It was not until 1916 that, sponsored by the Royal Colonial Institute, he undertook the mission that was to be, in his words, 'my war effort'. At the age of fifty-nine, he again travelled to South Africa, Australasia and Canada, this time to discover what arrangements could be made for the after-war settlement of ex-soldiers in the Dominions. His journey round the world took six exhausting months, during which his diary became much more a record of his own activities and private thoughts. Although, after his return home, Rider Haggard began again to report and comment daily on the incidents of war, his diary continued to include more details of his private life.

On 11th November, 1918, as the bells announcing the peace were 'rung out of time (for lack of ringers)', Rider Haggard wrote:

I am thankful that I began to keep this diary, imperfect and full of mistakes and misjudgments as without doubt it is, and have been able to continue it through the weary years, with scarcely a day missed up to the present hour. At any rate it is a record of what an average not unobservant man, whose lot it has been to endure those years, thought and experienced in the course of them, and therefore perhaps of some value, at any rate for future time.

Four days later Rider Haggard spent the day at Batemans with his friend, Rudyard Kipling. That evening in his diary he wrote:

> I took this diary over, as R[udyard] had asked me to do, and read him passages out of it till I was tired. These interested him greatly. He thinks that it must be a very important work some day; of much value indeed to the generations that are to come. His chief anxiety is as to its preservation, concerning which he made various suggestions — that I should hand it over to the British Museum in a packet not to be opened for fifty years, (which is the time he thinks should go by before its publication); that I should deposit it with one of the 'Safe Deposit' companies; that I should put it in an iron box enclosed in a lump of concrete and bury it, and so forth. I told him what I am doing, namely depositing one typed copy with Longman's and keeping the other, also the original, myself in different places.

Perhaps it was Kipling's enthusiasm that encouraged Rider Haggard to continue with what he had for so long thought of as his 'Private Diary of the War'; perhaps he went on just because after four and a half years it had become a habit. Certainly there were times when he wearied of the daily task, but these were during the increasingly rare periods of hectic activity. On 6th February, 1920, when, for example, he was engaged in his anti-Bolshevik activities with the Liberty League, he wrote:

> This diary alone, together with the reading that is necessary for its composition, takes me at least an hour a day, often more. Soon it will have to end.

But he continued to make entries almost every day until prevented from doing so by illness in the months before his death.

So for nearly eleven years, Rider Haggard kept his diary. The entries were first written either by him or, as he dictated to her, by his secretary, Ida Hector. It was, however, always Rider Haggard's hope that at some time his diary would be published and so he had two typed copies made. These at intervals he went through and corrected carefully. Only when this had been done did he post one copy in batches to Longman, his publisher.

On 15th November, 1918, Rider Haggard expressed concern that his diary might eventually be published in a 'highly-Bowdlerised version'. Later, as the work grew in length, he realised that it would have to be edited before publication. He discussed this with Rudyard Kipling at a Royal Garden Party on 22nd July, 1921:

> K. held forth about this diary, saying that he wished that I would make him my literary executor with discretion to publish such portions of it as he wished. (I suppose that rightly he expects to live much longer than I shall.) There is

something in the idea. The work 'edited' by Kipling would be a formidable document!

But it was not to be. Rider Haggard appointed his wife to be his literary executor. His autobiography, *The Days of My Life*, was edited and published posthumously by Charles Longman, who had last handled one of his books in 1911. But the sales were not high and it seemed unlikely that there was then a market for any further reminiscences by a writer whose popularity had waned. So Rudyard Kipling was not asked to edit Rider Haggard's diary and for over fifty years it has, apart from a few extracts, remained unpublished and all but forgotten.

Fortunately both the handwritten and the typed manuscripts of the diary have survived. The original, in the handwriting of Rider Haggard and Miss Ida Hector, is deposited in the Norfolk Record Office, Norwich. It consists of twenty-two bound volumes, each of about three hundred pages measuring 7¼ inches by 9¼ inches. The two copies of the corrected typescript are in the possession of Commander R. R. Cheyne, Rider Haggard's grandson. One of these, bound like the original in twenty-two volumes, has always been held by the family; the other, which was sent in instalments to Charles Longman, was thought to have been destroyed when the publisher's building was bombed during the Second World War, but it was found among the Haggard papers at A. P. Watt's, Rider Haggard's literary agent, and returned to Commander Cheyne. This unbound copy does not include the entries for 1925.

The complete diary is some two million words long and so at first the task of reducing it to about one-fortieth of the original seemed daunting. It was soon obvious, however, that, because Rider Haggard had not been as involved in world events as he would have wished, many entries were little more than digests of a day's newspaper reports and could readily be excluded. (I am, of course, aware that some of these omitted passages may be of interest to specialists such as military historians.) It was also apparent that drastic cuts had to be made to the entries written while Rider Haggard was travelling as a Commissioner in Canada in 1914 and on his world tour in 1916, for often these were but his notes for the official reports that he subsequently made.

In editing the diary I have worked throughout from the typescript that Rider Haggard corrected before sending it to his publishers. As a result I have had to make few alterations such as expanding abbreviations where necessary. I have chosen not to use ellipses to denote omissions. These are so numerous that any device would be intrusive. Great care has been taken, however, to retain the sense and flow of the original. As a result few linking passages have been used. Footnotes too have been kept to a minimum. A few of these were added to the typescript by Rider Haggard and in the text these end with his initials, H.R.H.

The diary as now published, although largely written while Rider Haggard was most concerned about his public duties and ambitions, reveals much about his private life and opinions. Although inspired at the diary's beginning by what he saw as the political and economic necessity of the war in which his country was involved, Rider Haggard became increasingly concerned about the resulting social upheavals. He records, in anger or bemusement, rising prices, shortages, the unreliability of servants, and the rapidly increasing organisation and political power of working people. In entry after entry he exemplifies, often unconsciously, the attitudes and conflicts of the landed middle-class. Rider Haggard's diary is then more than a comprehensive self-portrait of one of England's most successful writers during the last decade of his life. In its pages he also chronicles the demise of the ruling middle-class of which, desiring both to imitate and placate his father, he had striven with but limited success to be a part.

Born on 22nd June, 1856, Henry Rider Haggard was the eighth of ten children of William Haggard, a flamboyant, irascible Norfolk squire, and Ella, his long-suffering, gentle wife. His father seems to have dismissed him as a fool and so, having sent him to a variety of tutors and cramming schools, he was happy to dispatch him, in 1875 at the age of nineteen, to South Africa as unpaid secretary to Sir Henry Bulwer, the newly appointed Lieutenant-Governor of Natal.

Freed from his father's influence, Rider Haggard prospered in the adventurous atmosphere of colonial Africa. Having taken part in Sir Theophilus Shepstone's peaceful annexation of the Transvaal, he was in 1878 appointed registrar of the High Court there. Much of his time was spent in the company of the older, experienced administrators, and he especially enjoyed listening to their many stories and anecdotes. He also started writing, for in addition to keeping a notebook and writing long letters home, he completed a couple of articles that were published in English magazines.

In 1879 he threw up his post, returned to England, and the following year married Mariana Louisa Margitson, heiress to the Ditchingham estate in Norfolk. The newly married couple returned to South Africa just in time to witness the handing back of the Transvaal to the Boers. Certain that there was no future for him in Africa, Rider Haggard returned to England with his wife and baby son. He occupied himself writing a defence of Shepstone's policy in the Transvaal called *Cetywayo and his White Neighbours*, for the publication of which he had to pay £50. It was the first of over seventy books that he was to write.

While reading for the bar, he wrote *Dawn*, his first novel. It was well enough received, but sales were small. This too was the case with *The Witch's Head*, his second novel, although the African scenes in it did excite interest and comment. Inspired partly by this attention and believing that he could spin an adventure yarn as good as the recently published *Treasure Island*, Rider Haggard in a few weeks wrote *King Solomon's Mines* which, when it was published on 30th September, 1885, was an overnight sensation. Rider Haggard's future seemed assured, and he was soon able to take possession of Ditchingham House, which up to then had been let. During the next five golden years he completed a succession of best-sellers: *She* (1887), *Jess* (1887), *Allan Quatermain* (1887), *Maiwa's Revenge* (1888), *Colonel Quaritch, V.C.* (1888), *Cleopatra* (1889), *Eric Brighteyes* (1891) and *Nada the Lily* (1892).

Then in 1891 while Rider Haggard and his wife were travelling in Mexico, John, their only son, died. The unexpected tragedy seems to have unnerved Rider Haggard and for several years he lived a solitary life at Ditchingham, apparently doing little but brood over his loss. This period of withdrawal could not last — Rider Haggard was too spurred on by ambition — but during it he decided that he wanted to be more than a writer of popular romances. In 1894 he became a co-director of the weekly *African Review*. It was not a successful venture, but this spell spent in a London office rekindled his desire to be involved with men and matters of importance. The following year he contested as a Unionist the East Norfolk constituency. His defeat bitterly disappointed him. As he pointed out, 'A legislative career is about the only one of which the doors are not shut to the writer of fiction, as is proved by many instances, notably that of Disraeli.' But having been once rejected by the electorate, Rider Haggard was not the kind of man who was willing to try again.

But he had made a real effort to get back into the swim of things. In 1895 he was elected to the Athenaeum Club, and the following year he was chosen to be Chairman of Committee of the Society of Authors. These contacts with political, commercial and professional life seem to have refreshed him and he returned to the country and the writing of books with more enthusiasm than he had experienced for years. He felt, however, even more strongly 'the desire to do something in my day more practical than the mere invention of romance upon romance'. The subject that at the time was most on his mind was the state of agriculture and so in 1898 he kept a detailed diary of his experiences on his estate which, entitled *A Farmer's Year*, was subsequently published. Although the sales of the book came nowhere near those of his romances, Rider Haggard tasted and relished a new experience — universal critical acclaim; but another, and for him a more important, result was that his opinions on agricultural questions were eagerly sought by both individuals and official bodies.

More settled now, in the winter of 1900 Rider Haggard took his wife and three daughters to Florence and then set off to travel to Cyprus and the Holy Land. Once again he kept a diary and once again, after successful serialisation, it was published as a book, called *A Winter Pilgrimage*. He also used his researches to provide material for two novels, *Pearl-Maiden* and *The Brethren*, but like all his historical fiction they were far less popular than his African adventures. But this did not upset Rider Haggard; he was at last writing about the subjects that were of interest to him.

His position as an expert on rural matters was consolidated when later in 1900 it was negotiated with the *Daily Express* that he should travel through England and Wales reporting on the state of agriculture. *Rural England*, the result of his travels, which was published in 1902, revealed Rider Haggard as a tireless investigator, an astute observer, an incisive interviewer and an accurate reporter. His work was much more than a survey; with insight and acumen it presented a detailed programme for agricultural reform.

The next year, 1903, Rider Haggard spent at home, but once more he kept a rural diary, this time about his work in the garden at Ditchingham House. After appearing serially in *The Queen*, his delightful *A Gardener's Year* was published to wide acclaim. Immediately this was complete, Rider Haggard went to Egypt. The journal he kept there provided material for a series of articles printed by the *Daily Mail*, but they were not published as a book. He did, however, collect sufficient material about Egypt for two novels, *The Way of the Spirit* and *Morning Star*. On the way home he visited the south of Spain for the first time and there assembled data for another historical romance, *Fair Margaret*.

Rider Haggard seemed content with the pattern of life that had evolved, alternately spending long periods writing at home and then several months of purposeful travel that provided material for historical novels. His knowledge of agriculture brought him many invitations to lecture, so that he could indulge in two of his favourite pastimes — making speeches and meeting men of influence. Although he still had to write to earn his living, he felt more able to select those subjects that appealed to him.

Then in January, 1905, he received an unexpected letter from Alfred Lyttelton, the Secretary of State for the Colonies, stating that the Rhodes Trustees had agreed to pay the costs of sending him as a Commissioner to the United States to report on the labour colonies established there by the Salvation Army. This letter changed his life, giving him new ambitions and presenting the possibility of a new career. His trip was a great success. Wherever he went in America he was pursued by interviewers and fêted by those in high office. President Theodore Roosevelt welcomed him warmly and the two men became friends. On his return, Rider Haggard did not receive the same kind of treatment. When he went to the House of Commons to discuss his comprehensive report, Lyttelton spoke to him for less than half an hour, during which he said that Balfour, the Prime Minister, would not bother to read it. Eventually the committee appointed to consider his report rejected all his recommendations.

Though frustrated by this rejection, Rider Haggard had thoroughly enjoyed the experience and, when in 1906 he heard that a Royal Commission on Coast Erosion was to be appointed, he wrote to Lloyd George, the President of the Board of Trade, explaining how he had kept the sea back from his summer house at Kessingland by planting marram grass. His ploy worked and he was asked to serve on the Royal Commission. For the next three years he worked hard, only once missing a meeting. During this period he also conducted two private fact-finding missions: the first was a survey of the social work of the Salvation Army in England and Wales called *Regeneration*, and the second was an agricultural investigation of *Rural Denmark*. But when the work of the Royal Commission on Coast Erosion and Afforestation was complete, the Government, as had happened with his own report on the labour colonies, decided not to adopt any of the recommendations made and, much to his distress, Rider Haggard was not asked to serve on the Development Board appointed to consider the matter.

So after five years of strenuous activity during which he had travelled widely and felt he was playing an official part in planning the country's future, Rider Haggard had to return to Ditchingham. Later he described how he felt:

> I missed that Commission very much, since its sitting took me to London from time to time, and gave me a change of mental occupation and interests. Indeed I do not remember ever being more consistently depressed than I was during the first part of the following winter. I had nothing to do, except the daily grind of romance-writing, relieved only by Bench business, my farm affairs, and an afternoon walk through the mud with the two spaniels, Buckle and Jeekie.

He also suffered from a bad attack of bronchitis.

Some months later a press agency rang to inquire if he had died. The rumour was quickly denied but Rider Haggard, already depressed, was shocked by the inquiry. Being thus reminded of the certainty of his eventual death, he decided that the time had come to evaluate his life. He felt convinced that all his real achievements had been accomplished and, at the age of fifty-three, therefore, he prepared to write his autobiography. He collected together his notebooks and batches of letters he had received and, having determined that *The Days of My Life* would not be published until after his death, he began to write. But before he had covered more than half his life, things once again suddenly changed.

In December, 1911, he was offered and accepted a knighthood, and then a few weeks later he was offered an appointment as one of the six British Royal Commissioners selected to visit the Dominions and report on them. The intention was that over the following three years the Commission would make three visits — one of three months to Canada and Newfoundland, another of six months to South Africa, and another of six months to Australia and New Zealand. Rider Haggard was overjoyed at the honour bestowed upon him, although he was very aware that such long periods of travel would make it difficult for him to earn his living. But restored in spirits, he made another visit to Egypt in an attempt to shake off his bronchitis. Then on his return he rapidly completed his autobiography, wrote *The Holy Flower* — another in the Allan Quatermain series — and spent some busy weeks setting his affairs in order. On 29th November he set off for Australia and New Zealand on the first of the visitations made by the Royal Commission. It was while on the third of these that Rider Haggard began the diary in which he recorded the final years of his life.

Acknowledgements

The following books have provided essential background information:

Cohen, Morton: *Rider Haggard — His Life and Works* (Hutchinson, 1960)
Cohen, Morton: *Rudyard Kipling to Rider Haggard* (Hutchinson, 1965)
Haggard, Lilias Rider: *The Cloak That I Left — A Biography of the Author Henry Rider Haggard K.B.E.* (Hodder & Stoughton, 1951)
Haggard, Henry Rider: *The Days of My Life* (Longmans, Green & Co., 1926)
Scott, J. E. *A Bibliography of the Works of Sir Henry Rider Haggard, 1856-1925* (Elkin Matthews Ltd., 1947)

I should like to thank the many people who have helped me with this edition, especially Professor Angus Wilson, Professor Malcolm Bradbury, Dr Richard Shannon, Mr John Ridgard, Mr Norman Scarfe, Mr Michael Horniman of A. P. Watt & Son, Mr P. H. Muir, and Mrs Jean Lawrance.

For access to holograph and other material I am indebted to the staffs of the Norfolk Record Office; the University of East Anglia; the Henry E. Huntington Library, San Marino, California; and Columbia University Library.

I should like to thank the National Trust for permission to quote letters written by Rudyard Kipling most of which have been published previously in Morton Cohen's *Rudyard Kipling to Rider Haggard* (Hutchinson & Co.).

Finally I am especially indebted to Commander and Mrs R. R. Cheyne of Ditchingham House. I thank them gratefully for giving me so much of their time, hospitality and encouragement.

The Private Diaries of Sir H. Rider Haggard
1914-1925

1914

While the Dominions Royal Commission was sitting in Canada, the United Kingdom declared war on Germany. The Commissioners were ordered to return home. Once back, Rider Haggard waited with growing impatience to be called upon to serve his country. He even moved up from Ditchingham into a new London flat. But no call came.

Meanwhile, Mameena, *a play based on his novel* Child of Storm, *was, against his wishes, produced in London. But it was the tragedies of war that affected Rider Haggard most. Mark, one of his nephews, was killed. So too was the son of his friend, Charles Longman. Others he knew had lucky escapes. He was also disturbed by the frequent tales of German atrocities.*

These matters and the changes taking place as the country adjusted to being at war were carefully recorded by Rider Haggard, but, as he was not actively involved in events, it was a frustrating time for him. The many newspapers he read contained too many rumours and far too little news. This he attributed to unnecessary government censorship. The country's unpreparedness for war deeply concerned him and he continued to advocate, as he had done for years, that compulsory military service should be introduced.

Rider Haggard arrived in Newfoundland on 28th July, 1914. He and his fellow Commissioners started their investigations the same day.

St John's, Newfoundland   *29th July, 1914*

Today we heard that there is a grave peril of a European war, news which racks us all with anxiety. It is strange how suddenly clouds spring up in what seemed to be a spotless international sky. Poor England — without an adequate army! I am *very* anxious, and wonder whether Armageddon has come at last. Well, we ought to know more in a day or two.

Port au Basques, Newfoundland   *2nd August, 1914*

In the train on our way here the Commission held a meeting at which we discussed our future action in case of a declaration of war by Britain. The Colonial members present were in favour of continuing our Canadian mission. Lorimer and Garnett[1] said that in the event of war they must go home. I said that I also wished to return for obvious reasons, especially as I lived on the East Coast, but that I would do my duty and obey whatever orders might reach me. So matters were left — for a time.

Halifax, Canada   *5th August, 1914*

This morning we learned that England had declared war against Germany on the ground of the violation of the neutrality of Belgium by that Power. It is terrible, and of this business none can foresee the end. For years some of us have known that such a war must come, although millions at home have mocked at the idea. But always one hoped vaguely that it would not be in our day, knowing how ill we were prepared, owing to the madness of our nation which has steadily refused to bear the burden of any form of National Service. Now the thing is on us in all its horror and, ready or unready, we must fight — and win, or go under! God save England!

I have cabled to my belongings at home to look after themselves. Doubtless they would do this without my telling them, to the very best of their ability; but it relieves my mind, as I am terribly anxious about them so far away.

We arrived at Halifax and put up at a very crowded hotel. There is some firemen's fête going on, which seems to involve the consumption of a good deal of liquor. Thus poor old Bateman[2], when he retired to rest, found a drunken and be-ribboned extinguisher of flames in his bed, boots and all! We had another private meeting of the Commission and wired to our Chairman, D'Abernon[3], at home for instructions and information.

---

[1]William Lorimer and Tom Garnett were two of the six Commissioners representing the United Kingdom.
[2]Sir Alfred Bateman was the Vice-Chairman of the Commission.
[3]Lord D'Abernon (formerly Sir Edgar Vincent) had not made the trip to Canada.

6th August, 1914

It is very hard to have to sit here taking evidence on canned lobsters and such matters when the Judgement Day of nations has dawned upon the world.

Digby, Canada   *9th August, 1914*

This morning I put a proposition by wire before Longman[1] to the effect that I should write a History of the War — of course I mean if we live to see the end of it and are victorious, since in the other event no one would wish to read a history of it. It was an expensive business, as the cable companies have withdrawn all weekend privileges and full 'urgent' rates must be charged for everything that is cabled.

St John, Canada   *10th August, 1914*

In the evening there arrived a peremptory telegram from H.M.'s Government recalling us home after we have completed our work in the maritime provinces, a week hence. But how are we to get home under present circumstances? No British vessels are advertised to run, and I do not want to be obliged to travel by an American line, which would betray a lack of confidence in our ability to keep the seas open.

11th August, 1914

This morning Bateman, as acting Chairman, formally communicated the cable of recall to the Commission at a meeting in his bedroom, as there was no other piace where we could sit in private. A scene followed. The Colonial members (and one or two of the English) did not wish to be recalled, the former alleging that this could only be done with the actual consent of their own Governments. They desired to complete the Canadian journey. One of them, whose name I will not mention, was very violent, abusing H.M.'s Government and the absent Chairman in no measured terms. Had I been in the chair instead of Bateman I think I should have been unwise enough to answer him very sharply, as I hate to hear the absent attacked, and when all is said and done we are the servants of the Crown, not its masters, and appointed, every one of us, under the sign-manual of the Crown.

12th August, 1914

This evening we were entertained by the Mayor at a large public dinner in the Union Club. The Commission ordinance of 'No speeches' (which I hear from various sources is giving considerable offence in Canada) made this feast a

---

[1]Charles Longman published many of Rider Haggard's books and was a personal friend.

4

somewhat slow affair, for it is dull work listening to toasts to which no answer is vouchsafed. At last Bateman was forced to murmur a few words, in which he complained of the breach of the contract as to the matter of speaking. He sat down, and suddenly from all round the room there arose a veritable storm of cries of 'Haggard! Rider Haggard!' Still I kept my seat, till at last Bateman, growing disturbed, motioned me to rise.

I did so, and spoke for about three or four minutes only, but 'with my heart', as the Zulus say. Indeed everything that had been simmering in my mind for days seemed to rush to my lips, the difficulty being to know which thoughts to choose and in what words to clothe them.[1]

Charlottetown, Prince Edward Island   *16th August, 1914*

Here we are established in an hotel which is about as uncomfortable in the matter of service as are the majority of Canadian hostelries. However, we have managed to get some whisky, for which one must be grateful in a 'dry' State. The tyranny of these liquor laws is really overpowering. It is a perfect insult to travellers that they should not be allowed to drink what is necessary to them because the inhabitants of any given place are afraid that if tempted they may exceed.

Moreover the restrictions are quite ineffective, and only result in the pernicious habit of drinking between meals. The people who gulp down tumblers of iced water or cups of tannin essence (proper tea they seldom make in Canada) with their meat, often enough consume whisky or brandy before or after, when of course it is harmful. With the rest this total abstinence seems to produce a certain flatness and tameness of mind as to tend to a strange lack of imagination. This may be fancy, but it strikes many besides myself. I think that for the most part water-drinkers are dull dogs.

S.S.'Virginian'   *21st August, 1914*

At Quebec (on the 19th) I received letters from England telling of the state of affairs on the declaration of war. These speak for themselves. Alas! the world has become a hell, a place of wholesale murder!

Yesterday we were sent to the quay at three o'clock, but had to sit there on a wooden bench (there is no waiting-room) until six, till the boat came in. However, we secured some tea from the emigrants' reception shed. At length we came aboard this very comfortable ship, which is so empty that I was given a private sitting-room in addition to my cabin. It seems a perfect haven of rest after all our hard travelling, rough food, and knocking about over vast expanses of country.

[1] In his speech Rider Haggard said: 'The Angel of Death appears in a dawn of blood: the Armageddon which has been so long foretold has at length fallen upon us. . . We believe that by the aid of God we shall conquer, and that through us the world shall be free.'

So ends our Canadian trip, or as much of it as we can do. What between the absence of the Chairman, dissensions, anxieties, and uncertainties, I consider that it has been a failure, although interesting in a way. Of news we have practically none. We do not even know by what route we are to sail, or whether or not we are to be escorted by war-ships. Our funnel is being painted black, and the stewards are pasting brown paper over the cabin window-lights. Pleasant preparations for an ocean journey!

28th August, 1914

I write this off the coast of Ireland. We are expecting to reach Liverpool late tonight, and I have sent a Marconi home saying I hope to be in London tomorrow. It has been a strange and depressing voyage, rushing through ice and reek in this dumb and shrouded ship. It has been perhaps the worst so far of any of the hazardous voyages I have made[1], and I shall be thankful if and when we land at Liverpool, as I have been each morning to see the light again. Fighting is one thing, but to be sent to the bottom in a tin pot without the chance of striking a blow is quite another.

A poor young woman died on the voyage from the effects of quinsy, and was buried at sea after an operation. She had been a governess and housekeeper in Canada and was coming home to be married.

Ditchingham   *1st September, 1914*

I came to London on Saturday, 29th August, and thence home, where I found all well and the harvest up. On Monday I returned to town from Ditchingham to see my Chairman, Lord D'Abernon, as to Commission affairs. He had made an appointment for me with Mr Harcourt[2], whom I saw at the House of Commons at four o'clock. He welcomed me warmly, and seemed to be anxious that we should present a brief report as to the best way to secure German trade, whether the matter is or is not within our terms of reference. He said that there would be no Colonial Conference next year, and thought it would be most inadvisable that we should attempt to write a final report at present, or indeed till after the war.

Today I saw Charles Longman as to writing a history of the war, if we should all live so long. I found him very depressed. He said nothing could be sold and no money collected and it was difficult to know how to meet outgoings. Also his boy Freddie is somewhere at the front, and he knows not what is happening to him.

---

[1]Rider Haggard had several 'hazardous voyages'. On 25th June, 1888, the *Copeland*, on which he was returning from Iceland, was wrecked in the Pentland Firth. Ed.
[2]Lewis Harcourt (later 1st Viscount Harcourt) was from 1910 to 1915 Secretary of State for the Colonies. He was responsible for the Dominions Royal Commission and had appointed Rider Haggard to it.

But there, we are all in the same boat. Both Mark and George[1] are in Belgium, the first fighting in the Welsh regiment, the second trapped as a civilian. Mark, I hear, announced that he would never live to be taken prisoner. His poor young bride is in a sad state of anxiety.

I called at Watt's[2], and told him to inform the publishers that I thought they should postpone the issue of *The Holy Flower*[3], also Oscar Asche[4] that the production of *Mameena*[5] should be put off. At Barclay's Bank I find that no securities are saleable. Thank Heaven I have a good balance there.

9th September, 1914

On Thursday, officers arrived here. We have put up three. The whole district is full of soldiers. We are to have artillery camped on one field near Mann's Malting. The Cheshires are by the other maltings, but are being moved because of the damp mist at night. Poor people! they have been sent here without blankets, tents, or even great-coats, and have to walk about at night to keep themselves warm. Thus do we prepare our volunteer forces for service!

On Friday, after returning from seeing the Wills[6] at Bradenham, I attended a recruiting meeting in Bungay. My speech was well received, to put it mildly, and I am glad to say that then and after the meeting we got seventy-five recruits. This was good for a little town, whence many had gone as Territorials etc.

13th September, 1914

On Tuesday, the 8th, I went to town to attend the Royal Commission. Today I was present at a rehearsal of *Mameena*, which seemed to go very well under the direction of, so far as the native business is concerned, James Stuart[7], my

---

[1]Mark Haggard was the third son and George William Bazett (Copeman) the eldest son of Rider's elder brother, Bazett Michael Haggard.

[2]A. P. Watt was Rider Haggard's literary agent. Walter Besant had introduced him in 1885 to the firm's founder, Alexander Pollock Watt. Rudyard Kipling and Wilkie Collins were among his many clients.

[3]*The Holy Flower*, which Rider Haggard had finished writing in July, 1912, was at the time running as a serial in *The Windsor Magazine*. The book was published by Ward, Lock & Co. on 31st March, 1915.

[4]Oscar Asche was an actor and producer whom Rider Haggard had met in Australia in 1913. *Chu Chin Chow* was Asche's most successful show.

[5]*Mameena* was a dramatisation of Rider Haggard's *Child of Storm*. For Asche's spectacular production thousands of pounds had been spent on purchasing Zulu costumes and properties.

[6]Sir William Henry Doveton Haggard, Rider's eldest brother, lived with his second wife, Emily, at Bradenham, the Haggard estate that he had inherited in 1893.

[7]James Stuart had been Assistant Secretary for Native Affairs in Natal. *Child of Storm* was dedicated to him. At Rider Haggard's suggestion, Asche hired Stuart to purchase costumes and supervise the Zulu dances in the play.

companion in Zululand. Whether the public will patronise any play in the midst of all this excitement remains, however, to be seen.

London seemed much as usual, but the attendance at the Athenaeum is not what it was, as I am glad to say that all our unmarried servants here volunteered.

On Thursday morning a leader in *The Times* put it into my head that a Royal Commission should be appointed to enquire into all these allegations of atrocities. I wrote at once to this effect to Harcourt, as my chief, sending the letter by special messenger. He laid the matter before the Cabinet that morning. On Friday I received a private letter from him saying that the Government had decided not to appoint a Commission at present.[1]

On my return from town I found that our officers had departed under canvas at Kirby.

18th September, 1914

I have just heard over the telephone from my daughter Angie that her brother-in-law[2], my nephew Mark Haggard, 'died of wounds' on the 15th. It is a great shock, for I was fond of him. He was a good officer (Welsh Regiment) and a very gallant man. He said before he left that never would he live to be taken prisoner by the Germans. Well, he has not lived. All honour to him who has died the best and greatest of deaths! But his poor young wife, whose marriage I attended not a year ago![3] R.I.P.

My speech at Bungay had been issued as a leaflet by the recruiting authorities, and I have been doing my best to circulate it.[4] But without a publishing organisation this is practically impossible.

21st September, 1914

I hear from his mother that the King telephoned personally to Mark's widow to express his thanks, sorrow, and sympathy. I don't know why this was done, as it is not likely that His Majesty has any information about his end which has not reached us.

25th September, 1914

I have heard more details of Mark's death, supplied to his mother by an officer of his regiment, Lieutenant Somerset, who was in the next bed to him at the hospital

[1]But see the diary entry for 13th May, 1915.
[2]Agnes had married Thomas Barker Amyard Haggard, her cousin and Mark's elder brother, in 1907.
[3]Mark had married Doris Elizabeth Vaughan on 15th October, 1913.
[4]10,000 copies of the leaflet, entitled *A Call to Arms,* were printed at Rider Haggard's expense and distributed by him to various press agencies and prominent people.

in France. It seems that he got ahead of his men and killed the three German gunners serving the gun he was charging with his own hand and then was struck down.

We have heard over the telephone from Angie this morning that Reggie[1] is coming from India on General Pirie's staff, and that Dolly and the children are returning home. No doubt Cheyne will be delighted, for he is the keenest of all soldiers, but I confess I am not so pleased. We seem to have enough of our family in this war. God be with him!

4th October, 1914

Last night I returned after spending the week in London on the Royal Commission. It is a curious place just now. The lighting is about as bright only as that which I remember as a boy, when the gas lamps were few and burned dully and electric lamps were unknown. This is to avoid attracting Zeppelins, though whether it would have the effect if they were to come is another matter. Consequently the town looks melancholy, and so are its inhabitants. Outwardly things are much the same, but there is a gloom in the air. Business is shocking. Even at the smart hair-dresser's next to the Junior Army and Navy Stores they told me that they were doing nothing, and indeed the place was empty. Walking to Garland's Hotel from the Athenaeum at about eleven at night, no longer do I see the lines of magnificent motors into which enter jewelled ladies and fine gentlemen dispersing half-crowns to a huge and glorious hotel porter. At the Savoy, where I went to dine at a party given by D'Abernon to the Royal Commission, I observed also that the restaurant was only half full. Indeed I believe that today one can actually lunch at this hotel for five shillings! All of which means that the war is beginning to come home. Well may it do so, with search-lights stabbing the skies, and a dim something floating aloft which I took to be a guardian air-ship. (Perhaps it was nothing but a cloud with the moon behind it.)

This is the time that Asche has chosen to bring out *Mameena* in spite of my protest. I went to see it. The scenes are beautiful and the incidents interesting, but the drama as he conceives it is nowhere. However, it is of no use arguing with actor-managers. I should imagine that its career will be short.[2] I had long talks with Curzon[3] and Bryce[4] at the Athenaeum, but neither of them seemed to know much more than other people.

[1] Major Reginald Cheyne was the husband of Dorothy, Rider Haggard's second daughter.
[2] It played at the Globe until Asche's lease expired on 14th January, 1915.
[3] George Nathaniel Curzon, 1st Marquess Curzon of Kedleston, and Rider Haggard had known each other for many years. At this time Curzon held no political office.
[4] James Bryce, 1st Viscount Bryce of Dechmont, who was then seventy-six, had been Ambassador at Washington from 1907 to 1913.

14th October, 1914

To the outward eye things go on much as usual, at any rate in Norfolk. The bulk of the population do not seem at all to understand the seriousness of the crisis in our national affairs. One of the effects of the war is that numbers of the elder women, being better off, are drinking a great deal, while the young ones rejoice whole-heartedly at the presence of so many soldiers in their midst and are to be met with them in every lane. In Norwich they say the thing has become such a scandal that no woman under twenty is allowed in the streets after ten p.m. No stranger arrived from another planet would guess that there was a life-and-death war in progress, though he might suspect autumn manoeuvres. For instance, as I write, the guns of the partridge-shoots are popping merrily in the fields.

17th October, 1914

Yesterday, I went to London to attend my Royal Commission. London at night is very strange in these times. About six o'clock I went for a walk down Piccadilly, and when I reached the Ritz Hotel came back again, as I could scracely see my way about. Many lights are put out altogether, and most of the others blacked or veiled, while even the shop fronts no longer look gay. Indeed in walking to the Hampstead Tube at Charing Cross, on my way to dine with Angie, I fell over a high curb and was lucky to escape a sprained or broken ankle. Also these wide crossings are dangerous to negotiate in the gloom. It is strange too to see the great search-lights wheeling about the sky in their quest for hostile aircraft. As yet these have not come, but many people, especially old ladies, are in terror of them and a proportion sleep in their cellars. Personally I know of one case where this is done. For my own part I prefer to take the risk of sudden and fiery extermination.

I returned from Hampstead before the hour of closing public-houses, and looking into one which I passed on my way to Garland's Hotel I noted that the bar was crowded, one division of it with women, most of whom seemed to be young. If I had my way I would shut every one of them at sun-down, let the publicans say what they might and vote as they would.

When we were lunching together at the Athenaeum today, Sir Ian Hamilton[1] and I talked about the Censorship and generally of the methods of supplying war information to the public. He agreed with me that these were very bad indeed. I told him that I would gladly help in the matter if I could be of any use, thinking as I did that a clear and connected account of what was going on should be published day by day. He seemed rather to jump at the idea, which he said he would bring to the notice in the proper quarter, as he has no authority in that direction. On reflection I rather hope I shall hear no more of it, as what between red tape and the public it would be putting one's head into a hornet's nest, in which the stings would be many and thanks few.

The first batch of Canadian troops have landed — I think about twelve thousand

---

[1]He was the general who led the disastrous Gallipoli expedition in 1915.

men — and been encamped on Salisbury Plain, together with thirty-four chaplains and a hundred and five nurses. I am sure that the country is very glad to have them here. Among them is my nephew and godson, Lance Rider Haggard[1], who has pluckily thrown up his billet in Canada, where I missed him, and come over as a private, for which I honour him. I hope he will get through the war unscathed.[2] This once more brings up the number of my nephews in the war to six, plus my son-in-law, Major Reginald Cheyne. Old, gentle-born families like our own bear a large share in the national defence. Would that I were not too old and full of ailments to take my share! I should like to carry a rifle again!

23rd October, 1914

Freddie Longman of the Royal Fusiliers, the son of my old friend Charles Longman, has been killed. We knew the poor boy well, and he has stayed here; he was a charming young man, and took great interest in all that had to do with his profession. At the commencement of the war he was slightly wounded and got four bullets through his clothes. After a short time in hospital in France he rejoined his regiment, and now he is gone. I fear his family will be desolated, for he was their idol. Such is War.

I have received a gigantic type-written communication from Hall Caine[3], who is getting up some kind of war book to be presented to the King of the Belgians, and is anxious that I should write some sentiment — heaven knows what about! — to be included therein. When confronted with these demands — I think this is the third or fourth that I have had — my mind becomes a blank; in short I am no hand at this business; yet one does not like to be ill-natured and refuse.[4]

For many years the subject of war has been more or less taboo in England. For instance, how often have I been violently attacked for writing stories that deal with fighting rather than with sexual complications. Once or twice I remember I have been provoked to answer that I was not in the least ashamed for trying to inculcate in the mind of youth the ancient and elementary fact that their hands were given them to defend their head — also their King and Country. A lesson I hope has been learned by some of my young readers. Now everything is otherwise in this same England. It is war, war, war, from morning till night, and even sound Radical papers continually bewail that dreadful state of unpreparedness in which our hour of trial has found us, but what kind of treatment has been meeted out in

---

[1]Rider Lancelot Haggard was the second son of Rider's youngest brother, Edward Arthur Haggard.
[2]He was killed during an attack near Passchendaele in 1917, being then a Captain in the Princess Patricia's Canadian Regiment. H.R.H.
[3]Sir Thomas Henry Hall Caine, the novelist, was made an Officer of the Order of Leopold for his work in putting this book together.
[4]*King Albert's Book*, including Rider Haggard's message on 'The Desolation of Belgium', was published in December, 1914.

the past to those who have tried to tell the country that it was its sacred duty to be prepared.

27th October, 1914

I walked up to lunch at the Hall[1], where they were shooting pheasants. Some gentlemen from the neighbourhood gave a bad account of the recent recruiting in Norfolk. According to them it is drying up.

28th October, 1914

The *Evening Standard* asks me to write a series of articles on the war. I have declined, both because of my official position as a Royal Commissioner and because I am too outspoken a person in these days of censorship. If I wrote at all I should say what was in my mind, and that would never do.

30th October, 1914

Today I went to the Club[2] in Norwich, which seems much changed. Instead of country gentlemen discoursing about pheasants, it was filled with territorials and other officers talking about the war.

6th November, 1914

On the 2nd I went to town to sit on my Royal Commission. We agreed in the end to suspend our meetings till after the conclusion of the war and to issue no final or semi-final report at present. This is rather sad and against the wishes of one or two of the Colonial members. But what else could be done? I wonder if we shall ever meet again after signing the Newfoundland Report next week?

My train was an hour late, being blocked by a troop-train, so I lunched at the Anthenaeum before going to Scotland House. Here I met Sir William Richmond[3], whom I have known of for thirty years. (Lang and I dedicated *The World's Desire*[4] to him.) Although he wears his hair long and has a floppety tie, Rich-

---

[1]Ditchingham Hall was owned by William Carr, the village squire.
[2]The Norwich and Norfolk Conservative Club, 36 St Giles's Street.
[3]Sir William Richmond was then seventy-two. He was a well-known painter and from 1878 to 1883 had been Slade Professor at Oxford.
[4]*The World's Desire* was first published by Longmans on 5th November, 1890. Andrew Lang (1844-1912) was an influential critic whose penchant for romance and demand for 'more claymores, less psychology' made him an admirer and strong advocate of Rider Haggard's early work. The two men became close friends.

mond is really a most patriotic and war-like man. We had a long talk and discussed the advisability of starting a public movement to advocate compulsory military service. I thought, however, that the time had not quite come for this. Subsequently, while I was lunching, Richmond came to tell me that he had just seen Lord Roberts[1], who had come into the club, and told him of our conversation. Roberts also was of the opinion that the right moment had not yet arrived, since the War Office still had as many recruits on its hands as it could manage and equip. Soon, however, this would be otherwise.

Afterwards I saw Ian Hamilton, who told me that he had spoken to 'K. of K.'[2] himself as to my suggestion that the public should be supplied with better news, properly edited and written by competent persons instead of by War Office clerks or superannuated Army officers. The dictator, however, he said, only 'snorted'.

I dined with my brother Arthur[3], who told me stories of German atrocities, which he had collected at his Veterans' Club, until I implored him to stop. They are no good sauce for mutton cutlets.

7th November, 1914

In the paper appears a statement from Lance-Corporal Fuller, who, it seems, carried Mark back to the trenches. He describes him as 'a brave man and a fighting soldier from his head to his feet'. He adds: 'He never complained of his wound. Always he said he was all right. His last words were "Stick it, the Welsh!"' I received a very nice communication from Mr and Mrs Roosevelt[4] about Mark's death, in which they say, 'our sympathy goes to your family in this sorrow where pride and grief are mingled!'

Windham Club, London   *10th November, 1914*

I came to town today, and tonight saw Sir Bartle Frere[5] at the Club. He has been

---

[1]Frederick Sleigh Roberts, 1st Earl Roberts of Waterford, although then eighty-two, was the Colonel-in-Chief of the Overseas and Indian Forces in Europe.

[2]Horatio Herbert Kitchener, 1st Earl Kitchener of Khartoum, was Secretary of State for War.

[3]Arthur was the Founder and Chairman of the Veterans' Club.

[4]In 1905 when Rider Haggard was inspecting Salvation Army settlements in the United States, he met Theodore Roosevelt, who was then the President. The two men discovered they had much in common and, although they subsequently met only a couple of times, they became close friends.

[5]Sir Bartle Frere was made the High Commissioner for South Africa in the autumn of 1878 — three years after Rider Haggard had arrived in the country. In *The Days of My Life* Rider Haggard writes: 'In my opinion Sir Bartle Frere was a great administrator and *almost* a great man. But I do not think he was suited to the position in which he found himself.'

on a visit to Antwerp, and was in the trenches at the time of the surrender. Why I don't know, as he is not serving in the war. He says that some of the Marines Churchill sent to Antwerp were literally unarmed, or at any rate without ammunition and other necessaries.

11th November, 1914

Today we had our last meeting of the Dominions Royal Commission, and adjourned till the conclusion of the war. We signed the Newfoundland report, and then lunched in a queer old room at the 'Cheshire Cheese', one of Dr Johnson's haunts, where we ate lark-pudding and toasted cheese. I wonder if we shall all live to meet again and finish our work?

This war lacks the grandeur and picturesqueness of those of old time. There are no great battles, only one long hideous slaughter in the trenches. In the same way, where now is the majesty of Nelson's battles on the sea? In the place of them we have mines and sneaking submarines.

Montague Mansions   *12th November, 1914*

I saw Charles Longman today. Poor Freddie was killed by a shell. I did not like to pursue the subject, seeing that it distressed him beyond bearing. I thought he looked thin. The old gentlemen at the Athenaeum play their afternoon bridge as usual in the smoking-room. Probably they are wise so to do, but I admire their detachment of mind. Came to this flat. It seems a comfortable place.

15th November, 1914

Poor Gussie Williams, the son of Williams, the carpenter at home, has been killed. He was a nice fellow, a reservist, and leaves a widow and two children, one an infant born three days before he left.

16th November, 1914

This afternoon we heard that Dolly and her boys had landed and were due at Paddington at 8.45. Louie and I went to the station, where we met Tom and Angie, only to find that owing to the line being blocked with thousands of troops who had left for France today, the train is not likely to arrive for another two hours So, fearing bronchitis, I returned, leaving Louie and Angie in the ladies' waiting room. I hope they will get in all right.

17th November, 1914

Dolly and her children arrived very late, but safe, thank God! I have seen her today. She had an awful voyage, five weeks on the sea, after a long wait in the great heat at Bombay. The ship, in addition to the five hundred passengers for which it was designed, had two thousand soldiers on board. It is a vessel that has been employed on the North Atlantic trade, and built for cold weather. No fans, no windows that will open wide, and, above all, no cold storage. So most of the food was tainted, and there were deaths. The heat as far as Port Said was terrific, a hundred and twenty degrees in the soldiers' quarters, and the nurse Dolly had hired, a soldier's wife, having received her pay in advance, struck work altogether as soon as they were at sea, leaving her to look after the children alone. So bad was her conduct that those in authority on the ship suggested that she should be put ashore at Port Said and left to shift for herself, but to this Dolly, a soft-hearted person, would not consent.

18th November, 1914

I have applied for seats in St Paul's at Lord Roberts'[1] funeral tomorrow for Louie and self, but do not suppose that I shall get them.

19th November, 1914

I did not get the tickets, and therefore cannot set down any description of the ceremony as I hoped to do. Harding's letter was not answered, although sent from the Office of the Royal Commission. Probably the War Office clerks send any spare admissions to their own friends. Personally I am glad, as I hate funerals, and it has been awful weather.

20th November, 1914

I went to Gosling's, or rather Barclay's Bank, to send in an application for some of the War Loan, which I think everybody ought to support who can.

25th November, 1914

We went to *Mameena* again last night. It is much improved and a fine spectacle, if not the play that I should have liked to make of it. I saw Oscar Asche between the acts. He told me that he would be obliged to withdraw the play after another five weeks, when the lease of the theatre (two hundred and fifty pounds a week) expires, with the intention of reviving it in happier days, as I suggested that he should. The thing would have been an enormous success, but the times are too

[1]On 14th November, Lord Roberts died of inflammation of the lungs, while at the front.

much to fight against. The darkness of the London streets is, he says, their greatest enemy. Then comes the withdrawal of the licence to sell drink after nine o'clock, which keeps people away, then the general lack of cash, and lastly the ever-increasing lists of killed, which put so many into mourning among all classes, especially those who patronise theatres. Also there is the all-prevailing anxiety that at present does not predispose to entertainments, since to it the country is not yet accustomed. He tells me that he has been obliged to reduce all salaries by one half, and that further curtailments may be necessary. The actors bore it very well, he says.

Another anxiety. I have received a dirty slip of paper revealing no adequate authority, which informs me that Ditchingham House is to be valued today by some person from Norwich of whom I never heard. I suppose this is done under some of Lloyd George's schemes for tormenting everybody who owns anything. Let him value and be damned!

26th November, 1914

The kitchen-maid has had a letter from her mother, Mrs Savage, whose husband is in charge of my house at Kessingland.[1] Every one in the village has been warned to hold himself in readiness to remove to Bungay if the raid which seems to be expected should occur. The inhabitants of Lowestoft are to shift to Norwich. These orders seem to have occasioned great alarm. What foundation there is for them I cannot say.

My nephew George has escaped from Brussels by bribing his sentry.

27th November, 1914

I met my nephew George at lunch today. His adventures escaping from Brussels were many and peculiar. They included bribing a sentry (an old Carlton Hotel waiter) with a sum of eight pounds, a forged passport with his own photo attached etc., etc. Luckily for him that it was examined by the German officer in a dim light, for I could clearly see the erasures on the document. He seems to have found many friends, who provided him with clothes carefully marked with his own name etc., also with a guide across country.

[1] Rider Haggard had owned Kessingland Grange for about ten years. Lilias in *The Cloak That I Left* says the property 'had been two coast-guard cottages, which some later owner had joined together with a long passage, forming a sprawling, two-storied house shaped like an E without the middle stroke. It faced east, stood almost on the very edge of the cliff and from its windows nothing was visible except sea and sky.' The house contained sixteen bedrooms, four public rooms and two furnished halls. In the surrounding ten acres of land there was a croquet lawn and a tennis court.

16

This morning came Mr Edward Brown, head of the Poultry Organisation, on behalf of Mr H. T. Cadbury of the *Daily News*, to ask me to join a small committee of which the object will be to restore Belgium after the war. I consented, thinking this a very worthy business. It appears that the Belgians have lost thirty million pounds worth of stock and crops, the Germans have killed or stolen every head of the former, and consumed or destroyed all the latter. The idea is to raise voluntary offerings in kind from British agriculturists to help them to sow and stock when the time comes. I suggested that a letter should be obtained from the King of the Belgians approving this notion, which he will set about at once. Something I hope may come of this to the advantage of the poor Belgians.

25th December, 1914

I went to see Rider Greiffenhagen[1], who limps a bit with a piece of shell in his foot, which the doctors hesitate to extract bacause of intervening arteries. He also had a small fragment taken from his back, which he showed me.

Arthur (my brother) came to see us this afternoon. Lance, his boy, has gone to the front with 'Princess Patricia's Regiment' — I believe the only one out of the Canadian lot that is as yet sufficiently trained to be sent, and of course his father is anxious about him. Arthur gets a lot of information from wounded soldiers belonging to the Veterans' Club. These tell him that many of the casualties among the rank and file have not yet been reported, and that two of our regiments have been practically destroyed.

26th December, 1914

I went today to see Archie Cheyne, Reggie's brother, who is lying wounded at 10 Carlton House Terrace. The place is a palace, marble stairways, marble statues, painted ceilings, etc., which I believe belongs to Lady Ridley.[2] I wonder what the butler, a very nice fellow, and the footmen think of their changed duties. He was lying in a gorgeous saloon with eight or ten others, nice Red Cross nurses about, and a doctor attending to one patient behind a screen. Luckily Archie is but lightly hurt, a bullet through the foot — that is all — and looks quite well. He expects to be back at the front in a few weeks.

31st December, 1914

The old year closes for England in gloom as deep as that of this December day in

---

[1]Rider Greiffenhagen was Rider Haggard's godson. He had been injured while serving on H.M.S. *Hardy* in the North Sea.
[2]Lady Ridley was, until her marriage in 1899, the Hon. Rosamond Guest. Her father was the first Baron Wimborne.

London. Yet I believe that victory will come as surely as the sun of summer. But it must be hardly earned, and what are we to say of these leaders of our nation, of both parties, who, because of misjudgement, greed of votes, and refusal to listen to the voices of men like the late Lord Roberts have brought us into this sea of troubles? Had National Service been instituted ten years ago, it is probable that there would have been no European War.

1915

Rider Haggard continued to be concerned about the censorship of news, the heavy losses at sea, and America's refusal to join in the war. As tales filtered back from the trenches, he fully realised the horror of the conditions and the extent of the losses. As he sat at home daily reading his batch of newspapers, his major concern, however, was that he was still not involved in any public service, apart from the two agricultural committees on which he sat. Having failed to persuade the Government to appoint someone responsible for information, he wrote to The Times *stating the case for a Minister of Food Supplies, but his letter was not published. Still by the end of the year his persistence had been rewarded. Although the Government seemed not to require his services, the Royal Colonial Institute decided to send him in 1916 as its representative to conduct an investigation in various of the Dominions. Only the tragic death of Kipling's son cast a shadow over Rider Haggard's justifiable pride in the importance of the mission on which he was to embark in the New Year.*

1st January, 1915

Thank God that 1914 is dead and done with! It has been a year of misery and world wide disaster. May we never see such another in our day!

5th January, 1915

Caton Woodville[1] has been here to enquire about material for a large drawing of Mark's death which the *Illustrated News* wishes to publish. He, like myself, has aged much since last we met twenty-seven years ago.

11th January, 1915

Stivens[2] has just been here doctoring me.

13th January, 1915

Today I have been visited by Corporal Fuller, of the Second Welsh Regiment, who received his Victoria Cross, which he earned by carrying Mark out of action, from the King this morning.

He described Mark as a man who would 'fetch you a clout if you didn't do what he told you' — a circumstance which seemed to endear him to Fuller. He says that there was no hand-to-hand struggle between Mark — who by the way was quite thirty yards ahead of him when he fell — and the Germans, so as such a struggle is clearly described by others I can only suppose that either Fuller did not see it or that it occurred elsewhere.

The study of the hero at home is rather amusing. It appears that in private life Fuller is interested in breeding canaries, also that he has no yearning desire to return to mingle in the joy of battle. In short, he seems to have had enough of it, and informed me that his nerve is not what it was, nor his weight either. Like myself he has been enjoying the influenza, and lay awake all last night at the lodging which was given him at Scotland Yard, coughing as I do with this difference, that there, as he remarked pathetically, he was not allowed to spit. He showed me his Victoria Cross, which he had just received from the King, in a little white cardboard box, but objected that they had put 'Corporal Fuller' on the back of it, when at the time of Mark's rescue he was 'Private'.

16th January, 1915

In some ways I think the war is doing good in England. It is bringing the people, or

[1]R. Caton Woodville illustrated the serialisation of Rider Haggard's *Cleopatra* which appeared in *The Illustrated London News* between 5th January and 29th June, 1889.
[2]Dr Bertie Lyne Stivens had been Rider Haggard's friend and doctor for many years.

some of them, face to face with elementary facts which hitherto it has been the fashion to ignore and pretend are non-existent. To take one very humble example. How often have I been vituperated by rose-water critics because I have written of fighting and tried to inculcate certain elementary lessons, such as that it is a man's duty to defend his country, and that only those who are prepared for war can protect themselves and such as are dear to them. 'Coarse! bloody! brutal! Uncivilised!' such has been the talk. Well, and today have I done any harm by inoculating a certain number of the thousands who are at the front with these primary facts, even although my work has been held to be so infinitely inferior to that of Oscar Wilde, Bernard Shaw, and others? The worst of it is that here in England we have not as yet half learned the lesson, nor will it ever be fully learned unless the nation is forced through a strait and narrow gate of misery that I hope and pray it will never be called upon to pass.

18th January, 1915

Reggie Cheyne is home on a few days' leave looking extremely well, although his toes were frost-bitten in the trenches and are still black. He gives a very flourishing account of things, being sure that the Germans will be finished in the spring, when the knowledge of the true state of affairs soaks into the nation.

3rd February, 1915

I was at a meeting today of the Belgian Agricultural Restoration Committee, at which I took the chair. We are in a difficult position, as the Royal Agricultural Society, of which I am a member, has suddenly started a scheme of its own, after having had ours explained to it, with a request for its co-operation. We are going to write them a letter suggesting collaboration and offering that three of us should meet them to discuss the business.

Kipling[1], to whom I was talking yesterday, is of opinion that the best course with the States is to let them go their own way and take as little notice as possible, which he says they hate more than anything else. As he has lived there so long he ought to know. Kipling is also of opinion that our present policy of sitting tight in trenches and allowing the Germans to exhaust themselves in futile attacks is the wisest that the Allies can follow. With this I agree, since to attempt to drive them out of their trenches would cause horrible loss of life.

16th February, 1915

Yesterday while I was walking down the Harrow Road about three in the

---

[1]Rudyard Kipling and Rider Haggard had first met in 1889. They might well have been bitter rivals, but from the start, discovering how much they had in common, they formed a friendship that seems to have grown deeper during the period covered by these diaries.

afternoon, I noticed a group of women, all young and all with children, outside a public-house. There they stood, drinking very strong-looking beer, while their poor babies shivered in the bitter cold. For aught I know the fathers may have been doing likewise, but in the warmth of the bar.

St Leonards   *24th February, 1915*

I have come to St Leonards to recover from the effects of influenza.

26th February, 1915

I went to London yesterday to attend what I expect will be the last meeting of the Agricultural Restoration of Belgium Committee. Practically we have been absorbed by the Royal, in accordance with the King's wish, which has put me on its Executive Committee. But when shall we be in a position to commence the re-stocking of Belgium and the other lands desolated by the Germans?

6th March, 1915

Yesterday I attended the Executive Committee Meeting of the Royal Agricultural Society's Allies' Fund, at which we did a good deal of business, and at the request of the Duke of Portland[1], brought back with me to St Leonards the appeal to re-draft.

My old Aunt Fowler[2] is to be buried today, in the ninety-fourth year of her age. Her long life began, I think, in the year that Napoleon died, and ends in the midst of the greatest war that has overtaken us since his day. She kept her mind almost to the last. Indeed I had a letter from her at Christmas.

16th March, 1915

Mr Frank Harris[3], the malicious man who did me so much harm years ago, has been distinguishing himself by reviling his own country in America and belauding the Germans. The *Globe* speaks its mind very frankly, and I may add most libellously, as to his proceedings. I do not presume, however, that he will take advantage of this to hale the editor before a Court of Law.

[1]William John Arthur Charles James Cavendish-Bentinck, 6th Duke of Portland (1857-1943).
[2]She was his father's sister.
[3]Frank Harris was the editor of the *Fortnightly Review* when in 1890 it published an article, 'King Plagiarism and His Court', accusing Rider Haggard of wholesale plagiarism.

23rd March, 1915

The total casualties among officers in the recent fighting[1], according to last night's *Globe*, now amount to seven hundred and twenty-four. As Kipling, who was here yesterday, said, 'Heaven save us from more such victories!' Neither of the Kiplings look so well as they did at Kessingland.[2] He is greyer than I am, and, as he says, his stomach has shrunk, making him seem smaller. I expect that anxiety about the war is responsible. Their boy John, who is not yet eighteen, is an officer in the Irish Guards, and one can see that they are terrified lest he should be sent to the front and killed, as has happened to nearly all the young men they know. He does not take a cheerful view of things, either as regards our prospect in arms abroad or the labour question at home. When I remarked to him that it was nothing less than providential that it should have chanced to be a Liberal Government that declared this war, since had the Conservative Party been in power all the Radical extremists would have been on its back, he replied, with his usual wit, that this fact was the one thing that made him believe that we should win in the end. In it he saw the hand of the Almighty himself, who had created the Radical Party and borne with it during its eight long years of rule, merely that it might be in power when the great crisis of our fate arrived, and thus constrain its louder-voiced and more unpatriotic elements to silence. He does not blame the workmen so much for striking[3], because, he says, they are only doing what they have been taught to do for years by the Government and its press, who have steadily belittled patriotism, lessened and attacked the army, and so on, but now are pained and surprised to find their lessons bearing fruit. Also he said that a large ship-building friend of his had told him on the previous day that Lloyd George's speech[4] as to the public purse having no bottom had done an enormous amount of harm. 'You say that!' cry the workmen. 'Then you are in a position to pay me anything I ask.' 'But,' added R.K., '*I* am the public and *I* have a bottom.' I remarked that this was the case with all of us! He declares that it is not Kitchener who is to blame about the suppression of news, but the Government, who are hiding behind Kitchener and making use of him. In time to come, when he had served his turn, they would declare that Fate gave them this military despot for a bedfellow, forcing them into participation with his evil deeds, which all along they loathed and hated.

I asked him what he was doing to occupy his mind amidst all these troubles. He answered — like myself — writing stories, adding, 'I don't know what they are worth. I only know they ain't literature[5].'

[1]The battle of Neuve Chapelle,
[2]The Kiplings had stayed at Kessingland Grange during the summer of 1914.
[3]There had been a week-end strike of Liverpool dock workers.
[4]Made in the House of Commons on 15th February.
[5]Kipling was working on two war stories, 'Mary Postgate' and 'Sea Constables: A Tale of "15"' that were to appear later in the year. Rider Haggard was writing *The Ancient Allan*, which was not published until after the War.

Like all big men, Kipling is very modest as to his own productions. Only little people are vain. How anybody can be vain amazes me. I know that in my own small way I grow humbler year by year.

25th March, 1915

I have been lunching with the Kiplings at Batemans.[1]

31st March, 1915

I have been in town attending my two committees, that under the Chairmanship of Earl Grey[2] on Land Settlement at home and in the Colonies after the war, and that of the Royal Agricultural Society on the re-stocking of the devastated countries. I do not think that the first of these has at present the slightest idea of the complexity of the problems with which it proposes to deal. As I told it, I know all about them, having come to grief over something of the same kind through the action of what I must call a packed Government committee. However, things are changed now, and we shall see what happens. At the meeting of the Royal Agricultural Society Committee we voted two thousand pounds for the supply of agricultural implements of Serbia.

6th April, 1915

The King has ordered that from today nothing alcoholic is to be drunk in any of his houses. The motive is most good and kind, but I do think it a pity that His Majesty has been dragged into this matter. I don't know if we are all expected suddenly to change out habits of life in order to set an example to persons who drink too much while they are making ammunition, but of course what the King does many will imitate.

7th April, 1915

The drink controversy continues, and is likely to continue to rage. Personally I am inclined to try the experiment, not because of fashion or from terror of the law, but as an experiment and to see how it agrees with me.

[1]Batemans was the Kiplings' remote house near the village of Burwash, which was some fifteen miles away from St Leonards.
[2]The Rt. Hon. Albert Henry George Grey, 4th Earl Grey, was from 1912 to 1917 President of the Royal Commonwealth Society. His committee, which was to consider after-the-war empire settlement and rural employment, replaced the Society's standing committee on emigration which had secured the inclusion of emigration as a subject for the Dominions Royal Commission.

12th April, 1915

Yesterday I visited some houses of great interest in this neighbourhood, and among other places Winchilsea Church. In the churchyard I was astonished to come across the grave of Mr Inderwick, K.C. whom I used to know so well when I practised in the Probate Court, about twenty-eight years ago. I have never forgotten him, with his prominent eyes and soft whispering voice, and once I caricatured him as 'Fiddlestick, Q.C.' in my skit *Mr Meeson's Will*.[1] He was a kindly man, and a good antiquarian. Peace be with him!

Ditchingham   *16th April, 1915*

We have moved here from St Leonards. In London I attended the meeting of Earl Grey's Committee at the Colonial Institute, and yesterday that of the Economic Branch of the British Association at Burlington House. Speaking generally, I do not think that either of these has the slightest idea of the complexity of the problem with which it proposes to deal, namely the settlement of ex-soldiers on the land at home and abroad. I tried to show both of them the difficulties, which I think they began to realise.

21st April, 1915

I have been to town today to give away Phoebe at her marriage with Dan.[2] It was a cheerful wedding, but I could not help thinking on the shadows which overhang these war marriages. In a week or two Dan will be at the front with his regiment, and then — who knows? Even in my own small circle of acquaintance there have already been some sad bereavements of that sort. Good fortune go with them! They made a handsome pair.

After a fortnight of it I have been obliged to give up my teetotalling experiment, which has thoroughly disorganised my liver. Henceforth, I shall obey the Pauline maxim and take a little wine for my stomach's sake. Nearly sixty-one is too old for these violent changes of the habits of a lifetime.

22nd April, 1915

There are races on Bungay Common today. Motors toot past this house; flags fly; merry-go-rounds bray; bookies shout. And out there on Hill 60, a hundred and fifty miles or so away, our soldiers are dying, or, if they are unfortunate enough to

---

[1]Rider Haggard wrote the story early in 1888. It was published by Spencer Blackett.
[2]Phoebe was the second child of Rider Haggard's elder brother, John George Haggard, who had died in 1908. She married her cousin, Daniel Amyand Haggard, who was the fourth son of Alfred Hinubar Haggard.

be taken alive through wounds or the accidents of war, having their brains dashed out by the butts of German rifles. We are a strange people, one that does not suffer from the terrors of imagination. But let us remember how gloriously those soldiers are fighting, and take comfort. Probably the race-course crowds would do as much if once they *saw* the Prussians in front of them.

23rd April, 1915

The Society of Authors held its annual meeting yesterday, and discussed the effect of the production of charity books on authors. The blame for these books is largely laid upon the eminent hands that contribute the copy. In fact, however, they are absolutely innocent. A request comes to them in the name of the King, or some other royalty, which being practically a command, they are unable to refuse. For instance, in the time of King Edward, I was thus impressed to write a whole book by the direct wish of His Majesty, practically for nothing. By urgent representations I got out of the writing of the book, but was obliged to give a fortnight's work and study to composing the introduction.[1] Personally I think, and have always thought, the whole principle of these charity books extremely bad. People contribute to them because they must; the public buy them by the hundred thousand because they are fathered by Royalty, or for other reasons; and they compete most seriously with the work of those who live by writing, including that of their own authors.

25th April, 1915

Louie went to Norwich yesterday to see about moving the furniture from Kessingland to The Lodge. Bullen[2] told her this was impossible at present. All the motors are commandeered, all the packers are in Government employ, and the horses are liable to seizure at any moment. Norwich is full of troops; trains are standing in the station with steam up (she saw three of these) waiting to take them to destinations unknown; and in short something is expected to happen. Nobody knows what this is, but another raid is anticipated, also a great naval battle in the North Sea.

The spring is one of the coldest and most backward I remember. Today is particularly bitter, so much so that although the sky is black it cannot rain.

29th April, 1915

Yesterday I went to town to attend a meeting of Earl Grey's 'After the War'

[1] W. A. Dutt's *The King's Homeland, Sandringham and North-West Norfolk*, published in 1904.
[2] H. R. Bullen, antique furniture dealer of Elm Hill, Norwich.

Committee at the Royal Colonial Institute. The Committee decided to ask the Prime Minister to receive a deputation which will urge that the whole question of the settlement of ex-soldiers on the land in the United Kingdom and the Dominions should be referred to our Dominions Royal Commission. Today I have been drafting a letter to the Prime Minister, to be signed by Earl Grey.

30th April, 1915

I have been talking over the telephone with Mr Barratt[1], the wine merchant in Bungay, while buying from him some of that inebriating beverage — I mean claret. The wine merchant literally wept, and no wonder, for the poor man says he will be ruined.

2nd May, 1915

Yesterday afternoon I went to visit some wounded soldiers who are convalescing at Hedenham Hall[2], and to take them some of my stories to read. They are a very nice lot of men of different regiments, regular and territorial.

7th May, 1915

Yesterday I paid another visit to the wounded at Hedenham, among whom were some new and rather bad cases. They were delighted to see me, and *interalia* explained to me the various sorts of illegal bullets which are being used by the Germans. One man produced a Mauser cartridge which he had picked up, whereof the point had been filed off so as to make the bullet soft-nosed and expanding.

8th May, 1915

Kipling, who is in London and, therefore, in touch with men and things, writes to me: 'The news isn't as bad as it looks, and so far as I can make out Italy *is* coming in, and that right soon! We have had a tough time in the Dardanelles, but we have achieved certain results, meantime the Huns die! It don't much matter where they die, so long as they pass out!' This sounds well so far as it goes.

Yesterday I say some more wounded soldiers at Ditchingham Hospital.

[1]Gordon Barratt, Broad Street, Bungay.
[2]The Hall, some three miles from Ditchingham, was owned but not occupied by William Carr of Ditchingham.

10th May, 1915

My dear old friend, Bertie Lyne Stivens, is dead. He died yesterday; I don't know of what. Only a month or two ago he attended me constantly during my illness from influenza, as he has done for years, and although he was full of his accustomed jokes and stories I noted about him an underlying melancholy. The truth is that he has never been the same man since the sudden death of his little girl a couple of years ago. R.I.P. Had it not been for his skill I am not sure that I should be here to mourn him.

12th May, 1915

There is a bad piece of news for our family today. The Turkish official communiqué states that the Australian submarine A.E.2 was sunk by Turkish war ships while trying to enter the Sea of Marmora, and that the crew, consisting of three officers and twenty-nine men, were taken prisoners. Now this is the submarine of which my nephew, Geoffrey Haggard[1], was second-in-command. It is not agreeable to think of him and his companions in a Mussulman jail. As the Admiralty state that they have no confirmation of the report, there is still a chance that it may be untrue, but I fear the worst.

13th May, 1915

The Committee on German Atrocities has issued its report. It is a horrible document, on the details of which I will not dwell, further than to say that they amply bear out the worst accusations which have been made against these human devils, wherein at the beginning so many refused to believe. I repeat — How long, O Lord, how long? As I think I stated in my diary months ago, I believe I was, if not the first, at any rate one of the first to press upon the Government the necessity of such an inquiry. Although I had suggested it, I was not offered a seat on it, probably because I write novels and am known as a novelist on the Continent.

Today on the Bungay Bench we had to deal with a number of prosecutions of persons who in spite of repeated warnings steadily refuse to shade their lights. In fining the delinquents I told them that their conduct seemed to result from a lack of imagination, as does so much else in this country. Because they had never seen any one blown to pieces by bombs, they could not understand what such a thing really meant, or that their conduct was endangering the lives and properties of their neighbours. From their remarks I gathered that they did not in the least comprehend these things. The lower middle-class Englishman is a strange creature.

[1]Geoffrey Arthur Gordon Haggard was the eldest son of Rider's younger brother, Edward Arthur Haggard.

29

14th May, 1915

Earl Grey sends me a letter to him from Mr A. H. Asquith, in which he announces that he considers the question of settling ex-soldiers on the land very important and will be glad to receive our deputation on the subject; so I hope we may be able to get the business under way.

18th May, 1915

Horses are rising extraordinarily in price. Yesterday my steward, J. D. Longrigg, sold an animal of twenty-one years of age, with every conceivable infirmity, for thirty pounds. Six or seven years ago he bought it for twenty pounds, with a set of harness thrown in. The fact is the supply is running short.

19th May, 1915

In visiting the little Ditchingham dressmaker, Mrs Charles, Louie observed that her room was piled-up with work, and expressed surprise that it should be so in these times. Mrs Charles explained that the clothes were not being made for the gentry, but for the poor people, who were ordering many more garments than usual, owing to their having so much more money to spend. The Bungay drapers tell the same tale as to smart hats, etc. I believe that in this neighbourhood few of those in receipt of separation allowances are putting anything by. They spend what they get, and when the money ceases to come in will, I suppose, rely on charity, since it is sure there will not be work for all the returning soldiers.

20th May, 1915

We have received a wire from Rodney[1] at the Admiralty stating that there is no need to be anxious about Geoffrey as a prisoner in the hands of the Turks. Still, in view of the hideous atrocities which the said Turks are reported to be committing on the Christians who fall into their hands, I do remain anxious. All life is one long anxiety now-a-days.

22nd May, 1915

Yesterday I wrote a letter to Curzon begging him to try and enter the Coalition Ministry, because I consider him one of the best available men. After all, as I tried to point out, the choice is very limited. Few of the really first class men of the country are in the political line of life. To many of these the subterfuges, and humiliations, the renunciations of principles and judgement, and even of truth, are quite abhorrent and therefore they cannot touch politics. I know this is my own

---

[1]Rodney Kempt was the cousin of Rider Haggard's wife.

case; I tried it once[1] but never again, for when the thing was over I felt as though I had emerged from a mud bath.

11th June, 1915

I have been to London to attend the Royal Agricultural Society's Allies Relief Committee, where we voted a sum of money to assist in buying implements for devastated districts in France. The accounts written by the gentlemen we sent to Serbia are horrible. Every sort of terrible outrange seems to have been committed in the country on man, woman and child by the Austrians acting on the German model. I even heard of some wounded who were found buried alive.

Also I saw Sir Sidney Olivier[2] as to possibilities of Land Settlement for soldiers after the war, and generally talked over the agricultural position with him. He told me that Lord Selborne[3] is receiving a lot of fine confused advice from farmers.

I am completing the insurance against war risks of all my property. It is a heavy pull but one, I suppose, that should be faced. I should never be surprised to hear that one of the coast towns had been burned and its population massacred. Moreover we have to deal with an army of spies and uninterned Germans, who, as is admitted in Parliament, can still be counted by the thousand. No doubt all these gentry have matches and know how to use them.

15th June, 1915

In a letter from Roosevelt which I received this morning, he writes, 'As for the *Lusitania*[4] affair, you know what I have said: you know what I would do if I were president.' I do and I wish to heaven that he were.

(My birthday)   *22nd June, 1915*

Kipling has been making a good speech, a report of which appears in the *Morning Post*. It says exactly what we all think, neither more nor less, pointing out the terrible things that defeat would mean to this nation. The speech was made at a recruiting meeting and its first words were: 'I am here to speak on behalf of a system in which I do not believe. . . the system of voluntary service. It seems to me

---

[1]In 1895 Rider Haggard stood unsuccessfully as the Conservative and Unionist candidate in the East Norfolk constituency.
[2]He was Secretary to the Board of Agriculture.
[3]William Waldegrave Palmer, 2nd Earl of Selborne, had recently been made President of the Board of Agriculture.
[4]The American liner *Lusitania* was torpedoed by the Germans on 8th May. Over 1500 people were lost.

unfair and unbusinesslike that after ten months of war we should still be raising men by the same methods as we raise money at a charity bazaar.' The audience said 'Hear, hear,' to this, as I do very heartily.

I have received a letter from Watt enclosing one from Cassell's[1], in which the latter request that any authors writing fiction for them will avoid all mention of the war. This is a curious little sign of the times, but what it means exactly I cannot pretend to say — that the public is 'sick of the war' I suppose. If so I am not certain that this attitude is healthy, although personally the last thing I want to read or write fiction about is the war.

23rd June, 1915

Yesterday my brother Will came from Bradenham to lunch and brought with him his wife's sister-in-law, Mrs Hancox, the wife of Colonel Hancox who is at the front and the mother of Lieut. Hancox, R.N. who is in the Dardanelles. Will gave me on what he said 'ought to be good authority' an account of the origin of Churchill's[2] action in the Dardanelles. He said he was told there was a meeting between Kitchener, Fisher[3] and Churchill before operations were commenced. Churchill asked for 100,000 men as a land force. Kitchener replied that he could not spare them from the front and that those in England were not sufficiently trained. Fisher said nothing one way or the other. Churchill insisted; Kitchener politely declined to find the men. At last Churchill sprang up shouting out, 'The fleet will be in the Dardanelles next week,' stamped from the room and slammed the door behind him. Such is the story.

24th June, 1915

Rose[4] has brought me a patent anti-gas respirator which I am to keep by my bedside, a peculiarly hideous article that looks somewhat like an executioner's mask. Such are the birthday gifts in this year of Count Zeppelin 1915.

25th June, 1915

I have received a polite letter from Lord Selborne explaining nebulously why he,

---

[1]Cassell and Company had published several of Rider Haggard's books, including in 1885 his first success, *King Solomon's Mines*.
[2]At the time he was 1st Lord of the Admiralty. After the Dardanelles disaster he served for a time with the Army in France.
[3]He was the First Sea Lord.
[4]Rose Hildyard, Louie's cousin, had lived with the Haggards to help look after the children since 1900.

or rather the permanent officials at the Board of Agriculture, finds it impossible to make use of my services in any capacity. It would appear that men like myself who have life-long experience and much accumulated knowledge are practically of no value to the country. Yet foolishly enough perhaps, I feel sore, and not altogether for my own sake, since I know well enough that I could still do good work for the nation, if only I were given the chance. At present the only opportunity I have been offered — tentatively — is that of investigating the claims of soldiers' dependents to allowances!

28th June, 1915

Yesterday I invested money, which now grows scarce, in the purchase of a sporting Lee Mitford from Willie Carr who had the foresight to buy several at the beginning of the war, and this afternoon I am going to be instructed in its action. In my youth I was accustomed to rifle shooting in Africa, but then we always used Martinis and Westley Richards falling-blocks and I do not understand these new-fashioned magazine rifles. We have a kind of Volunteer Corps here and this I propose to join, if only nominally, for since I hurt the muscles of my leg a couple of years ago jumping out of the way of a taxi-cab I am too lame to do much drilling. But I can shoot and am still man enough to fight Germans from ditch to ditch until knocked out. I would sooner die in putting up a fight against them than in any other way. Alas! that such a thing should have happened when one has grown old and useless. How I envy all my nephews who can go to the front.

A cutting has been sent to me *a propos* of some comments on my birthday in the *Evening Standard*, wherein a certain Mr J. M.S. Brooke writes as follows: 'Sir, my cousin, the late Major General E. T. Brooke R. E., has often told me that he, and he alone, hoisted the Union Jack at Pretoria.[1] He also added that Sir R. Haggard asked him to be allowed "to put his hand on the rope". I really thought that this controversy had been settled long ago.'

I cannot believe that the late General Brooke, who was a close friend of mine until I lost sight of him, ever said anything of the sort, except perhaps as a jest, for he was a great joker. Also at an important public ceremony, as was the hoisting of the flag at Pretoria in 1877, in which all of us on Sir T. Shepstone's Staff had our allotted parts, it is, of course, ridiculous to suppose that I could have somehow cut in and begged Brooke to allow me to lay my hand 'upon the rope'. The truth is that as the youngest member of the Staff I was ordered, in conjunction with Colonel Brooke who was its senior Military member, to formally hoist this flag, though whether I lifted it from the ground and Brooke ran it up, or Brooke lifted it and I ran it up, I cannot now remember, but I think I did the latter. When I was in

---

[1]Rider Haggard (who was then twenty) and Colonel E. T. Brooke were two of the small party that in 1877 accompanied Sir Theophilus Shepstone when he was sent as Special Commissioner to the Transvaal. On 24th May, Queen Victoria's Birthday, the Union Jack was hoisted to mark formally the Annexation of the Transvaal.

Pretoria the other day I met people who quite well remembered the incident. Jeppe, the Administrator, also recalled to my mind what I had forgotten — namely — that when the late Sir Melmoth Osborne grew nervous in reading the proclamation, I took it from his hand and finished the business.

30th June, 1915

I have heard from Curzon who tells me that if he can hear of any suitable public work for me to do, he will bear me in mind 'since you are just the man who ought to be employed at such a time as this'. But I don't suppose he will hear of anything for 'at such a time as this' everybody is wanted collectively, but individually very few indeed are wanted.

1st July, 1915

I practised rifle shooting yesterday morning, and in the dim light under the trees found that my eyesight leaves much to be desired, as it was difficult to see either the fore-sight or the bull's eye. I must get some clearing glasses.

5th July, 1915

I went to Norwich this morning to be fitted with glasses for rifle shooting; also to try to buy some cartridges for practice purposes. The difficulty of obtaining these appears to be almost insuperable, although Mr Rudd[1] had plenty in his shop. It does seem absurd that volunteers, such as I am now, should be unable to buy a few ball cartridges, even of the sort that are used in rook-rifles, to enable them to perfect themselves in shooting at a target. Mr Rudd was extremely emphatic on the subject. He may not even sell rifles that he has in stock to equip volunteers. He says that the War Office is responsible for these silly regulations.

12th July, 1915

Yesterday I drilled with the Ditchingham and Bungay Volunteer Defence Corps on the Common, whereof I am a platoon Commander. The spectacle was distinctly funny — that of a lot of determined old gents stumping about and doing their best to execute manoeuvres which they did not understand. However, if only rifles and ammunition are given to them, I am convinced that they and tens of thousands like them would be most useful stuff in the event of invasion. Even if one is over 40 one can still hold a gun straight enough to shoot a German and we have the advantages of knowing the country. But the ammunition seems to be the trouble.

Athenaeum Club   *17th July, 1915*

I have come to town to stay with D'Abernon till Monday.

[1] Arthur James Rudd, gun and fishing tackle depot, 54 London Street, Norwich.

34

Esher Place   *19th July, 1915*

At Esher I met Lord Crowe[1] who was staying with D'Abernon. He had recently been acting as Secretary for Foreign Affairs, during the absence of Sir E. Grey, whose sight he tells me is much better, although for a while at any rate he will have to depend much upon others in the way of reading and writing. I had several talks with him. He strikes me as an able, painstaking and most industrious man, but not one, for instance, who could be trusted to settle the Welsh Mining crisis. The Hon. George Lambton[2], who was also staying in the house, told me that he had known him intimately from a boy, but to the best of his recollection he never yet heard him express a decided opinion about anything; that he walked round and round a matter without ever getting to the centre. For the rest he is a very perfect type of the section of the English nobility which serves the State, courteous, well-educated, well-informed, averse to strong views, unwilling to believe strong statements. I do not think one meets such men anywhere else in the world, at least I never have.

It was curious to me to watch all these brilliant and exalted folk, Mrs Winston Churchill — a very handsome young woman — among them, playing every kind of game (golf and tennis in the day time and bridge at night) there in that soft lap of luxury and wealth, with its wonderful gardens, priceless pictures and the rest, at this somewhat dark hour in a struggle to which only light and casual allusion was made from time to time, and to wonder what would happen to these and their kind, and indeed to all of us, if we should chance to go down in the war. Then how fearsome might be the debacle; how many of the houses great and fair without inhabitants! But I think that the thought of such catastrophes is as yet far from any of them, which is comforting, since they are in a position to know the facts. At any rate the shadow of it does not yet lie thick upon their Sunday bridge and tennis.

D'Abernon told me that the Canadian Government is anxious that our Royal Dominions Commission should go to Canada at once to finish our investigations there and that Bonar Law seems to favour the notion. I do not quite see how it is to be done but we must meet and discuss.

Ditchingham   *23rd July, 1915*

I went to London yesterday and took part in the Royal Colonial Institute 'After the War' Deputation to Mr Bonar Law and Lord Selborne, making one of the speeches on Oversea Land Settlement of soldiers and sailors at the end of the war. Sir John Taverner, the ex-Australian Agent General who also spoke, suggested that I should be sent round the Dominions to find out the minds of their governments on this and kindred matters, a remark at which Mr Bonar Law

---

[1]This is a mistake of Rider Haggard's. It was Sir Eyre Crowe (he was never given a peerage). He worked at the Foreign Office.
[2]He was the fifth son of 2nd Earl of Durham and the younger brother of Admiral Meux.

nodded his head. Whether anything will come of it, I neither know nor greatly care. In the course of his reply Lord Selborne went rather out of his way to pay a heavy and evidently premeditated compliment to Mr Christopher Turnor[1] and myself, whom he described as two of the greatest agricultural experts in the country, or words to that effect. But as Lord Sydenham[2] said to me, as we were walking away together, if he holds that opinion of us, as I believe he honestly does, why in Heaven's name does he not put us on his Committee?

The aspect of the crops on the way to London is deplorable, which in this year of struggle is most unfortunate. Where there are decent fields of corn, in many instances they lie as flat as though a steam roller had passed over them.

Windham Club, London   *27th July, 1915*

Came to London. Lunched here with Bateman, who says he is willing to make the Canada expedition, so I suppose we shall go.

I went to the British Museum after the sitting of R. A. Belgian Relief Committee and saw that many of the more valuable exhibits (for instance the Rosetta Stone and the Elgin Marbles) have been removed to the vaults for fear of Zeppelin attack.

29th July, 1915

At our Royal Commission meeting yesterday we found that only Sir Alfred Bateman and I, out of the 11 members present, were willing and able to proceed to Canada. The Canadian Government is to be cabled and we must await its decision.

Ditchingham   *3rd August, 1915*

Watts[3] has been to cut my hair. He says one of his men was at Southwold, I think on Saturday, and saw a torpedo fired from a German submarine at two patrol vessels, which it missed. He watched the bubbles made by its course as it travelled along parallel with the shore till ultimately it struck the beach or something else and went off a fearful bang.

4th August, 1915

We have been at war for a year today. How much has happened since I chronicled its declaration in my pocket book in Newfoundland and how many prophecies

[1]In 1919 Turnor made an overseas tour to investigate progress made in land settlement.
[2]George Sydenham Clarke, 1st Baron Sydenham, served on many Government bodies. He wrote many books.
[3]Edgar Watts, furniture dealer, Broad Street, Bungay.

have been falsified. Much do I wonder whether August 4, 1916 will find us still struggling for our national life, also whether I shall still be keeping this diary. From a telegram I received this morning I imagine that I shall soon return to Canada. Bonar Law, however, writes to D'Abernon that he is not prepared 'at present' to recommend that a mission should be sent to enquire into land settlement for soldiers in the Dominions. This means of course that enough pressure has not been put on by the Dominion Governments. Indeed it is doubtful whether these really want immigrants, especially in the case of the Australasian Labour Governments. Also the end of the war seems some way off!

7th August, 1915

I have signed a petition for National Service which is being circulated by the *Daily Mail*.

Yarmouth   *8th August, 1915*

Came to Yarmouth to spend the week-end with Angie and Dolly. Notwithstanding the war the place seemed crowded though not, I should say, with the best class of visitors. I see a great number of lusty young men on the beach who have apparently escaped the attentions of the recruiting sergeant.

Angie and I attended the intercession service in the splendid parish church, the largest in England. It was crowded with some thousands of soldiers and civilians, Mayor in robes etc. The service was very impressive, a brass band supporting the organ and choir. We had special prayers (with intervals for private devotion) for the King, the soldiers and sailors, the fallen, our Allies, and even for the political leaders of the nation who, it is probable, need them just now. A very fine sermon also. I am glad to have been present.

A long telegram from Harding[1] about our Canadian journey. It is now suggested, apparently, that I and perhaps one other Commissioner should go ahead and inspect middle Canada. I don't know what will be arranged.

Ditchingham   *9th August, 1915*

Last night at Yarmouth we had an amusing instance of what the spy mania can do. The venetian blinds and curtains in Angie and Dolly's lodgings are not of the newest or best. The latter feeling warm, opened the window behind the blind. Presently there arose murmurs from the esplanade without, which I should explain is plunged in the most intense darkness in these dark and moonless nights and yet seems to be the haunt of hundreds who wander about in the gloom, feeling their way from post to post. Next the landlady's daughter arrived saying that

[1]Sir Edward Harding was Secretary of the Dominions Royal Commission.

37

soldiers and police had called complaining that light was escaping from the window; that the esplanade was filled from side to side with a mob who swore that signalling to the Germans was going on from the house and that there was much excitement. She added that the same thing had happened to them some weeks ago when the rooms were occupied by Army officers and that they were always being worried by police and soldiers and boy scouts. Indeed this was the third time that it had happened since Angie and Dolly had been in the house. Well the windows were blocked up with old rugs and whatever could be got but the crowd would not disperse. Indeed some hours afterwards when I was in bed in my room next door I still heard the police urging them to move on. And the whole thing is a madness for how could anyone signal with a lamp or a candle over the Yarmouth Roads filled with mine sweepers to the deep water miles away? In Yarmouth I am informed this spy hunting has become an absolute mania, so much so that the unfortunate land-lady of number 59 thinks she will have to leave the house.

10th August, 1915

War comes very near to us. Last night about 10.30 we heard the heavy detonation of bombs from the direction of the coast, so heavy that windows shook and clocks were stopped at the Lodge. Personally I heard about 12, but observers on the Common counted 30, though some of these may have been anti-aircraft guns. It is hard on people like myself, with Angie and Dolly and Dolly's children at Yarmouth, not to be able to discover whether these accursed machines did or did not visit the town. We wired early but have had no answer. All I can gather from railway guards, P.O. offficials etc. is that the Zeppelins attacked the front at Lowestoft, killing soldiers and others.

11th August, 1915

Angie and Dolly returned from Yarmouth last evening. After wiring that they meant to stay they went to Lowestoft and saw the terrible damage done by the bombs: the wrecked houses, the shattered windows, the bed from which a poor girl had been hurled and killed etc., etc. This changed their minds and they hurried to Ditchingham, which they should never have left, after wiring to me that they intended to stay as they were enjoying the excitement of it. Well, it shows a good spirit.

13th August, 1915

Yesterday I was summoned to London to discuss the question of Canada or no Canada. As a sequel to volume of cables over the earth, the Duke [of Connaught] wires agreeing to our proposals but, after all his implorations, throwing the onus of decision as to a Canadian tour at this juncture on to the shoulders of the

Commission. Their judgement being thus freed, none of them wished to go at such a time! Indeed I was the only one to vote for it, on the ground that I did not want to change my plans any more — an insufficient reason. So the thing is put off indefinitely and I think with wisdom. Still I wish I had some public work to do!

I have written to Reggie to find out if it would be possible for me to visit the front.

15th August, 1915

Yesterday I motored to Southwold and Lowestoft. Southwold is deserted. No one on the beach, except a few soldiers and their girls. Barbed wire defences everywhere, also trenches and sandbags though what the use of them is I do not know as they look to me as though they could easily be turned by an invading force taking advantage of the deep water to land here — if it can. At Lowestoft I saw the bomb-shattered houses. In one of them a poor old landlady sat disconsolate by her broken window — a melancholy sight. The proprietor of the tea-shop told me she was shutting up her place and going away.

17th August, 1915

I went to Diss last night to speak at a volunteer meeting. A Diss audience is not inspiring. Line upon line they sit in solemn silence, looking as though they wondered when the plate was coming round, while the poor speaker must ply their solid ranks with precept upon precept that they do not seem to understand. Bungay with all thy faults I love thee still — a Bungay audience is very different.

19th August, 1915

Old Mr Woods[1] tells me that signals are being made nightly to Zeppelins from a road just outside Bungay. An innocent-looking market cart is used. Apparently it has candle-lights but inside are powerful acetylene lamps which are used to signal to the Zeppelins in the Morse code. Last night the signallers could get no answer but the night before they were answered. Woods has been collecting the evidence in his official capacity and is going to make an effort to catch the signallers tonight. I fear, however, that they will have got wind of his intentions. I have no doubt but that the real object of these Zeppelin visits is to collect information. The bomb dropping is a mere by-the-way amusement.

21st August, 1915

I went to Norwich today to attend a farmers' meeting about the purchase of a Shire

[1]Woods worked for Rider Haggard and was, during the war, a special constable.

stallion and travelled with the Bishop of St Asaph. He had just seen Churchill and said that he found him 'very shaky' and somewhat unnerved by the Dardanelles news. It appears that there has been a bad upset there.

26th August, 1915

It is curious how little we hear of the King now-a-days, except that he has been here or there to visit troops or hospitals. In all the private discussion on the war at which I have been present, I have never heard his name mentioned. No one asks what does the King think or what line is he taking? Personally I think this a pity as what the nation needs more than anything just now is a strong man somewhere. I think too that if Edward still occupied the throne it would be otherwise.

28th August, 1915

I went to Dalling today to see Lilias[1] and watched the destroyers streaming past, also the aeroplanes flying over Norwich. During the light the place is much as usual, but as soon as dark comes, Lilias says it becomes as armed camp. I passed through Stalham where I was besieged and stoned during the election of 1895 and looked with interest at the spot where our coach was dragged across the road by a mob of hired Radical roughs.[2]

30th August, 1915

This morning at the Bungay Bench I presided at the trial of 11 cases of exposed lights. We inflicted various fines and I hope that more care will now be taken. Here again there is a lack of discipline. No one will pay heed to the orders or to the warnings of the Police; at least many will not.

4th September, 1915

Yesterday I was in town giving evidence before the committee appointed to consider the settlement of soldiers and sailors on the land at the end of the war. The committee were so good as to say that my evidence was very interesting, whether it will encourage them to urge the country to spend a good many millions in a land settlement experiment of great size I do not know. Personally I have grave doubts of the success of the venture although nobody can hope more earnestly than I do that it may succeed.

[1]Rider Haggard's youngest daughter, who was doing war work.
[2]Following this 'Battle of Stalham Bridge', Lord Wodehouse and a drover named Saul were charged with common assault.

Leenane Hotel, Co. Galway, Ireland   *14th September, 1915*

I have just arrived with Lilias for a fishing holiday. We crossed from Holyhead last night in perfect safety, but I think that submarines and mines were present to the thoughts of all aboard.

Ledbury[1]   *30th September, 1915*

Last night I arrived in London from Ireland where our fishing was a fraud. Travelling to Ledbury today the train, usually so crowded, was almost empty. The guard told me the passenger traffic was falling off very much on the Great Western, he did not know why.

5th October, 1915

I am much puzzled. The *Yorkshire Post* makes the following announcement: 'Mr Bonar Law has received from the Governments of the Dominions promises to cooperate in making provision for settling returned soldiers on the land. Mr Law has accordingly appointed a small Commission, of which Sir Rider Haggard is chairman, to visit the Dominions with a view to drawing up a scheme.'

Now I have heard nothing from Bonar Law or anyone else, except casual correspondents who wish to be connected with the Commission, as to the truth or falsity of this report. I have wired to Harding to ask for the facts. If there is anything in it, which personally I doubt, the business will be large and important and involve more world-wanderings.

Ditchingham   *7th October, 1915*

John Kipling, Rudyard Kipling's son, whom I have known from a child, is wounded and missing, but there is still hope that he may be a prisoner as he was not severely hurt when last seen. Poor Kipling, I know how great have been his anxieties about this boy ever since he entered the Irish Guards about a year ago; now they must be terrible. I know too what view he takes of the world as a place of abode for mortals. I wonder what he thinks of it today! I wrote him a brief note from the Club, but perhaps he has gone to France. Personally I still hope that John may be alive. One wonders how he came to be abandoned in a wounded condition.

16th October, 1915

Watt sends me an extract from a letter from Mrs Kipling about John. It seems that at the beginning of the month, according to a communication received from his Colonel, he was with his men in advance under a Captain of the Scots Guards.

[1]Rider Haggard was visiting his elder sister, Mrs Ella Green.

There were 200 men and but one man returned. 'They were enfiladed, and John was seen to fall, get up and go into a small shed which was almost immediately surrounded.' He was in advance of his men at the time and up to last Tuesday nothing more had been heard of him. Still he may be captured and alive. It is terribly anxious work for his family. If perchance he is dead, it would be better to know the worst at once. Yet his is only one of hundreds of similar cases which excites my particular interest because I happen to know him and his parents.

18th October, 1915

It seems that Miss Edith Cavell, the daughter of the late Rev. F. Cavell, Vicar of Swardeston, near Norwich, who has been murdered at Brussels by the Germans for assisting Belgians to escape from that city, met her end bravely. She fainted, however, in the presence of the firing party, whereon the officer in charge blew her brains out with his revolver. May Heaven avenge this noble woman, whose fate, perhaps, will help to bring home to the civilised world what German dominion really means. So would our wives and daughters be dealt with if ever the Huns got a footing in England.

19th October, 1915

I see that John Kipling is included in the list of *missing* only, not among the 'missing and wounded', or 'missing believed killed', so there is good hope that he has been taken prisoner.

29th October, 1915

Today I went to London to attend a Committee Meeting at the Royal Colonial Institute on the question of Empire Land-Settlement. It is obvious that the Government will do nothing to help this forward and the question arose as to whether the Royal Colonial Institute should not undertake the work and send me to the various Dominions to interview their Governments. As nothing could be settled then, I defer any comments. This attending of committees from so great a distance is tiring and expensive work but perhaps it is as well that I went.

I passed St Paul's Cathedral in a bus about noon, not without difficulty because of the great crowd that had gathered to attend the memorial service to Miss Cavell. It was not till 3.30 in the afternoon, but I was told that people had been waiting to get in since 8 or 9 in the morning. This shows the public interest in the case. I observed that there are still plenty of young men unenlisted in London. In the bus alone I think I counted six.

13th November, 1915

Today I was at Norwich elected Chairman of a local committee which gives me a seat on the Norfolk War Agricultural Committee. But what the said committee is to do remains somewhat vague. Apparently its objects are to increase the output of food stuffs and to deal with the question of agricultural labour.

26th November, 1915

Today as a Governor of the Bungay Grammar School, I attended a meeting as to the volunteering of the headmaster and his assistant, both of whom are of military age, the latter an unmarried man of 22. The governors present, leading tradesmen of the town and a non-conformist minister, wished to advise the assistant to apply to be enlisted in a lower group which would have the effect of postponing his call to the colours. I said I thought this wrong under our circumstances but was entirely outvoted. The truth is that in this country there are still very many who put convenience or the advantage of any institution with which they are connected before the needs of the nation. So it must be unless and until we have some system of conscription. The headmaster, a married man of thirty-eight, we all, of course, looked on as indispensable.

10th December, 1915

I have just been on the telephone with Sir Harry Wilson[1], the Secretary of the Royal Colonial Institute. Mr Bonar Law will not help officially about Land Settlement in the Dominions but Sir Harry says that there is no doubt that it will be arranged for me to go to Australasia, though nothing definite can be said until the money for expenses is subscribed. Doubtless I shall hear more before long.

13th December, 1915

Labour difficulties on the land are increasing. Here is an instance. This year we are very much behind with our best lifting; indeed never in my life have I known mangolds pulled within ten days of Xmas. To make matters worse the weather has been wet and stormy with frosts. The nett result is, so far as I am concerned, that I have about 150 loads of mangold which will probably rot in the ground — also that none of my kales are earthed up. On one field only 10 or 12 loads remain to get, but as Saturday morning was wet the pullers did not come. At breakfast time it cleared and became beautifully fine, but for the whole of the rest of that day those men loafed in public-houses, although well they knew how great was the emergency. Result — before Monday the frost had set in and those beet will, I suppose, be ruined.

Such are the troubles the farmer has to face, and such is the spirit of the agricultural labourer in England. I have made up my mind that as soon as I can I shall get out of farming.

[1] Sir Harry Wilson was from 1915 to 1921 Secretary of the Royal Commonwealth Society.

22nd December, 1915

I have been in town for the last day or two attending a meeting of the Council of the Royal Colonial Institute and of the Committee as to my going to Australasia on behalf of the former. Everything seemed to be satisfactorily arranged, but a new point has arisen which I confess I overlooked. I am a Royal Commissioner and though unpaid more or less, I presume under the control of the Government even while the Royal Commission is indefinitely adjourned. Now the Colonial Office is against this mission, fearing, I imagine, with the prescience of officials that it might result in giving them trouble in one way or another at some future date. Therefore it is quite possible that Mr Bonar Law will put a spoke into our wheel and stop me from going. At any rate, as the point has been raised it must be followed up which means more delay. Somehow, I begin to doubt whether I shall ever get off to Australasia, nor do I really greatly care. I think it would be a good bit of Empire work which I should be very glad to put in as my offering, since I am too old to fight, but if the Government chooses to thwart it, as up to the present it has thwarted it in every way, notwithstanding all the representations that have been made to it from different quarters, well, I have nothing to say. Then I shall stop at home and attend to my own affairs.

I saw Kipling in town. He has heard nothing of John and evidently has practically lost hope. He says that from all the accounts he can gather, the boy made a good end in his first action, that he liked his men and was liked by them. Poor lad! He added that he was very fond of me and asked me what I had done to make his children so fond of me. I answered I didn't know except that young people like those who like them — a fact, I think, to which I owe the affection of so many of my nieces and nephews. Rudyard Kipling expressed his opinion of the Government and individual members thereof in language too strong to write down even in a private diary. His vigour on the subject is amazing.

24th December, 1915

This is Xmas Eve and in reflecting on all that has happened since last Christmas, I have come to the conclusion that had I been an agnostic at Christmas 1914, I should have come to believe in God by Christmas 1915. For nothing short of the goodness and protection of God could, in my opinion, have preserved this country during the last twelve months from reaping the fruits of ruin from the seeds that it has been busy sowing for over a generation.

27th December, 1915

Today I interviewed a young wounded soldier of the Irish Guards, named Bowe. He was near to John Kipling (within forty yards) when they entered the wood near Givenchy where the latter vanished. What became of him remains a mystery.

44

He may have rushed ahead in charging the German Maxims and been captured. If he fell it is a marvel that he was not picked up as the wood remained in our hands for days. Bowe and another man named Frankland who was with him were of the opinion that he was either blown absolutely to bits by a large shell, which they had seen happen several times, or taken and murdered in the German lines during the two hours that elapsed before they finally rushed the wood. These possibilities, however, I did not put down in the signed statement which I sent to Rudyard Kipling. There is still a faint hope that he is a prisoner. He has just vanished. Bowe said that the poor boy was much liked.

28th December, 1915

Lilias has received a letter from Frankland, the soldier who accompanied Bowe here yesterday — a very well educated man. He writes that Bowe, who is a very nervous youth and shy, now remembers certain other things about John Kipling. 'Bowe *did* see Lieut. Kipling after the wood was taken under the following circumstances. The Irish Guards had dug themselves in on the edge of the wood when they heard a loud shouting from a body of men in their rear. The Sergeant in charge, thinking the Germans were making a flank or rear attack, ordered them to retire from the wood. This they did and found the noise to be the cheers of the Grenadier Guards who had come up to support the Irish. Bowe now says that as they left this wood he saw an officer who *he could swear* was Mr Kipling leaving the wood on his way to the rear and trying to fasten a field dressing round his mouth which was badly shattered by a piece of shell. Bowe would have helped him but for the fact that the officer was crying with the pain of the wound and he did not want to humiliate him by offering assistance.' I shall not send this on to Rudyard Kipling — it is too painful, but, I fear, true. Still it makes J. Kipling's disappearance still more of a mystery. A shell must have buried him, I think.

1916

After weeks of preparation, Rider Haggard set off on 10th February as the honorary representative of the Royal Colonial Institute to ascertain by local inquiry the possibilities of after-the-war settlement of sailors and soldiers. He saw the mission as his war offering. During the next four months he travelled to South Africa, Tasmania, Australia, New Zealand and Canada. Although he had not been sent by the British Government, which seemed less than enthusiastic about his mission, he spent his days badgering officials, giving interviews, and compiling a detailed report. His aim was to obtain from each state government a promissory letter detailing the help that would be granted after the war.

On his return to England, Rider Haggard was warmly welcomed but he was not surprised to discover that his achievements were not rated as highly as they had been in the Dominions. At home the war was still dragging on with the same problems of wrecked ships, strikes, spy-scares, food shortages, and heavy troop casualties. And in Ditchingham Rider Haggard met a new danger — Zeppelins. Having travelled safely right round the world, he faced bombs in his own home.

Asquith fell, to be replaced by Lloyd George; but neither of the Prime Ministers called upon Rider Haggard to serve his country officially. Perhaps it was just as well, for his health had been adversely affected by his long, tiring journey, and he had still his living to earn. So Rider Haggard wintered in Budleigh Salterton and wrote.

The weather on this first of January is as dreary as the news and the immediate outlook. Still for my part I enter on this year with high hopes, believing as I do that it will see the downfall of Germany and the triumph of the Allies. But even if that happens, what else it will see in this country is more than I can guess, since here *after* the war will be worse than the war itself.

3rd January, 1916

Yesterday I received my marching orders from the Royal Colonial Institute. South Africa, Australasia, Canada, a long and arduous business! I can only hope that the mission will be fortunate and fruitful. At any rate it is my duty to take the risks, go ahead and do the work to the best of my ability. Here is my war offering!

Queen Anne's Mansions, London   10th January, 1916

I write this at night after a long day in London. First I saw Sir Owen Phillips, the Chairman of the Union Castle Line, who told me that if any emigration scheme was inaugurated in Rhodesia or S.W. Africa he would undertake to bring out the wives and families or sweethearts of settlers free for a period of two or three years. Then to lunch with D'Abernon and afterwards to the offices of the Dominion Royal Commission at Scotland House, where we met Harding and went into all the matters that the Royal Commission would like to enquire into in the various Dominions — plenty of them, especially the Cape Route to Australasia. As to these I am to have letters. Then to the Royal Colonial Institute where the farewell lunch to me was arranged and other things. So here to dine tired.

Ditchingham   12th January, 1916

In a letter from Rudyard Kipling today, he asks, 'Have you observed in your correspondence that the percentage of d---d, vacuous, idle, unconnected idiots rises steadily with every month of the war?' *Yes, I have.*

14th January, 1916

I have had a letter from John Ward[1] thanking me for mine. It is extraordinarily to his credit that a man who writes like a child and cannot spell should have risen so high and done such good work in the world.

15th January, 1916

After a long delay, so Lord Sydenham writes to me, some secret Committee at the

[1]John Ward began work at seven. He became a trade unionist (founding the General Labourers Union) and a socialist. In 1914 he recruited five labour battalions. He became a lieutenant-colonel.

Foreign Office has declined to allow Mr Corbett[1] to accompany me on my tour. Moreover, it seems that the tribunal to which he should have a right of appeal does not exist. Therefore he must stop at home and I must search for another secretary at the last moment.

18th January, 1916

All day I have been employed telegraphing, telephoning, writing letters over the Corbett affair, with what success remains to be seen. I have now been driven to advertising for a secretary, a dangerous experiment. But I must get a man somehow.

20th January, 1916

I have had a very nice letter from Sir W. Robertson Nicoll[2] about his review of *The Ivory Child*[3] in which he says, 'There is something of profound and awful truth in the way you speak of love at the end of the book.' A high compliment from such a source. Am awfully busy making preparations and over the Corbett affair.

22nd January, 1916

At length the complication about my secretary has been cleared up, but not until I had used every ounce of interest which I possess. He has just wired that his passport has been granted. What an infinity of trouble it would have saved us all if this had been done a fortnight ago.

28th January, 1916

For the first time in my life I have been cinematographed today. A photograph in which you are told to move about and talk, instead of sitting like a lay figure, is something of a novelty.

Great Eastern Hotel, Liverpool Street   *31st January, 1916*

I arrived in London with Louie on Saturday night and have been very busy ever since. This afternoon I went to the last day of Raemaeker's[4] war cartoons. Here I committed a great extravagance, buying for twenty-five guineas his cartoon of

[1]A. R. Uvedale Corbett appears to have been recruited by the Royal Colonial Institute to serve as Rider Haggard's secretary.
[2]He was the editor of *British Weekly* and the *Bookman*.
[3]It had been published by Cassell and Company on 6th January, 1916.
[4]Louis Raemaeker won world-wide fame with his vicious anti-German war cartoons.

President Wilson which appeared in *Land and Water*. Also I met Mr Raemaeker himself, who knew all about me and had read my books. He is a jolly-faced, little Hollander of genius. I told him that if he gave them to me I would not have most of his cartoons (which are nearly all sold) in the house — too horrible.

I have arrived back at the hotel to be told that the Zeppelins are coming. If so, it is likely to be warm work here at Liverpool Street, but we are all in the hands of Heaven and must take our chance.

1st February, 1916

We had an extraordinary time last night over those Zeppelins. Cochrane and Stuart came to dinner. Cochrane came by the tube, which he found packed with thousands who had taken refuge there, with also some waiting for trains that did not appear. He had great difficulty in fighting his way out. There was no panic, he said, but it would have been easy for one to develop, if for instance the lights had gone out. People think them safe, but in fact the tubes are terribly dangerous in such emergencies.

We proceeded to go down to dinner, but in the hall found that the lights were out in the dining room and dinner was 'off'. Instead we were informed that the Zepps. would arrive in a few minutes, and were conducted to a marble Masonic Chapel on the lower floor, which was supposed to be bomb-proof. Here, in a dim religious light, with the rest of the hotel guests we remained in cold storage (it was *very* cold) for about two hours. At length, able to bear no more we broke away upstairs, creeping through miles of dark passages with the help of an electric torch. By now we were ravenous, and tried to get something to eat. In the end we did secure some cold meat in the dining room but, as it was ten o'clock, under the new regulations nothing to drink. (I told D'Abernon today how we cursed him — he was delighted.[1]) Cochrane had to sleep in the hotel and so ended our Zeppelin adventure. No doubt they came very near London but not, I think, over it.

The lunch given to myself by the Royal Colonial Institute at the Hotel Cecil was a great success, and a still greater personal compliment, one, I confess, that moved me much. About 250 were present, among them many well known and public people. Curzon presided and spoke most handsomely of me, as did D'Abernon. The former declared I was a 'great Empire servant' going on a great errand and the latter bore very generous testimony to my public work.

During the next ten days Haggard was kept extremely busy speaking to people about his mission, writing letters (including two to The Times*) and attending various meetings.*

[1]He was the Chairman of the Liquor Board, which in an effort to restrict drinking had introduced the Licensing Laws with which Great Britain is still afflicted.

7th February, 1916

Went to Lucoque's[1] to see films, including that of myself from the cinematograph taken at Ditchingham the other day. Very good and amusing, especially the ones with my spaniel Jeekie and Dolly's children. Met Miss Hector[2] at Lucoque's and signed agreement with Ward Lock for *Finished*.[3]

Kenilworth Castle   *11th February, 1916*

Yesterday I departed from London — a melancholy business. Louie, Angie and Lilias came to see me off at Paddington, also D'Abernon, Sir H. Wilson, and many others. Well, we steamed away and it was over, leaving my heart sore for starting on so perilous a journey. I wondered if we should ever meet again. Oh! it is a sad world, so full of partings. I enter on this great undertaking without illusions, for estimating the risks of my non-return at from thirty to forty per cent. The seas are very dangerous in these times and it will indeed be fortunate if we get back to England without accident by torpedo or otherwise. Still I take the chance gladly because I hope to do good work for the Empire. We (Corbett and I) slept at the Duke of Gloucester Hotel at Plymouth; it was pleasant to see a town brilliantly lighted again.

 Last night I wrote several letters home etc., and this morning we came aboard the *Kenilworth Castle*. She seems a full ship. We sit at table in life-saving waist-coats. What hateful times we live in!

16th February, 1916

On Monday night about ten we reached Madeira which looked beautiful beneath the moon, with its bright lights shining in squares and lines and clusters and running high up the encircling mountains. One could judge by their brilliance how necessary darkness is to cities that can be raided by Zeppelins. I could make out most of the localities in the island which I know so well, including the site of the Quinta which figured as the home of Mildred Carr in *Dawn*.[4] How long ago it is since first I saw it and wrote that book, so long that this Mildred has become quite as real to me as many persons whom once I knew in the flesh. She has joined the company of my dead that is all, as have a number of the creatures of my brain.

---

[1]H. Lisle Lucoque was later to film *She* (1916), *Dawn* (1917) and *Allan Quatermain* (1919).
[2]Ida Hector, the daughter of the Irish novelist 'Mrs Alexander', was Rider Haggard's secretary from the 1890s to his death. During the war she lived in London.
[3]The book was published on 10th August, 1917. In this, the last of his Zulu trilogy, Rider Haggard describes places he had revisited in South Africa early in 1914.
[4]Rider Haggard and his wife spent a couple of weeks in Madeira on his way back from Africa in 1881. *Dawn*, his first novel, was published in three volumes on 21st February, 1884.

I have been employing my time in correcting MS. of *The Ancient Allan*[1] and am now doing ditto with that of *Finished*.

Also I have read some stories to amuse myself. Have had some lumbago which the doctor has tackled. It is better now that the weather begins to grow warm.

Near Groot Schur, South Africa   *28th February, 1916*

Reached Cape Town about 10.30 p.m. (on the 27th). Received letters on board from His Excellency the Governor (Lord Buxton) and Merriman[2] warning me that the political situation is very strained and that I must be most careful in my public utterances re land settlement which would be instantly seized on by the Nationalist party.

Received also following cable from the Chartered Board of the British South Africa Co. 'On further consideration Board has decided to offer land not exceeding 500,000 acres free to approved soldier settlers from oversea. Will also undertake to provide expert advice and supervision.' This is a really handsome offer and I consider something of a personal triumph for myself, at least had it not been for my interview with the Board and the attitude I took then[3], begging them for something *definite*, it would never have come about. Coupled with Sir Owen Phillips' promise of free passages for families, sweethearts etc. there is now a prospect that something may be done in Rhodesia.

Captain Lawrence, one of Lord Buxton's aide-de-camps, met me and took me at once to Westbrooke, the Governor General's country house. Here I saw His Excellency and after a talk accompanied him and Lady Buxton to a luncheon at Parliament House. Then to Government House where I had more talks with the Governor, and thence back to Westbrooke where I showed him my instructions from the Dominions Royal Commission, which we discussed. In the evening there was a dinner party to meet me — an agreeable function reminding me much of that in 1914 in the same house when I was here with the Dominions Royal Commission, only all the personnel (except some of the guests) was different. Botha[4] does not look very well, worried I think; also Mrs Botha is ill with her heart. Merriman was as evergreen and amusing as ever. I don't think there is much prospect of land settlement in the Cape or indeed the Union; all the conditions political and natural are too adverse.

A *Cape Times* reporter has been after me. Last night I told the butler to reply that I had just gone in to dinner, but today I shall be up against him. It is very

[1]The book was published by Cassell on 12th February, 1920, after appearing serially in *Cassell's Magazine* in 1919. [The contract was not signed until 14th November, 1917.]
[2]John Xavier Merriman, the South African statesman, was an old friend of Rider Haggard's.
[3]Rider Haggard had visited the Chartered Board on 3rd February.
[4]General Louis Botha was the Prime Minister of South Africa.

awkward for one must say nothing in this country. 'Interviews — speeches — *nein*' as Botha said when he heard I was coming.

29th February, 1916

Went into Cape Town and entered on our new office at Government House with which H.E. has kindly provided me. Got onto the British South African Office and asked if they would kindly cable as follows: 'Delighted Board's generous decision. Please inform Wilson.'

At four I returned to Parliament House to see General Botha, the Prime Minister. He found an empty committee room and in it we had tea together.

I read him my instructions and then tackled the question of the Cape Route to Australasia setting out D'Abernon's and my own arguments as well as I could. He listened attentively and then explained that it was the same idea as had often struck him. He had even tried to urge it in the past but had been obliged to abandon it because of 'hostile feeling'. He said that if the thing could be carried through it would do 'enormous good and help to tie the Empire together'. 'Yes,' I answered, 'it would be a true Empire bond.' 'Exactly so,' he replied. Finally he declared with some enthusiasm that it was 'a thing we must discuss and carry out'. We agreed that the Union Castle Line might be asked to undertake this extended work, and that failing them a subsidised or even a State-owned line might be considered. We then passed on to my mission which I explained. Here too I found him most sympathetic if somewhat helpless in the grip of circumstances.

He dwelt at some length on the prevalence of racial feeling in South Africa, which he believed, however, would die down if and when we were victorious in the war. He is deeply anxious to get British population into the Union, but dare say nothing openly. I told him I had received his hint and acted on it — lying very low indeed, as the last thing I wished was to make trouble for him. He replied with much warmth that he knew it well that 'you could not do any such thing'. He added that he wanted to start industries in the Union but could not as there were no people to work them and he could bring none in: it made him ill to think of it or words to that effect. With emphasis he declared that he wished me to understand that he was working whole-heartedly 'on Imperial lines'. Then he said that I must see all his ministers. Finally he told me that I had his 'heartiest sympathy' and good wishes on all matters of which we had spoken together. Indeed he was most cordial and evidently anxious to be helpful in every way.

My admiration for Botha grows continually. I believe him to be entirely whole-hearted and reliable — earnest in the Empire's cause. He is, I think, one of the few really big men that it can boast at present. Altogether a most satisfactory interview, although I fear I have forgotten much of our talk. Botha strikes me as looking harassed and even nervous: he has a queer team to drive and they are taking it out of him. I have written him a note bringing to his notice certain points I forgot to put. Now I am tired and can write no more; so to bed.

Merriman's home, Schoongezeigt   *4th March, 1916*

I had a pleasant dinner yesterday at the Kotzes'.[1] The judge is well but very white, his wife whom I have not seen for thirty-seven years is now a handsome old lady, but deaf. The unmarried daughters are curiously early Victorian in appearance. They were all *very* glad to see me and it is strange that we should meet again after all this time — more than a generation.

Mount Nelson Hotel, Cape Town   *8th March, 1916*

I had a long talk with my old friend, Sir William Beaumont[2], in which we spoke of many whom once we knew in 1875 and later. They are nearly all dead, but a few remain, retired like Beaumont himself. Everybody seems to have retired in some sense or another, except myself, whose lot it is to go on working rather harder than usual. So we parted, I reminding him as he went down the steps of how he had been married in my frock coat. And now he has eight grandchildren. After all these years I recognized him from his back as he walked in front of me — there is much character in backs!

9th March, 1916

I saw Hertzog[3] today; a dangerous face, that of a fanatic, brooding, intense and rather cruel. A thin dark-eyed man. Why are all or nearly all who think much thin?

10th March, 1916

I went to lunch at Parliament House. Here, amongst others, I met an old lady, Mrs Pagan of Heidelburg in the Transvaal, who said I stayed in her house when I accompanied Sir T. Shepstone on the annexation journey in 1876.

General Botha was present also and I had a long talk with him. His views about the war were interesting. He said that the failure of the German onslaught at Verdun showed that neither side could hope to pierce the other's lines. In France therefore the war must come to an impasse. Under these circumstances he thought we should withdraw some of our great army from Egypt and attack from Salonika, mopping up the Bulgarians as it were, turning the Austro-German flanks. He thought also that all the threats we were uttering as to what we would do to the

[1]John G. Kotze was a judge in the Transvaal when Rider Haggard first went there. The two often travelled and worked together.
[2]He was the Resident Magistrate of Newscastle when Rider Haggard went out to the Transvaal.
[3]Dr General James Barry Munnik Hertzog had resigned in 1912 from Botha's Cabinet and established the National Party.

Germans after the war were a profound mistake (and I agree with him). 'Do what you like after you have conquered, but till then hold your tongue. Don't try to skin the bear till you have killed him. Threats will only make him hold on till the very last kick, since if he knows that he must die, he will prefer to die fighting.' These were, I think, his actual words and sound ones too. I told him he had better go and take a command at Salonika. He shook his head and answered pointing towards the Chamber, 'No, I have to take command *there*.' I happened to remark that I should like to live on a Natal farm. He replied that so would he. I said that at any rate he was having an interesting time. 'No, no,' he answered. 'I would like to be quiet on the farm.' I believe him; it was not a pose, but truth.

S.S. 'Turakina'   *13th March, 1916*

This morning we bade goodbye to the Mount Nelson Hotel at nine a.m. and drove down to the docks where we found the *Turakina* finishing coaling and in an awful mess. We have quite decent cabins and the ship seems very comfortable with some nice people on board. We got away in a fog at 10.30.

I have this evening begun my chapter on South Africa for my book *The Empire and its Land*[1], dictating to Corbett in his cabin. So for the fourth time I bid farewell to the shores of South Africa[2], leaving them as usual peopled by problems and political trouble. I think that I have done everything possible in the time and am fairly satisfied with the results of my visit.

16th March, 1916

On a ship like this there is little to record. One watches the albatrosses sail, sail, day and night and that is all. How wonderful are these lovely birds, that, as the Captain has been telling me, have been proved to follow a ship for thousands of miles. They neither rest nor stay. At midnight by the moon, I have still seen them sweeping ghost-like about the vessel.[3]

I have written my two chapters on South Africa for *The Empire and its Land*. There is a good deal of information in them; indeed I propose this book shall be all information with no attempt at anything fine or flashy about it. I want it to be useful and for this reason it must not be long. People in a hurry who need to learn about countries in which they or their friends may make a home do not desire long books; they desire something which tells them the truth as to matters of which they seek to acquire information briefly and with authority, or so I think. The details they can find in guides and handbooks.

[1] I never wrote this book. H.R.H.
[2] The three previous occasions were in 1879, 1881 and 1914.
[3] His observations apparently inspired Rider Haggard to work on the plot of the story referred to in the next entry.

I have evolved the plot of a new story to be called *The Fatal Albatross* of which the scene would be laid in some of the desolate islands we are passing, the Maori group perhaps. Or it might be called *Mary of Marion Isle.*[1] Have written a synopsis of the tale to Miss Hector, so I need not set it down here. It seems pretty but one can never tell how a book will work out.

The cold is very sharp now, and the worst of this ship is that there is nowhere to go. Peculiarly shrill-voiced children occupy the smoking room, and indeed almost the whole ship, and in the cabin one feels like frozen mutton. Passenger boats on this route ought to have special accommodation, a kind of heated winter garden or greenhouse on one of the decks for instance.

The Tasmania Club, Hobart, Tasmania   *3rd April, 1916*

Our apparently endless voyage came to a conclusion this morning when we arrived at Hobart about 5 a.m., coming up the channel in dense darkness caused by a thuderstorm and heavy rain.

After lunch I saw the Premier, Mr Earle, in the Town Hall. He seemed fairly sympathetic on the subject of land settlement. He is a thick-set man with a rather forceful but not very clever face. Then I went to Government House and dined with His Excellency Sir William G. Ellison-Macartney, a cultured and most agreeable gentleman. After dinner I had a long talk with him. He does not think that I shall get anything done here about land settlement because of prejudice, jealousies and the power of the caucusses. I daresay he is right. However, one can only try.

6th April, 1916

I went to lunch at Government House. Sir W. Ellison-Macartney was very agreeable and said that he intended to write to the Colonial Office that my visit here had been very useful.

7th April, 1916

This morning I went to see the Premier, Mr Earle. We discussed the pros and cons of nationally-owned steamship lines: also he again promised me a letter on the subject of soldier land settlement. On my return from the town I was conducted to the luncheon given to me by the local members of the Royal Colonial Institute. In the midst of this function I received Mr Earle's letter formally undertaking to provide land for and to look after a minimum of 300 soldiers (and their families) on behalf of Tasmania. This is most satisfactory, as I have accomplished what Sir

[1]Under this title the book was published posthumously by Hutchinson and Company on 4th January, 1929 — the last but one of Rider Haggard's books to appear.

W. Ellison-Macartney declared to be impossible in the present conditions — political and otherwise — of this state. It has been a struggle but I have won.

S.S. 'Lungana'   *8th April, 1916*

Left Hobart at 8 a.m. On the whole I am well satisfied with my visit. The promise of the Government does not go into as much detail as I could wish, but in their circumstances nothing more definite could be obtained.

Melbourne Club, Melbourne, Victoria   *9th April, 1916*

Arrived at Melbourne early. My round begins again — new interviewers, new ministers and the same old arguments.

12th April, 1916

This afternoon, together with Mr Hagelthorn[1], I saw Mr Pearce, the acting Federal Prime Minister, and expounded my mission to him. He is pleasant and kindly, but I should say a politician, rather than a statesman. I could see that all the while he had his eye on the political rather than the Empire side of the matter. I do not think that he will oppose me, however, although I did not get much out of him. Also I laid my Dominions business before him, especially as to an Imperial steamship line. Further I submitted to him the letter I have received from the Publishers' Association as to the ousting of British works in Australia by American publishers.

13th April, 1916

Last night before I went to bed, at Hagelthorn's suggestion I drafted my idea of the letter I should like to receive from his Government — it occupied me till 12.30. This morning I took it round to him. He seemed to approve of it. Whether this is really the case I shall know in due course. Afterwards I took up my quarters in the new office and saw a number of people on a number of subjects. I also wrote letters to the Governors of Western Australia and New South Wales and others.

The burden of this work is hard for one man to carry. Speech making, diplomacy, interviews, bores, endless arrangements, and negotiations fill the day very full, to say nothing of the constant strain of thought. I hope I shall pull through the job all right, but it is very, *very* tough. Especially trying are the continual new names and faces and the difficulty of remembering them all and avoiding mistakes and *faux pas*. Then the speeches! These are a nightmare but so far I have managed all right. And the cranks! Corbett had almost to wrestle with one lady

[1] He was Vice-President of the Board of Lands and an old friend of Rider Haggard's.

today who tried to force her way into my office. She wanted me to write her life, which she declares has been remarkable. I do not doubt it! At last he got a glass door between himself and her and carried on the conversation through the panes.

14th April, 1916

Corbett has been getting out our itinerary. It looks as though we could just get in everything in the time. Sydney (4 days) to Brisbane; back to Sydney to take ship to Fremantle (Perth); from Perth to Adelaide; thence through Melbourne by train to Sydney; sail from Sydney to Wellington, New Zealand; from Wellington to Auckland; at Auckland take the *Niagara* to Vancouver. A pretty programme! I only hope I shall get through all right. The work is very hard and not made easier by its social side. Also there are the telegrams and the multitudinous arrangements of extended travel.

15th April, 1916

This morning I saw Hagelthorn and settled draft of letter from the State Government (Victoria) to myself. But there is many a slip etc. At four this afternoon he rang up to say that he had been reading the draft to the Premier[1] over the telephone. The Premier on reconsideration thought the matter so important that it ought to be formally accepted at a meeting of the Cabinet.

17th April, 1916

I have been through an anxious time. An appointment was fixed with the Acting Prime Minister, Senator Pearce, for 11. We went and the letter was read to him. He appeared in favour of postponing action (he is a very indeterminate kind of man). Finally he agreed to cable to Hughes in England for his views. It seemed to me then impossible that the letter could be read. We returned to Hagelthorn's office and by great industry and the constant use of the telephone he got nearly all the Ministers into his office one after another and to each read and explained the letter. To my relief they all approved although some made alterations. The end was that it was signed *on behalf of* Premier Peacock (a most unusual proceeding) and a covering letter given to me authorising me to make public use of it was also signed by the Chief Secretary. I cannot tell with what relief I saw those signatures attached; the whole success of my Australian mission depended on them and it was run very, very fine.

Government House, Sydney, New South Wales   *18th April, 1916*

Last evening started for Sydney, spending a night in a shaky train. At Sydney this

[1]Sir Alexander Peacock.

morning I was received at the station by the Lord Mayor, representatives of the Government and a number of others. Came up to Government House and saw His Excellency Sir Gerald Strickland.

19th April, 1916

After breakfast I was caught by some cinematograph operators who took pictures of Corbett and myself which they said would be all over Australia in a week or two.

21st April, 1916

Corbett and I dined with the Governor General, Sir R. Munro Ferguson, at Admiralty House. It was an awful job getting there in the pouring rain by the launch and up the garden. I had to borrow a pair of dry shoes.

Brisbane, Queensland   24th April, 1916

The journey to Brisbane was long and wearisome, the train shaking terribly and making sleep difficult, a wretched Easter Sunday. At length, after 25 hours of it, we arrived and were met by the Mayor, Mr Hetherington, and some others — also reporters. These depressed me by saying that nothing was to be expected from the present Queensland Labour Government.

This morning I went to write my name in the book of the Governor, Sir H. Goold Adams, who by the way has taken no notice of my existence. His callers do not seem to be many as I observed that the last name was a week old and, if I remember right, a good deal more. I understand that he lives very isolated.

26th April, 1916

I went by appointment to see Mr Theodore, the Acting Premier of the Labour Government. He is a Roman Catholic of alien blood, Roumanian it is said, and a very tough proposition to tackle, the toughest indeed that I have met in Australia. Being alien he is not to be easily influenced by arguments about patriotism and being Labour immigration does not particularly appeal to him. Naturally therefore he made much of the money difficulty. Still I think I shall get something out of him, not because he wishes to give, but for reasons of expediency. It would scarcely do for Queensland to be left behind. (The interview ended in sherry and bitters that I thought it wise to swallow.)

I was motored to Government House in the Governor's car. He is a nice old gentleman — with a young wife — who evidently is looking forward to his pension and retirement. He said he would have asked me to stay with him but that he lives so far out. Indeed it would have been impossible for me.

I have received a cable from Louie which tells me that my brother Alfred is dead.[1] *Requiescat!* He was, I think, intrinsically the ablest of us, yet the lack of some qualities and the over-plus of others made his abilities of no avail.

27th April, 1916

Today I lunched with the Queensland Ministers and made a speech which I could see influenced them. This afternoon I received a letter from them. They will give a million acres of dairy and agricultural land for soldier settlements, if they can raise the funds to build railways and to develop settlements. They stipulate also that their Government (or its representatives) shall select the men. There are loopholes of course in this letter, but considering all the extraordinary local difficulties and the Labour Government in power it is really wonderful to have got so much out of them. I do not think that anyone could have done more, and perhaps few would have done as much.

Sydney, New South Wales   *29th April, 1916*

A busy day. At 9.30 I met Mr Holman and his ministry at the Premier's office. At once I felt that the atmosphere was unfriendly. They all argued against me, especially the Minister for Lands. They said that the matter had been settled at the Interstate Conference. They said that they had more obligations towards their own returned soldiers than they could fulfil etc. etc. At length I replied that it was no use debating further and I regretted that I must wire to the Royal Colonial Institute that New South Wales would do *nothing*. Indeed I took a piece of paper to draft the cable. Then the tone changed somewhat, and in the end Mr Holman sent for a shorthand clerk and dictated a letter. It has ambiguities, but appears to give 1000 farms in the irrigated Yarroo district to British soldiers, subject to selection. I thought it well not to bargain any more but to take what I could get while I could.These Labour Governments are not easy to deal with and if I had given them further time to debate they might have backed out. As it is, I have something and public opinion and the criticism of the opposing Party and other States may be relied on, more or less, to keep them to their promises.

Adelaide, South Australia   *4th May, 1916*

Yesterday I wrote a long letter to Rudyard Kipling. We arrived at Adelaide early this morning (having travelled by train) and wrote our names at Government House. I did not see His Excellency as he was off to an Executive Council. Went to see Mr Goode, the Minister for Lands, and had a talk with him. I *think* I shall get something out of South Australia.

---

[1] Alfred Hinubar Haggard was the third of the seven sons. He was a barrister who served in the Bengal Civil Service.

Perth, Western Australia   *8th May, 1916*

Arrived at Perth after an uneventful voyage. Here we are the guests of Sir Harry Barron, the Governor.

9th May, 1916

This morning I met Mr Seddon, the Premier, and other members of the Ministry. I put my case before them and after an interview of an hour and a half obtained a promise of a letter on the lines of those given me by Victoria!

11th May, 1916

This afternoon I received the letter from the Premier of West Australia. In its terms it is similar to that of Victoria. Very satisfactory. Only one State now left to bag. It was worth while taking this long journey. Indeed without a *personal* effort and appearance, nothing could be achieved.

Off Albany, Western Australia   *14th May, 1916*

We came on to our ship, the *Katoomba*, which we boarded in a tender. She is a splendid boat with every modern comfort, glass-enclosed decks etc. The company has kindly given us a beautiful deck suite, large bed and sitting room oak-panelled with bath-room attached, so we are in luxury. What a comfort all this would have been on board the *Turakina*, or for any long voyage.

Adelaide, South Australia   *17th May, 1916*

Arrived this morning at Adelaide after an uneventful voyage and were motored to the club. On our way got our mails — letters for me from home. Very glad to have them after weeks with none. The great gale has worked havoc among the trees at home, also done fearful damage at Bradenham.

18th May, 1916

I hear today that the South Australian Government will give me an undertaking similar to those of the other states; indeed that it is being drafted.

Henry James[1] is dead. I see that Gosse[2] writes of him as a 'hero', I suppose because he became a British citizen. But at heart he was British long ago. I was in

---

[1]He had died on 28th February. When war broke out he became a British subject and shortly before his death was awarded the O.M.
[2]Sir Edmund William Gosse, the poet and critic, had been a friend of Rider Haggard's since 1887.

the United States at the same time as he was, in 1905, and remember that Roosevelt protested about him as a man whose own country was not good enough for him. The last time I saw him some time ago at the Athenaeum, he declaimed to me with positive passion, as others might talk of great affairs which really moved them, on a system he had discovered, or adopted, of the prolonged chewing of food. It is an indication of his love of detail and of the little things of life. He was a kind old boy, however, and if personally I did not find his novels entertaining it is my own stupid fault. I wonder how many of them will be widely read twenty or even ten years hence?

20th May, 1916

Today after various hitches I got my letter from the Government of South Australia. Luckily I sent Corbett round to see how it was getting on. He found that the Secretary had drafted a lot of windy stuff with nothing of value in it, and was able to persuade him to simplify it and put point thereto. It has still to be rewritten to rectify one or two errors, which they *promise* to do on Monday. However, as it stands it is good enough, but my word it is not easy to extract these letters. Indeed without infinite perseverance and harrying they never would be extracted.

Well that finishes my work here — except for meeting the Premiers' Conference, if this can be managed on Monday morning — and today I was able to cable Wilson that there is an open door throughout Australia for our ex-service men. I think the Royal Colonial Institute may be proud of the result of its efforts, that is so far as they have gone. If they ever result in anything really useful will depend upon how the matter is handled at home in the future. It is quite a toss up, with odds against, as the Government or the permanent officials, or both, are sure to be openly or secretly obstructive, unless indeed distress and tumult force them to action.

His Excellency Sir H. Galway, the Governor, somewhat tardily became aware of my existence this morning — I have sat outside his gate since Wednesday — and asked me to come to see him.

21st May, 1916

I dined at Government House where I met Sir Ronald and Lady Munro Ferguson (the Governor General). I don't think that either he or Sir Henry Galway really grasp or understand the full significance of what I am trying to do. Lady Galway is a clever and well informed woman.

Melbourne Club, Victoria   *23rd May, 1916*

Yesterday morning Corbett went round to get the revised letter from the South Australian Government which he succeeded in doing, waiting until it was typed and the Premier caught to sign it. After this I met all the Premiers and some of their Ministers in the Conference room — an important moment![1]

S.S. 'Manuka', en route New Zealand   *26th May, 1916*

Yesterday I had talks with Sir G. Strickland who is very anxious that I should be appointed a Governor in Australia. Then we bade a hurried farewell to all the Government House party who, I think, were truly sorry to say goodbye to us and motored off to this ship, where I am accommodated in the hallowed bridal cabin! So ends my Australian adventure.

30th May, 1916

We have had a terrible voyage so far. We should have reached Wellington yesterday morning, and now we shall be lucky if we see it by tomorrow night, on Wednesday instead of Monday! All the way there has been a heavy head gale. Yesterday, however, the wind changed and blew from behind us. Then after lunch it veered round again and set in a cyclone. All the afternoon and night the seas were fearful, driven on by hurricane and to go on deck even with guide ropes to cling to was dangerous. I have never seen anything more tremendous and awe-inspiring, except perhaps in the Bay when Angie and I made that fearful voyage on board the *Macedonia*.[2] All night and until about midday today we had practically to lie to, only keeping steerage way. Then there was a little lull followed by more wind and tropical rain which still continues. We are now, I should judge, doing seven knots or so. The glass seemed lower than ever I have seen it, but I think it is rising a little. Our run for the twenty-four hours (till noon today) was 104 miles and for the previous day only 200 miles. It was difficult to keep in bed last night and still more so to sleep. I was almost thrown to the floor and all the drawers from the elaborate bridal chest suddenly flew out and sprang at me like tigers! Oh! I am weary of these voyagings for which I grow old. However, it is in a good cause.

Government House, Wellington, New Zealand   *1st June, 1916*

Yesterday morning at 9.30 we got into Wellington with no other damage than the carrying away of a portion of the ship's rail, after the worst voyage that has ever been experienced by one of the ships of this line, or so I understand. Indeed from information that came to me from Mr Paterson, who had it from one of the ship's officers, it appears that there was a moment on the night of the 29th-30th when it was just touch and go as to whether any of us ever saw land again. It seems that the

[1]The Conference passed a motion thanking Rider Haggard 'for the manner in which he has discharged the great Imperial work in which he has been engaged during the past few weeks'.
[2]On his trip to Egypt early in 1904.

Manuka got hung up between two gigantic seas, her bow on one and her stern on another, with nothing underneath, and for some seconds the question was whether she would capsize or break her back, as it is said had she been a longer boat she would have done. If this had happened it would have been — goodnight! Well, thank God, it did not happen, the water seethed in time to support and save her. But I never want to encounter such another sea.

On arrival we were met by the aide-de-camp, Mr Helmore, and motored to Government House where we were very kindly received by Lord and Lady Liverpool. At 12.30 I went to Parliament House, where Mr Massey, the Prime Minister, came out from a Cabinet Council to see me for a little while. I gave him a copy of my Conference Memo. and attached letters. Am to meet him tomorrow at eleven.

2nd June, 1916

This morning I saw Mr Massey. Notwithstanding some rather contrary remarks he made in the House last night, I gathered that he is going to give me a satisfactory letter on the usual lines, if a little limited by the smaller facilities of New Zealand. However, until I get the letter it is useless wondering about its exact contents. He was very cordial and sympathetic. Went for a walk in the town in the afternoon, but cold here today. Home-sick!

3rd June, 1916

I received a letter from Mr Massey this morning. It is full of sympathy with my cause and general promises of help, but contains no definite undertaking to do anything. I have written acknowledging and asking if he cannot make it stronger and clearer, but am doubtful of success.

5th June, 1916

Got an English mail today — letters up to 20th April which I was very glad to receive after so long a silence. There has been disaster on the farm — the fine young grey mare dead foaling, also another foal. Labour is getting very short and Longrigg talks of selling the cows. Louie has taken to gardening — real gardening. The *She*[1] film is going very well, nearly two million people having paid to see it already.

Have been in all day (except for a civic reception) because of my cold and aches, but hope it is better tonight. I suppose I ought to see a doctor but dare not do so, although I am feverish, fearing lest it might be cabled home that I am ill.

[1]Made by H. Lisle Lucoque and starring Alice Delysia, the film was first shown in February, 1916.

6th June, 1916

This morning I received a week-end cable from home, which says that they are well and that the farm progresses, also that Tom is now doing work as an Army doctor and that Angie is at Ditchingham. I was very glad to get it.

In train to Auckland   *10th June, 1916*

Yesterday noon we bade goodbye to Lord and Lady Liverpool and Government House and started in His Excellency's car for Auckland where we have just arrived. On the road I have been bombarded with telegrams asking me to speak at a memorial service to Lord Kitchener[1] tomorrow. One, two or three addresses am I requested to make. *Nein!* as Botha says. I got my letter from Massey. It is not very definite but full of goodwill both as regards land settlement and employment, and in every way as much as can be expected in New Zealand where the Government is under the thumb of the landowners.

Auckland, New Zealand   *11th June, 1916*

On arrival at Auckland yesterday morning we were greeted by a very different air to that which nips one's bones at Wellington. Auckland is the only place I should care to inhabit in New Zealand. To me it seems far to surpass all the other cities in beauty, climate and general attractiveness.

This morning I attended the Memorial Service to Lord Kitchener at the Pro-Cathedral (why 'pro' in a rich city like Auckland?). It was very crowded and had not a place been reserved for me I could not have got in. The Dead March was played and the Last Post was sounded, also the Bishop preached a good sermon, all about Kitchener and his career. For my part I could not help thinking of the six or seven hundreds of good men and true who went to doom with him. But of these we heard little or nothing. Such is the world.

S.S. 'Niagara'   *13th June, 1916*

This morning I spent in receiving interviewers to whom I delivered a farewell message, and in getting to this boat which, however, did not sail till 4 p.m. So ends my visit to Australasia. Well on the whole it has been extraordinarily successful, much more so than I could have hoped. I trust that the results may prove enduring and for the good of the Empire.

16th June, 1916

We are through the black northerly gale and in tropic seas where the flying fish

[1]Kitchener was lost when H.M.S. *Hampshire* hit a mine off Orkney on 5th June, 1916.

flash from wave to wave. Unfortunately we shall not reach Suva till after dark and depart again before dawn, which is a disappointment to me.

17th June, 1916

We reached Suva about 6.30 last night. For some hours previously we have been passing various islands of the Fiji group and approaching the largest of them. The mountains of which it is full looked black and grim in the evening light, but I am informed are really for the most part green to the top. As, winding our way through the fine harbour towards the pier, we approached the town of Suva, which is situated on what looks like a promontory and climbs up the hillsides, the full moon rose over it, a lovely sight. On the jetty were gathered a dense crowd, all of them apparently clad like the Blessed — in white garments. The arrival of the mail steamer is an event in Suva. I did not go on shore as we were advertised to leave at nine (in fact we did not get away until eleven) but after dinner arrived an interviewer; then appeared the Bishop, a very nice man; then Mr Headstrom — who I understand is the Mayor — and his family; then others with whom I conversed till in that heat my throat was like a lime-kiln.

I have declined the invitation to give a lecture on this ship. It seems to me that I have heard enough of my own voice of late. Had a tooth pulled out by the doctor this morning. I never can get myself to like or even to tolerate the process.

22nd June, 1916

Today is my birthday; a very lonesome birthday amidst all this crowd of strangers in which I take no interest and who take no interest in me — except as a penny peep-show to some of them.

Today I have definitely entered upon old age, for at sixty a man is old, especially when he begins young as I did. Let me look round: of my early friends but two remain and one of these is broken-hearted. For me the world is largely peopled with the dead; I walk among ghosts, especially at night. Well ere long I must join their company; ten years more the Psalmist would give me, but with my weakened health I cannot expect as much, even should I escape accidents. My work, for the most part, lies behind me, rather poor stuff too — yet I will say this: I *have* worked. My talent may be of copper not of gold — how can I judge of my own abilities? — but I have put it to the best use I could. My opportunities have not been many, and for the most part I have made them for myself; the book writing, the agricultural research business, the public work for instance. Of course I might have done more in the last line by going into Parliament. But this really I have never been able to afford, since, except in the case of Labour members, it has designedly been made to suit the rich alone. Especially has this been the policy of the Conservative Party which wants wealth and does not want ability. Also it is scarcely a place for a self-respecting man who sets store by honesty of purpose and would call his soul his own, though the narrow party politician may find in it a congenial career. Therefore such as I must remain mere hodman Peris, labouring and suffering without the Gate.

23rd June, 1916

We reached Honolulu this morning and had the usual bother with the farce of 'doctor's inspection'. The new game is to make you show not your tongue but your hands!

When the ship was leaving a native band played very well upon the wharf, ending up with 'God Save the King', yet this in an American possession. But the real joy was a native woman who in a rich and thrilling voice sung the famous South Sea farewell song. I don't know when anything has stirred me so much. Of course I could not understand it, but there was no need to understand. Being tired I was asleep in my chair when she began, but woke up at the first line and *knew*. It was the very spirit of mournful, resigned 'goodbye'; it had in it all woman's love, all life's futility and sadness. A truly moving thing which it was worth visiting Hawaii to hear. The woman waited for no money and would sing no more in answer to applause. She just wailed her farewell with a sad, quiet face and vanished.

24th June, 1916

Last night I sat on deck till eleven. There was dancing and, after the dancing — just noise that made my head ache. I have rarely heard such female screams, even from a kitchen, or such high-pitched and continuous laughter. I remember that it was the same on the *Katoomba*. All very harmless, of course; just young men and women working off their superfluous excitement. But heavens! how common the world — our world I mean — has become even in my time. I can remember nothing like this in my youth — even in South Africa. The 'advance of civilization' I suppose. Listening to those Maenadic young persons, I bethought me of a little party of Japanese women in their national costume that, earlier in the day, I had seen going round the Honolulu Museum, grave, polite, interested, dainty. I bethought me also of the sad-faced native singing her heart-stirring farewell upon the quay.

Andrew's home, Victoria   *29th June, 1916*

We reached Victoria about 5 yesterday afternoon, after steaming for a long while past beautiful wooded hills and — on the main land — a mighty range of snow-clad mountains, one of which is, I think, called Olympus. As we made fast I caught sight of my brother Andrew[1] on the quay looking thin and of course older, but

---

[1]Andrew Charles Parker Haggard gave up his apparently successful army career and emigrated to Canada where he wrote many works of fiction which, to his great chagrin, were not as popular as those written by Rider Haggard.

otherwise just the same as ever. Presently he came aboard and with him Ethel and a whole crowd of distinguished citizens to greet me. With them was Mr E. H. Scammel[1] sent by the Government from Ottawa to conduct me through Canada.

A hurried and tumultuous consultation ensued and in the end it was decided that Corbett should go on to Vancouver to fetch the letters etc., returning today, while I stopped with Andrew. Accordingly I was motored out to this pleasing little house where presently three reporters joined me.

The war news seems better. But I must get on (for life is very real and earnest for me just now) and I have no time to comment on all these matters.

Empress Hotel, Victoria, British Columbia   *1st July, 1916*

I am in the thick of it again. Yesterday I left Andrew's house and came to this hotel. Then I went on to the meeting of the local branch of Mr Scammel's Commission, where a number of gentlemen were in attendance. There I discovered that British Columbia has already passed an Act to deal with and benefit her returned soldiers by means of land settlement etc. which, by implication, expressly excludes anybody who is not a British Columbian. This is a fact that no one seemed to have grasped so I am 'right up against it', as they say here. Either I have to get that Act altered or I can do nothing in British Columbia. The meeting was long and the speeches were many. At length, however, I got a resolution passed asking the Government to amend the Act.

Then with Mr Scammel I went to lunch at Government House with the Governor, Mr Barnard, and his wife. She is of German descent and was in some risk during the anti-German riots here, a very intelligent woman with a great love of flowers. The view from the house is lovely.

This morning before I was up Corbett returned from Vancouver whither he had been for our mail, bringing a number of letters from home which I was very glad to get with all the news. Alas! my godson, Rider Greiffenhagen, has been drowned in a submarine which was lost a couple of months ago, the disaster being kept concealed, as I understand many like it are, relatives receiving requests not to publish the deaths. Miss Hector sends me a letter from his poor mother. He was a nice lad and I was fond of him. It seems only the other day that I was present at his christening and now he is dead in a lost submarine! Longrigg writes that the authorities seem to make a particularly dead set at milkmen. One of ours who is a humpbacked has even been taken. He has got two women now but they swear so much that the remaining men complain of them. The result of all this is that many cows are being sold and butchered and where stock is to come from in future no one knows. The season seems good for farming.

[1]Mr Scammel was the Secretary of the Military Hospitals Commission and the son of a member of the Royal Colonial Institute Committee.

Off Victoria   *3rd July, 1916*

At 12 went to see the Premier, Mr Bowser, and put my case before him. Convinced him so thoroughly that he promised to introduce legislation to amend the Homesteads Act of 1916 and to place Imperial ex-service men on the same footing as British Columbians, also to let me have a letter, which half an hour later was put into my hands. A great triumph as I was up against an existing Act.

Came onto the ship where I write this after bidding farewell to Andrew. I wonder if I shall ever see him again. My visit to this beautiful place has been successful indeed.

Vancouver Hotel, Vancouver   *4th July, 1916*

Reached Vancouver this morning and came on to this Great Canadian Pacific Railway hotel, being cinematographed en route. At 12.30 there was a luncheon given to me in the hotel, attended, I should think, by about five hundred people, the galleries also being filled with ladies.

Prince Rupert   *7th July, 1916*

Here I received cables from Wilson and D'Abernon, the latter informing me that the Royal Commission has made up its mind to come to Canada this autumn. I cannot imagine what induces them to take this step, to my mind so foolish and useless, also contrary to what we had arranged, unless it be that they are tired of the whole business and wish to shut it down. I weary of Royal Commissions and their ways, also of the infinitesimal results of so much ponderous and costly labour, and wish to have no more to do with them. Probably I shall never be asked since I am too energetic for such official bodies[1]; also the fact of my being so generally known is not always pleasing to my colleagues when we are travelling the Dominions. (Of course I except D'Abernon who being a most able man is correspondingly large-minded.) Therefore, I hope that they will not be too anxious for me to journey through Canada again in their company. I am, however, distressed that we are not to wait till the end of the war..

On train to Edmonton   *8th July, 1916*

A racketty night and I have utterly lost my eye-glasses and gold chain. Put them away carefully when I went to bed and can't imagine where. The human mind is a strange thing, refusing to register the trivial. The Grand Trunk Pacific Railway Company wants, if the Geographical Board of Canada consents, to name a great Alp in the Rockies after me — *Sir Rider Mountain* and *Haggard Glacier*, a great

[1]In June, 1924, Rider Haggard was asked to serve on a Committee to consider problems concerned with East Africa.

70

and unusual compliment![1] Can write no more; shaking too dreadful.

Edmonton, Alberta   *9th July, 1916*

Arrived here this morning and were driven to Government House. Dr Brett is the Governor. A good house, expensively furnished with imitation old furniture (which cost £10,000 Mrs Brett tells me) that somehow gives one the idea of an hotel.

Calgary, Alberta   *11th July, 1916*

Here there was a luncheon at 11.30! (by true time, daylight-saving being in force) attended by some 300 people. It really was a great success. I made some play with the Alp, Mount Sir Rider, which has been named after me (that is if the Geographical Board of Canada consents), saying it would make the best and most enduring of tombstones and exciting laughter by speculations on the possibility of its being taxed as an 'improved lot', with the result that my descendants would be ruined etc., and then turned to the serious subjects. I never had a better audience, but oh! what a bore is this water drinking by compulsion and how dreary! The luncheon ended with rousing cheers for myself followed by 'God Save the King'. It is a curious world. Here they give my name to a towering Alp; in Norfolk they would not bestow it on a 'pightle'![2] Truly no man is a prophet in his own country.

Regina, Saskatchewan   *12th July, 1916*

In the afternoon I had a long interview with the Government (Mr Walter Scott, Premier). As a result they have promised me such a letter of support as I desired. We dined at Government House. It was a great treat to get a quiet dinner and a glass of light wine after a long hot and tiring day. I have rarely enjoyed anything more than that Sauterne.

Ottawa, Ontario   *17th July, 1916*

In Winnipeg I went to see the Government and had a satisfactory interview. They promised a letter which has not yet arrived. At five this morning we were shot out, weary and dishevelled on the platform at Ottawa. Really this is a land of trial for the traveller. The trains generally seem to start at midnight and arrive at dawn; meals are held at any hour (at Winnipeg I 'lunched' at 6.30 p.m., or rather looked at the slabs of tough beef in front of me). In most places one can get nothing to drink, in others nothing on Sundays even on the trains, a decree not calculated to

[1] I saw it. It is a wonderful and magnificent Alp, some ten thousand feet high and measuring many miles round its base. Snow lies on its summit even in summer and it has deep, ribbed glaciers and fir-clad ravines upon its flanks, while the crest has some resemblance to a lion. H.R.H.
[2] = a small meadow.

endear the Sabbath to many. On top of everything, living is extraordinarily costly, twice as dear as in Australia I should say, and domestic help only obtainable by millionaires. The climate too, except in British Columbia, seems to fulfil the conditions of Dante's two hells, a hell of fire in summer and a hell of frost in winter, though I believe it is beautiful in spring and autumn. However those who dwell in it seem to like it and certainly it is wonderfully wholesome for white people.

18th July, 1916

Yesterday morning, after interviews, I went to lunch with Sir Robert Borden, the Prime Minister. He was very polite and listened to what I had to say, replying little himself. In the end, taking my papers with him to read, he made an appointment to meet the Committee of the Privy Council which is dealing with this matter at eleven this morning.

19th July, 1916

Yesterday I met the Committee of the Privy Council and set out my case. They (i.e. the Government) can make no definite declaration of policy at present inasmuch as this will require legislation, but I think they are sympathetic and in the end will do all they can. A letter of sorts has been promised to me. Last night I received a wire from Roosevelt saying he would be delighted to see me to lunch on Friday.

S.S. 'St Louis'   *22nd July, 1916*

The last two days of my journey have been very busy and hot as only Canada and America can be at this time of year. On the morning of the 20th I received the promised letter from the Prime Minister, Sir Robert Borden. It is much better than I expected and indeed all that I can hope for in the circumstances. Also I had a conversation over the long-distance telephone with Mr Hearst, the Premier of Ontario, at Toronto, a place I did not visit owing to the non-delivery of a telegram. I understand him to promise everything I asked on behalf of his Government; the letter to be sent to me at home.

Then came the luncheon in a heat inconceivable, so much so that it seemed wonderful that several hundreds of gentlemen found courage to attend. But they did and another hundred could not get tickets. I spoke as well as I could in my melting state (after it my shirt was literally *black* with the dye from my waistcoat) and I noticed that the Prime Minister frequently applauded. At length I sat down amidst loud cheers, having read the letter from the Government and indeed my heart was grateful as I reflected that this was my last speech and that I had successfully accomplished the work I set forth to do throughout the Empire. It has been hard, very hard, but the end is attained; that is the great thing. In many ways also Providence seems to have fought for me and I hope sincerely that my efforts may result in some lasting good to my country, also that I have succeeded in opening the eyes of thousands of my fellow subjects to the responsibilities of our generation and to the dangers that lie ahead of us.

An hour after the conclusion of the luncheon ceremony we left Ottawa. At Montreal we dined at the station and started on for New York in terrible heat, indeed the train was like a heated oven and its woodwork almost burnt my hand. All night I had to get up to drink iced water. We arrived at New York at 7.30 and drove to the City Club, where I put up to escape reporters. After breakfast I started off in a crowded train, where everyone was gasping with the heat, to Oyster Bay about forty miles away and in due course arrived at Sagamore Hill, on the steps of which I was most warmly greeted by Theodore Roosevelt. Luckily there was no one in the house except Mrs Roosevelt, a married daughter, and the wife of Kermit Roosevelt, so we enjoyed a solid three hours of the most delightful intercourse I have perhaps ever had with any man.

Heavens! how we talked — I think without stopping for a single moment till I was obliged to go. The house is a pleasant building with some good rooms and situated in the midst of large grounds — many acres of them. Here Roosevelt lives in a dignified, modest seclusion. He has grown older and stouter since last we met about six years ago, and at times his burning manner of speech (I can think of no better description of it) is nervous in its intensity.

I went with him into his study — a large room filled with African and other trophies (including the hugest pair of elephant tusks I ever saw; I think they weigh about 200 lbs each). Here we began to talk about the political situation. He said, and this I have heard in sundry quarters, that he believes he would have been elected could he have secured nomination the other day.[1] As it is he means to support Hughes, taking all his enormous party with him, which probably means that Hughes will be elected. For certain reasons, however, he added, he must do this carefully and with discretion, not too violently and openly. Of Hughes he thinks well but, I gathered, considers him somewhat professorial and 'without experience of international affairs'. His opinion is that he will prove sound with reference to the Germans and their outrages but that he will not reopen any of the old issues such as the sinking of the *Lusitania* and the murder of Americans. Only if anything fresh occurs he will act. He said that Wilson is afraid of him (R) and never attempts to answer or refute his exposures of his policy, because he dare not do so. I said I was sorry that he had not stood again at the conclusion of his second term when he would have been certain of election. He answered that was so but it was well he did not, as nothing of importance with which he could have dealt happened during the four years that ensued on his retirement and he did not care

[1]The Republican Presidential nomination had gone to Charles Evans Hughes.

for Office, just for its own sake. What had pressed him on to make an effort now was that he believed it to be his last opportunity of serving his country and the world. He had suffered serious illness during his South American explorations from fever and thought his strength would not endure for very long. I answered that I had always considered this expedition of his rather foolish. He replied that at any rate he had discovered a new river; he seemed very proud of this river.

I found that he is fond of my stories, reminding me of incidents in passages in them I had almost forgotten. Allan Quatermain, he said, he had always taken to be myself, clothed in the body of Selous[1] — as many others have done. I told him that he was right as to the first but not as to the second, since at the time I conceived Allan Quatermain I did not know Selous. He said he was especially fond of the old boy's (Allan Quatermain's) reflections and moralisings, and seemed to think that some of my work would live.

At length I had to go to catch my train. We parted with what I think I may call real affection and understanding. He says he will not, he thinks, come to England any more, adding: 'The truth is that I cannot bear to go to crowded countries where I must hear criticisms of the conduct of my nation during the last two years which I know to be just and cannot defend. If I go anywhere again it will be to wild lands.' I said that I should like to end my days in Africa. 'So would I,' he answered, 'if I were not married.' Other things we debated also but it is too long to set them all down. 'Goodbye and God bless you,' I said as I got into the motor. 'I thank you, sir,' he answered with a curious and gentle courtesy.

So we parted. I wonder if we shall ever meet again. No, I do not wonder for I am sure that we shall *somewhere*. We have too much in common not to do so, though it may be perhaps in a state unknown. He gave me characteristic photograph of himself jumping a horse over a fence and promised to send me some of his books. A great man indeed, but oh! how much misunderstood by millions. It was well worth coming to America just for those few hours of comradeship.

This morning we came on to this ship which is crowded. It is a mercy to escape the excessive heat, which just before we left culminated in a thunderstorm.

27th July, 1916

A good voyage so far, though the heat was considerable at first, up to 90 degrees indeed, which is a good deal in a cabin like mine without any ventilation whatsoever.

Ditchingham   *1st August, 1916*

On Saturday (the 29th I think) we drew near to Liverpool and I got no sleep because a number of passengers, mostly American, who anticipated torpedoes, sat

[1]He was an explorer and big-game hunter whose books, especially *A Hunter's Wanderings in Africa* (1881), made him well known.

up all night by the boats and kept their spirits high by talking and singing at the top of their voices. We arrived safely early on Sunday morning, but owing to various contretemps did not get away for London till 6.30 p.m. arriving at Euston about eleven. Here I found Louie and Angie waiting to meet me, both well and glad enough I was to see them safe and sound after this long absence, during which one has run so many risks — oh! glad indeed and thankful to Providence.

I slept at the Hotel York and next morning I went on to the Royal Colonial Institute where I was greeted by Sir H. Wilson. Instantly I was whisked off to the House of Commons where a conference was sitting of representatives from the Colonies. I received a fine reception, all the gathering clapping when I came in with Sir H. Wilson and the Chairman called out my name.

Yesterday Louie and Angie and I came on home in the company of a great crowd of soldiers. Very thankful was I to see Ditchingham again at about nine o'clock (by daylight-saving time!), so tired that for the second night I could not sleep. Indeed now that the work is over I am feeling the reaction somewhat. We were greeted by a Zeppelin raid, several of these accursed machines being on the bomb in the neighbourhood.

The farm looks well and greatly did I enjoy a stroll over it with Longrigg looking at the foals and the crops. After so much rush and turmoil is seemed very peaceful and yet the war aeroplanes were droning away overhead and as I write I listen for the sound of bursting bombs. The Dominions Royal Commission is going to Canada but I have leave to skip the tour. I do not think I could face Canada again at present. Indeed I must have a little rest and look to my affairs. So ends my journey round the world as Honorary Representative of the Royal Colonial Institute. I wonder if any good will come of all the work.

2nd August, 1916

I saw Ransome[1] who prescribes rest and strychnine tonic and says I am not to travel again at present. That mission has taken it out of me.

3rd August, 1916

Last night Lilias and Joan went to a dance given by a Colonel in Bungay. (It is an odd thing that a trained military man should select moonless 'Zeppelin' nights in August for dances.) In the middle of the party rumours of Zeppelins arrived and some left, but not Lilias and Joan. They departed about 12 in the Carrs' motor which duly landed them here and went on to the Hall with Dorothy Carr. I saw them upstairs and returned to bed. A few minutes later there was a terrific explosion which nearly shook my window and followed rapidly by others all from the direction of the Hall. Confusion and scurryings ensued in the house till at length

[1]Dr Gilbert Holland Ransome lived in Bungay where he was physician, surgeon, medical officer and the public vaccinator.

we all found ourselves in the cellar, clothed with precious little. Well there we stopped till nearly three in the morning, servants and all while the Zepps, of which an officer tells me he saw three over the Common, disported themselves around. We must have heard over 50 bombs and how many more there were, or what damage they have done, I do not know. What happened was that the Zepp picked up the bright electric lights which the Carrs' chauffeur was forced by the police, in pursuance of some idiotic regulation, to turn on as soon as he was across the Suffolk border. It lost them up our drive, where the trees and the ivy-covered house saved us, found them again on the road and followed them in the belief that it was one of their own sympathisers leading them to a camp or works. At least so I am convinced, since no German could be made to believe that on the very best night of a Zeppelin season, an Englishman would travel about at night with blazing electric lights except for some secret purpose. After the motor arrived at the Hall, the Zepp seems to have given it three minutes to get away, since Dorothy tells me she had just time to get to her bedroom when the bombs began to come. The nearest fell about 100 yards from the house, smashing trees and windows and making a large hole, others, some of them incendiary, in neighbouring fields. Luckily none hit the house where the Carrs, like ourselves, were in the cellar, which abode I suppose we shall become familiar with in future. The terrific noise of these things and the uncertainty as to where they are coming next is nerve-racking, and it is odd that I should have emerged from all risks of a round the world trip in these days to run into Zeppelins at home.

In the Zepp raid last night everybody in the house behaved extremely well, including the servants; only when I went to rescue my wife, my energetic niece Joan[1] knocked the candle out of my hand and practically kicked me down the back stairs! She is amusing in these emergencies. Another ludicrous incident was that suddenly one of the girls swore that they heard an anti-aircraft gun. It turned out that the sounds proceeded from the cook's little boy being sick with terror!

5th August, 1916

Yesterday afternoon we walked to see some of the bomb holes made near Tyndale Wood and in the Lake Plantation. They are terrific, but only killed a rabbit (which I saw blown to bits) and stunned a golden-crested wren! I have corrected and returned the rough draft of my report to the Royal Colonial Institute.

Windham Club   *9th August, 1916*

I had a busy time yesterday. First I went to the Royal Colonial Institute where I saw Sir Charles Lucas and Sir H. Wilson. Thence to see Harding at the Dominions Royal Commission office and talk over the Canadian trip etc. Then to

---

[1]She was the daughter of Rider Haggard's brother, John G. (Jack) Haggard and his wife Agnes (Barber).

lunch with D'Abernon whom I found well and as amusing as ever. Then to see Curzon who was most complimentary about my work and very glad to see me. Then to the Deputation to Bonar Law (with whom was Lord Crawford, the new President of the Board of Agriculture). After we had been introduced by Earl Grey I spoke and was followed by the others. Then Bonar Law replied in a pregnant little speech. In answer to my expressed fears lest while our shipping was occupied returning soldiers after the war the Americans should remove our ex-service men he made the remarkable declaration that personally he would be prepared to extend the present passport regulations and thus to prevent them from leaving the Empire. He dwelt also on the terrible *future* danger to the food of this country through the action of enemy submarines, speaking of the matter in no reassuring way. Finally in practice he promised that some sort of Board should be set up to deal with the question of Oversea Land Settlement. Evidently the trouble is to know what Board.

I dined with Harding and met Mr Macnaghten, the Chairman of the Emigration Department of the Colonial Office. We had a very interesting conversation on all these matters and I gave them my ideas which no doubt will percolate. Really I begin to hope that something may be done.

Ditchingham   *12th August, 1916*

I got home with difficulty, the Waveney Valley train having been suddenly taken off in connection with troop movements. So I was obliged to hire a motor at Beccles (15/-!). In town I went to the bank and invested the money from the sale of the Great Eastern Railway shares (which I look on with doubt) in Government securities together with £200 that I had saved and some more from my general account. It may as well be earning some interest and at the same time help — as a drop helps a sea! I imagine that ultimately there will be a crash in English railway shares as, notwithstanding the promises of the men, there is more labour trouble ahead.

14th August, 1916

Louie has gone to Budleigh Salterton to look for a house for the winter.

15th August, 1916

I have been correcting the proof of my report to the Royal Colonial Institute and returned it. My share in the work is, I suppose, finished and it must go as is fated.

16th August, 1916

Longrigg tells me that the Loddon Tribunal was very rude as to our application to have some of our milkmen spared. The line taken was that I as a 'gentleman' could shift for myself while others were helped, while Louie's letter saying that we shall be obliged to sell the cows unless we could find milkers was publicly described as 'unpatriotic'. I think that this is a strange term to be used in view of what I was and am doing for the country. The truth is that there is great jealousy of 'gentlemen' who farm, although in my case I have done this for reasons the reverse of 'unpatriotic' and have never made anything out of the business.

Well this occurrence settles my mind. I shall give up my farming. I can no longer be exposed to all this pettiness for what brings me in nothing at all. The incident throws a lurid light on the difficulties that those who would help forward reforms in matters to do with English land must expect to encounter. It is an impossible effort and very disheartening, while as for gratitude it is not to be expected. As Meade[1] has been pointing out to me, one of the reasons that the farmers round here do not like my pursuing practical agriculture is that they consider that it gives me too accurate a knowledge of the details of the business. He says that he knows this to be the case.

17th August, 1916

I went to the Bench this morning, arriving half an hour late, because of the impossibility of driving through a mile long train of artillery which blocked the road. Ultimately I had to get out and run a mile. Mann[2] moved a vote of congratulation to me on my safe return from my Mission which I acknowledged. I wished to say something about Meade's loss of his young son killed in France, but he begged me not to do so. Too trying for him I think, poor fellow.

18th August, 1916

Today Simpson[3] came and we agreed that it is wisest to wind up my agricultural affairs. So notice is to be given in respect of the lands I hire. Thus end my efforts and experiences as a farmer. I have done my best, but the fact is that the adventure is scarcely possible for a gentleman in East Anglia. Too many forces are arrayed against him. I have not the patience to set out all the details whereof I have had a stomach-full today. So I will only add that there comes a time when one must throw up the sponge though it cannot finally descend to earth for another year.

I am in trouble about Kessingland. In spite of Mr Simpson's and Longrigg's warning, the soldiers who have taken possession of the place have been digging pits between the house and the cliff edge which will probably result in the Grange going into the sea as the water will gather in them and let down the cliff. Really this seems an unnecessary proceeding since the pits, if wanted for defensive purposes,

[1]Captain John Percy Meade, J.P., lived at Earsham Hall, Bungay.
[2]Robert Campbell Mann lived at Wainford House, Ditchingham.
[3]He was a land agent and auctioneer at 21 Butter Market, Bury St Edmunds.

could equally well be constructed on the waste land clear of the house. The question is what remedy have I? It looks as though my property would be ruined somewhat wantonly and I shall be exposed to losses that I cannot afford. The truth is that intelligent direction is lacking in all these matters. No one seems to be in authority and everyone passes on the responsibility to someone else.

Windham Club   *22nd August, 1916*

I came to town by the early train, went to the bank where they admitted their error in my accounts and then by a bright inspiration on to the *Field* office where I had promised to be interviewed. After lunch I went to the committee meeting at the Royal Colonial Institute where we got through a good lot of business. I hear indirectly that the Government is doing something about appointing a board, but I do not suppose I shall be on it.

Ditchingham   *24th August, 1916*

Yesterday morning I went with Corbett to meet Mr Hearst, the Premier of Ontario, at the office of the Commissioner for Ontario in the Strand. I missed him again as I had done in Canada, but I drafted the kind of letter I wanted him to give me and left it with Mr Reid, the Commissioner. Afterwards I lunched with Mr Reid at the Automobile Club and there met Mr Hearst and others. He promised the letter in the afternoon and today Corbett sends it on to me, obtained, he adds, with much difficulty — as usual. However, it is a quite satisfactory letter giving all I asked and they are managing to include it in the report which is to appear tomorrow or Saturday. Thus ends my work on behalf of the Royal Colonial Institute. By the way Harding tells me that the Colonial Office is stirring about the appointment of an Imperial board to deal with all this business. Obviously he knows a good deal of the matter, but informed me frankly that he was not at liberty to make disclosures. I wonder in a somewhat impartial fashion if they will offer me a seat on the board. Really I don't greatly care, having done my work as well as I can and not being particularly anxious for more arduous, unpaid labour. They may or they may not, and there it stands. But of course they *ought* to do so *if* they mean business.

On my return home last night I found a *very* nice letter from the Duke of Connaught[1], whom I missed in Canada, awaiting me — all written in his own hand. I have been engaged most of the day writing to the Comptroller of Lands at the War Office about the damage done at Kessingland, which the military appear to be turning into a kind of fortress. Already in London I conversed with him on the telephone.

[1]Arthur William, Duke of Connaught, was the third son of Queen Victoria. From 1911-16 he was Governor-General of Canada.

3rd September, 1916

We had a terrible time last night. Louie and I went to dine with the Carrs where we met General and Mrs Anderson. During the evening General Anderson got news that the Zeppelins were about. We got home in Lambert's fly about a quarter to eleven. Lilias and Mrs Jebb[1] had gone to bed. I sat down to smoke in the old study. A little after eleven Lilias called to me from the top floor, 'Dad, I hear a Zeppelin.' I called to them to come down at once to the cellar, but instead of doing so she and Mrs Jebb looked out of the window for the Zepp which they saw approaching from Earsham way. Louie also saw it out of the bathroom window. Mrs Jebb made a mess of getting down the stairs and they were passing the little window with Lilias when a bomb exploded quite near, about two hundred yards from the house and sixty or so from the stackyard pond, where it made a large hole but by some miracle did not kill the horses. Other bombs had already been falling on the common. There followed a veritable rain of them, the idea being that the guns at the Pulham sheds had hit this machine and that it was lightening itself. The next bomb fell in the little shrubbery over the Norwich road just by our front gate, nearly blowing in the farm, and terrifying the Longriggs almost to death; the next in the moat of the Nunnery Farm about forty yards further on; then others towards the House of Mercy[2] which is a good deal knocked about. By the goodness of God they missed both this house, over which the Zeppelin was hanging, and the cottages etc. near the gate. It was hellish — the whirr of the machine above, the fearful boom of the bombs, and the crashing of glass in the greenhouses and one pane in the garden door, also one of the kitchen windows. The accursed thing went over spawning shells, and we sat for hours in the cellar. The women wanted to go to bed — I resisted. Mason and the policeman arrived and said there was another Zepp coming. It came and went. They insisted on going to bed. I waited a little and Mason came in again. We talked. At 3 (daylight-saving time) I went to bed. Nearly an hour afterwards the girl ran up to tell me that Mason said that yet another Zepp was coming. It came and seems to have hung over the village, not departing till near daylight. Meanwhile we once more took refuge in the cellar. At last we went to bed but I found sleep difficult till broad day.

6th September, 1916

Williams is engaged making new 'bolt holes' in the basement, taking iron bars from in front of the windows and reopening the little stairs to the front door. Such are the necessities of the time.

---

[1]Rider Haggard had been friends with J. Gladwyn Jebb and his wife since they met in 1889. The Haggards were with the Jebbs in Mexico when Jock, their only son, died in 1890.
[2]This was opened in 1858 by the Sisterhood of All Hallows to serve 'penitent women from all parts of England'.

7th September, 1916

Hornor[1] has been here to assess the damages done to me in the air raid: I should think £20 or £30 will cover them. I have been raising the insurances on this house and its contents in view of possible occurrences. They are much too low.

Bradenham   *10th September, 1916*

I write this before getting up from bed in Hocking's old room at Bradenham Hall. (I asked them not to put me into either of the front spare rooms because they have such painful recollections for me. I watched my mother's long death scene in the one and saw my father lying dead in the other.) This little place only reminds me of dear old Hocking, that wonderful type of the family servant of the vanished sort, untiring, energetic, resourceful and above all faithful unto death. With dignity too: well can I remember her 'There lies what *was* your mother!' and the simple yet impressive gesture with which she said it. I can see her in this room now, in the midst of a mass of vast disorder, mixed up with apples, shoes, and bits of tape. Well she is long dead like the others whom she loved and served. God rest her. It is odd at the end of life coming back to houses in which one has spent its beginnings, for then such become one vast and living memory. Every bit of furniture, every picture on the walls, every stone and tree brings forgotten scenes before the eye, or finds tongues and talks. Scenes in which dead actors played, voices that can stir this air no more! Where are they all, oh where do they hide from the search-light of our love? Well, ere long the play of our generation will be finished and we too shall learn or cease to be eager and curious for ever and a day. Bradeham, where first I saw the light, you are a sad spot for me; the echoes from your old walls are too dear and many. Yet I slept well here last night, for the first time for a month.

Ditchingham   *11th September, 1916*

I went to church yesterday and saw Alfred's grave near that of my mother and father. Poor Alfred! Edward Winter has the living now. He tells me that he buried Andrew Lang at St Andrews and knew him well. We had not met for many years. I did not see one face in the church that I knew again; all have changed. Will is arranging his cellar for Zeppelin emergencies, making another bolt hole etc.

13th September, 1916

I received a letter from Roosevelt today thanking me for the replica of Raemaeker's cartoon of Wilson. In it he says, 'I trust I need not tell you how much I enjoyed your visit.' Well the enjoyment was mutual. He talks of books he has sent me, but these have never arrived: the Censor, I suppose.

[1]He was a land agent and valuer from Prince of Wales Road, Norwich.

14th September, 1916

I have been trying lighting cases in Bungay, five or six of them. One man who abused the police in very foul language and struck a match in the street when a Zepp was straight over the town was sent to prison for seven days. Boswell has been here to value the pictures; it is necessary in these times.

15th September, 1916

Mr Blackman[1], the Egyptologist, came to see me today. He has taken off all my Egyptian rings (Tiy's, Nefertiti's etc.) to show to the Ashmolean Museum and to publish.[2] I had a very interesting afternoon with him. It is curious how deeply everything to do with old Egypt interests me.

Windham Club   *18th September, 1916*

Today I left Ditchingham and came to town to draft a sub-report of the Dominions Royal Commission on the Agriculture and Forestry of the Empire, a very difficult task in the limits allowed, especially as I am asked to make it interesting. Louie and Lilias remain for a few days. I only trust that they will be safe as one can be anywhere in these times.

20th September, 1916

I have been working at the office of the Dominions Royal Commission. I dined with Angie at the Ladies Imperial Club. She is up to look after Julia, whom I saw this afternoon in a nursing home waiting to be operated on for appendicitis. I was talking to Coller[3] last night about all the terrific problems with which Western civilization is permeated and threatened and especially of its advancing death owing to the non-production of children. We discussed various possible remedies and he said that if I would put them into the form of a story I should be the most talked-of man in the Empire. I replied that I had no ambition that way; also that this was a matter on which it was very easy to do harm and one with which, for my part, I would not take the reponsibility of meddling.

22nd September, 1916

I attended the lunch to Hearst, the Prime Minister of Ontario. He made a long and eloquent speech, poured out like water from a jug, for it was I think learned by

[1]Aylward Manley Blackman.
[2]'The Nugent and Haggard Collection of Egyptian Antiquities', *Journal of Egyptian Archaeology*, 1917, Vol. IV, pp. 30-46.
[3]He was a Chief Justice in the West Indian Islands and a fellow passenger with Rider Haggard on the *St Louis* in July, 1916.

heart. Indeed I saw the reporters following it from pages of type-written copy. Afterwards at Angie's Club I met the Greiffenhagens. It was sad, for poor Mrs Greiffenhagen told me all about my dear godson, Rider, who vanished in a submarine. It seems that he *would* thrust himself into every kind of danger with a kind of nervous eagerness. They have never even been allowed to announce his death. Greiffenhagen came to dine with me here at the Windham and talked of him all the while, almost weeping as he did so, and therefore it was not a cheerful meal. Poor people, theirs is a very common lot now-a-days and all the harder, at any rate for him, since I do not think that he has any faith in a future.

At the luncheon I sat next to Lord Brassey.[1] He is a dear old gentleman, but he has become infirm and aged very much since last we met, also grown garrulous as old men do. It would be sad to live to reach that stage of natural decay.

24th September, 1916

I write this before getting up after another Zeppelin night. Last evening I sat in the drawing room where I thought I heard firing, till nearly 12. In the hall on my way to bed I met a member of the club in the uniform of a Special (I think) who told me the Zepps were out. I went to bed but did not take off my clothes. Presently it seemed to me that three bombs were dropped in the neighbourhood of Chelsea and others further off but the sound may have been of guns. From the streets round came a confused murmur of voices. At about two there was a good deal of cheering. I rose and looked out of the window. In the sky I thought I saw and indeed did see a light like a costermonger's flare and above it the outlines of a Zeppelin. The latter, however, may be a mistake. I wondered if it was on fire and going to fall! Finally I lit a candle and went downstairs to discover what was going on, but finding no one there got into the lift and came back again, after which I heard no more. I hope that they did not visit Ditchingham again and wish that Louie and Lilias would get out of it. But they are hard to stir.

25th September, 1916

It would seem that I *did* see a Zeppelin the other night from the club, for one of the papers describes a 'magnesium glare' that was let down by a parachute from an airship in order to enable it to discover its whereabouts. Now what I saw was exactly like a costermonger's naphtha flare, and above it the outline of a Zepp. I wonder why it was not fired at, as it seemed to be quite still in the sky.

Louie has come to town today (but Lilias stops with the Carrs). Angie and I met her at Liverpool Street.

[1]He was an expert on naval affairs, having been Civil Lord of the Admiralty. His father was an engineer who had built the Great Northern Railway.

26th September, 1916

I attended a meeting of the Allied Aid Committee of the Royal Agricultural Association today and made a short speech upon the Dominion offers of help. This afternoon I went for a walk with Louie and looked at shop windows.

27th September, 1916

Today I went to see the Somme War film with Louie, Angie and Mrs Jebb who dined with me afterwards at an Italian Restaurant in Panton Street where we got a very good and well-cooked meal at a most reasonable price. The film is not a cheerful sight, but it does give a wonderful idea of the fighting and the front, especially of the shelling and its effects. Also it shows the marvellous courage and cheerfulness of our soldiers in every emergency, and causes one to wonder if one would find as much in a like case. At their age I have no doubt the answer would be yes, but now at sixty I am not so sure. It is a young man's job! As usual all the pictures move too fast, even the wounded seem to fly along. The most impressive of them to my mind is that of a regiment scrambling out of a trench to charge and of the one man who slides back shot dead. There is something appalling about the instantaneous change from fierce activity to supine death. Indeed the whole horrible business is appalling. War has always been dreadful, but never, I suppose, more dreadful than today.

30th September, 1916

Went with Louie to see her Uncle William[1] at Clapton. The old boy talked all the time about the bombs that had dropped not far away from him but which, being deaf, he did not hear.

2nd October, 1916

Another night of it. As I was sitting after dinner here with Tom, who dined with me, we heard that the Zepps were out again and the general call came from the Special Constables. About midnight the fun began — guns and bombs at a distance. I was sitting up in the reception room alone, awaiting events, when the butler invited me to the basement. Thither I went and took up a position with a pipe and a novel in a kind of servants' hall. Presently the vegetable maid arrived and declared that she had seen a Zeppelin fall in flames and was not altogether believed. Then came two Club boys from Waterloo who had seen something. Meanwhile searchlights everywhere and aeroplanes sailing overhead. So on till 2.30 or so when it was reported 'clear'. Then the searchlights ceased their wanderings and stood up like sentinels of flame round London. I confess that I am

[1]William Hamilton died early in 1917. H.R.H.

heartily tired of Zeppelins and should like some good nights rest.

I have been sitting to Strang[1] this morning for my portrait and must return to-morrow. In the afternoon I went to Locoque's to look at the film of *She* which I had not seen. It is fair, considering all things, though somewhat distressing to an author.

Havercroft, Ledbury   *4th October, 1916*

Yesterday I sat again to Strang who finished the drawing of me. Of course it is good, but too 'pretty' I think. I look older than that. However, all being well, he is going to etch me next time I am in town. His etchings I think wonderful. I arranged for him to do Lilias. Such things are valuable in after years. I took the 4.55 train here.

I have received a formal letter from the Royal Colonial Institute in which I am informed that I have been elected an honorary life fellow in recognition of my services to the Institute and that a formal presentation is to be made on 14th November. Very flattering and kind of them.

11th October, 1916

I went to Worcester today with Nellie and after many years renewed my acquaintance with the fine cathedral and the tomb of King John. Some years ago I began a romance about King John and for that purpose read all the historical records extant, including those least consulted. I found the canvas so charged with gloom and wickedness, however, so utterly unrelieved by anything kindly or good, that I gave up the job as too depressing.

'Thornsett', Budleigh Salterton   *14th October, 1916*

I came here today from Ledbury. It seems a pleasant place and this house is comfortable and well furnished.

20th October, 1916

Lilias has arrived from town, bringing Strang's pictures of herself and me. I think he has made her rather too serious and a little scornful which is not her character — although she is determined. Mine everyone thinks as excellent likeness of me as I am today.

23rd October, 1916

Ted Hildyard[2], Louie's cousin, has died quite suddenly. He was my executor and I

---

[1]William Strang was a successful artist, best known for his strongly imaginative book illustrations.
[2]He and Rose were children of Louie's sister.

was attached to him. He seemed a strong man and yet some of us who are creaking doors have outlived him; even his delicate sister Rose R.I.P His was an industrious and a useful life.

31st October, 1916

Kipling finishes his articles on the Destroyers at the Jutland Naval battle in today's papers. Great as is my general admiration for his work, I cannot say that they have impressed me as much as I hoped they would, largely, I suppose, because of the strain of jocosity with which they are tinged. It may be, however, that he understands his business perfectly and knows what the public will read and that, as I suspect, I am hopelessly old-fashioned. Still I cannot help reflecting how the Psalmist, or any of the Elizabethan writers, or Gibbon, or even craftsmen of my own youth, would have dealt with matters so great and solemn as the struggle to the death between warships upon the seas at night. But now, as he himself says, we 'jest in Zion', and I daresay that in this mild criticism really I am criticizing myself, who at 60 years of age find that I am out of tune with some of the new developments of our day which loves to jest — even in Zion. To me the whole thing is too terrible, yes, for the most pregnant and wittiest jest. What is more, I am sure that in his heart Kipling feels it to be so himself. He is adapting his means to his end, that is all, and I daresay he is right. To him the great ear of the Public is open and he knows how to make it listen, which many of us would not do.

1st November, 1916

This morning I received from Theodore Roosevelt his book called *Fear God and Take Your Own Part*.[1] On the fly-leaf is the following inscription: 'To Sir Rider Haggard, who has both preached and practised fealty to the things of the soul. With the regards of his friend, Theodore Roosevelt. 23rd July, 1916.' Clearly the book was sent off on the day after our interview, but why it has taken all this time to arrive I do not know. Others from him have, I think, been lost.

8th November, 1916

Yesterday we went over to Sidmouth to lunch with the Lockyers.[2] Sir Norman has aged a great deal since I last saw him and has a nervous affliction of his right hand which he declares is due to his treatment in being turned out of the public service, no doubt because he had passed the age limit. He is an extraordinarily clever old

---

[1]The book had been published earlier in the year.
[2]Sir Joseph Norman Lockyer was a distinguished astronomer who had worked for the Science and Art Department. At the time he was eighty!

man, brilliant indeed. I was seeking some astronomical information from him to help me in my romance *The Glittering Lady*[1], which I am writing. He was full of suggestions and is going to communicate with me further. He said he thought that I had a great idea in this book; also that 'intelligent romance' is of wonderful assistance to science as it turns attention to problems and excites interest in them. He has an observatory near the charming house they have built there, but it is shut up at present as all the assistants have gone to the war. I should like to be an astronomer. In fact there are so many things I should like to be that about ten lives would be necessary to master half of them. What a little can we do in our brief span and that little alas! how imperfectly.

Windham Club   *13th November, 1916*

Came to town today for the function tomorrow at the Royal Colonial Institute. At Waterloo I met Lord Curzon and asked him if anything was being done about the appointment of a board to deal with my Colonial results. He said that he had spoken to Bonar Law who told him that he was going to appoint such a board. (I forgot to ask him if I was to be one of them.) I remarked that 'nothing had happened'. He replied with sarcasm, 'Nothing ever does happen!' He promised to stir Bonar Law up again.

14th November, 1916

Both yesterday and today I sat to Mr Strang who is engraving my portrait on a copper plate, a three-quarter size head. It promises to be very good, though one can never tell how it will print. He has done all he can until a proof is taken. It is a wearisome business, but I think worth doing in order that a faithful representation of oneself as one is now may be preserved. Also it is his venture, not mine.

Last night I attended the Royal Colonial Institute dinner with which they open their session, Louie accompanying me. At the commencement of the proceedings Earl Grey, who had risen from bed to attend, presented me on behalf of the Council with a beautiful illuminated address thanking me for my work on behalf of the Institute and conferring on me an honorary life-fellowship of the Royal Colonial Institute for my public services. Also he read a letter he had received from Mr Bonar Law which stated that he was in communication with the authorities in the Dominions as to setting up a Central Board to deal with all these matters of emigration which we had raised. This is satisfactory as far as it goes. It was a remarkable gathering and one in which I may legitimately take some pride. It is

[1] The book which was then entitled *When the World Shook* was published on 20th March, 1919. Rider Haggard sent the outline of the book's plot to Lilias in a birthday letter dated 22nd June, 1916 (i.e. when he was on the *Niagara* off Honolulu).

strange that so many people should be willing to turn out at night in these times. I did not enjoy the trudge home through the darkened streets — for no cabs were available; I lost Louie as she got into a bus and after a vain hunt came back here.

16th November, 1916

At the office of the Dominions Royal Commission I was shown the cable which Bonar Law had sent to the Dominions, also one from Munro-Ferguson, the Governor General in Australia, to the Colonial Office. Bonar Law suggested an Imperial board to arrange emigration to the Dominions. Munro-Ferguson replied that the attitude of the Commonwealth towards this question of the settlement of Imperial ex-service men had changed 'partly owing to Rider Haggard's work', to which Bonar Law's cable also alluded. I understand that favourable replies are coming in, except from South Africa, so perhaps the board will be finally established.

I went for a walk and happening on St Thomas' found there was a service and attended it. One lady and I formed the congregation! It was a restful, hallowed place. I dined at the Athenaeum off oysters and a chop.

Budleigh Salterton   *17th November, 1916*

The weather is horrible and very cold. I am glad to be out of London which is a dreary place now after 4.30 p.m.

26th December, 1916

Yesterday was Xmas Day, a sad, sad Xmas for many. I had not the heart to drink healths after dinner. That old custom reminds one of too much. Angie and Dolly dined here, so all the girls were present. They had just gone home when there was a ring and who should come in but Reggie, who had got his leave and motored from Exmouth. He was an impressive and war-worn figure, his khaki clothes covered with trench-mud, haggard, exhausted, almost unable to speak from bronchial laryngitis or some other form of throat common at the front. I don't remember anything that has, in a flash as it were, brought the war more home to me than his sudden appearance in that quiet drawing room in search of his wife whom he must have passed on the road — except perhaps the first Zeppelin bomb thundering down near the house at home. Well thank God he has appeared, for he has been a long while in the trenches commanding the 18th Durham Light Infantry and well under fire the whole time. He has been whispering incidents to me this morning (for he cannot talk).

Windham Club   *27th December, 1916*

I came up to town today. In mid-November I left it plunged in black fog and so I

88

find it again. At Waterloo porters were difficult and taxicabs an impossibility. At last by soft words I persuaded an old fellow who said that he had been on his wheels since six this morning with nothing but a glass of beer to support him to drive me here, where to my relief we arrived in safety through the numb streets. It is sad that this melancholy winter should be the worst climatically that London has known for a score of years and the most unwholesome. The fog never seems to lift. Yet I left Budleigh Salterton bathed in bright sunshine.

29th December, 1916

Sitting all day on the Dominions Royal Commission and at 4.30 went to see Mr Massey, the premier of New Zealand, at the Hotel Cecil. He says that very small progress has been made as to the appointment of an Emigration Board by the Government. He promised to make further enquiries.

30th December, 1916

I have been sitting on the Dominions Royal Commission all day and in the evening was interviewed on agricultural matters by the *Daily Chronicle*. Afterwards Bainbrigge[1] and I dined together at the Athenaeum, a very pleasant meal. I suggested to him that he should compile a short book of the actual sayings of Christ, dealing with all the aspects of human life, with a short preface and an explanatory epilogue. He was much taken with the idea and proposes to follow it up.

[1] He was the vicar of St Thomas's Church, Regent Street.

1917

During the long, cold winter Rider Haggard wrote When the World Shook, *his last truly original story. In March, on his way to Ditchingham, he stayed in London for a while. He was relieved and triumphant when America declared war on Germany in April; but his own efforts to become closely involved in the war continued to be frustrated, although he was asked to serve on the Empire Settlement Committee but not, as he would have wished, as Chairman. And so in late April he returned to Ditchingham, but it was not to be even there as once it had been. In September his farms were sold and, having thus started, Rider Haggard seemed determined to set all his affairs in order. He gave to the Corporation of Norwich the collection of his bound manuscripts. So aged sixty-one he went for the winter to St Leonards, seeming to have accepted that there were to be no further official calls upon him and that as a writer he could expect nothing more than the apathy of the critics. Then in December, quite unexpectedly, he was involved in a bizarre incident — the War Office asked him to write to his friend, Theodore Roosevelt, to discover what additional help America could provide if, as seemed likely, Russia withdrew from the war. In the end the letter was not sent, but Rider Haggard had discovered a new interest — the fight against the spread of Communism.*

It is New Year's Day. I pray that in the course of the present year it may please Him to put an end to this fearsome war and in a different fashion to that intimated by that earthly interpreter of the Divine Will, the Kaiser William of Germany.

2nd January, 1917

The interview I gave to it appears in the *Daily Chronicle* today with a complimentary leader. Dined with Louie at the Empress; she has come to town for a few days.

3rd January, 1917

Bateman and I entertained the members of the Dominions Royal Commission at dinner here at the Windham. It went off very well, I think.

5th January, 1917

I received this morning a very affectionate note from Kipling begging me to write to him and to come to stay with him. I have answered, pointing out that I have written twice and had no answer and that therefore I desisted not wishing to bore him. Perhaps he never got the letter. In a small way I was put out. How easy are misjudgements and misunderstandings. 'Why the deuce can't you send me a letter?' he asks. Well, I was wondering the same of him. I can't go down to Batemans at present.

Have been working hard all day on the Royal Commission and at the Royal Colonial Institute. I saw Balfour at the Athenaeum tonight. He looks uncommonly well, but no man with such a nose as his ever was or will be really great! I did not speak to him as I daresay he has forgotten me by now.

6th January, 1917

I see sad news in the evening paper: Selous has been killed in East Africa. Although he was not the original of Allan Quatermain as everybody says, I have known him for very many years and once he stopped with us at Ditchingham. The last time we met was a few years ago at the dinner of a queer club of which I forget the name[1], when, under the guise of speaking as an inhabitant of the earth 2000 years hence, which by the rule we were all obliged to do, I made rather a successful speech about population and the future of the Western world. I remember noting how wonderfully well and strong he looked. He was an odd but most gallant man, with a frame and constitution of iron — a mighty hunter before the Lord. And now the Germans have got him, just after he had received a decoration. Well, I daresay he would have asked no better end. It seems only the other day that I was

[1]It was the Delphian Club. H.R.H.

sending him a wedding present, I think a pair of fine old Sheffield candlesticks, but I daresay it is over twenty years ago. God rest him! He is one of the last of his sort, an African hunter of the Allan Quatermain stamp.

I have been working all day on the Dominions Royal Commission. The evenings are lonely. It is impossible to dine out at any distance and then be obliged to make one's way home in the dark or rain because no taxi can be found. I do not understand how some men can spend their whole lives in clubs, chatting to people whose names, for the most part, they do not know. It would have driven me to vice — or spiritualism — for a change!

8th January, 1917

Today Strang finished his copper engraving of my head. I am glad to be done with the job, but it may serve to show any who are curious in after days (should such be found) what I was like — more or less — in the year 1917.

9th January, 1917

We had a special meeting of the Land Settlement Committee of the Royal Colonial Institute this morning to hear the views of Mr Massey, the Prime Minister of New Zealand, on all my business of ex-soldier settlement in the Dominions after the war. He spoke very wisely on the whole matter, urging its vast importance. Of the formation of the proposed board he said that he thought the Dominions should be represented, also that I should be on the board, either as Chairman or at least in a very prominent position. He is going to advance these views in the proper quarter. I spoke also, as did others. Whether anything will come of it I do not know.

This afternoon I visited the second exhibition of Raemaeker's famous cartoons. When I was there on the final day of the show last year the place was crowded and every drawing sold. Now at the beginning of the show there were not half a dozen people in the room and only a very few of the drawings had been sold. Thus does fashion change in England. The pictures are powerful as before, but most of them dreadful; also as before I noticed that those which satirized Wilson had been bought.

12th January, 1917

Today the Dominions Royal Commission has risen for about three weeks. Thank heaven! I am not clear of it, however, as Harding (who dined with me tonight) and I have to draft a new chapter at Budleigh Salterton.

This afternoon I saw and passed the film of *Dawn*.[1] It is not so bad, but as I have remarked before to an author these cinema performances of his books are full of

[1]Made by H. Lisle Lucoque, the film starred Karina as Mildred Carr, Hubert Carter as Devil Caresfoot, and Madeleine Seymour as Mildred Caresfoot.

woe and grief. The women as usual are better than the men, but I doubt if Angela would know herself.

Lance came to say goodbye to me this evening before returning to France. Good fortune go with the boy who is a gallant young fellow. I have received a charming letter from Kipling.

Budleigh Salterton   *13th January, 1917*

I returned from London this morning after an absence of nearly three weeks. The weather in town during that period has, I think, been the worst that I remember during the whole of my life, and the intense darkness of the streets added to its misery.

18th January, 1917

I am working here with Harding on the Dominions Commission Report.

19th January, 1917

Kipling writes to me today: 'Your account of Roosevelt was *most* interesting. I don't think he need worry however about coming over. *Very* few people, I fancy, would care to discuss the U.S.A.'s attitude with citizens of those parts. It is beyond words, or explanation. Of course the interesting thing is the price the Gods will exact. *We* betrayed a poor 70,000 or 80,000 dead Frenchmen in 1870; and — behold the price today. What comes to a land that betrays all lands?'

20th January, 1917

I have been engaged for the last four days on the Introduction to our Dominions Royal Commission Report. It is a tricky piece of hack writing, of which the chief objects are to avoid giving offence and to conceal certain unpalatable facts. Moreover, one feels that it is to a great extent labour in vain, since few read these documents and fewer still follow their advice. However, it all comes in the day's work and thank goodness it is done.

22nd January, 1917

I hear today through D'Abernon, who has been recommending me for the Chairmanship of the new Emigration Board, that a Chairman has already been appointed. Indeed he encloses a letter from Mr Walter Long in which this is stated. I cannot say that I am surprised, although of course this is disappointing, as I should have liked to run that show. However, it frees me from responsibility and

I greatly doubt whether sufficient powers will be given to the Board to enable it to do anything effective. Very probably the permanent officials do not desire an energetic man as Chairman. I trust, however, that whoever is chosen will be one of ability.

The weather remains bitter and as depressing as is the news.

24th January, 1917

I have put all the balance in my investment account, and a little more into the War Loan, not because I like it very much, but because I conceive it to be the duty even of humble people like myself to help to the full extent of their power. But as to this borrowing to invest I will have none of it, for who can tell what they may be able to earn another year?

26th January, 1917

Last evening we were indeed distressed to hear that Hal, my nephew and godson, had been 'terribly wounded' apparently in the naval fight of last Monday. His mother writes that one of his feet has been amputated and the other operated on; also that he is much cut about in other ways. Her first letter suggested doubt as to whether he would live, but this morning's news is better. At the best his naval career, I presume, is finished. In short it is a sad business.

29th January, 1917

Desperate efforts are being made to popularize the War Loan. Thus this morning I received from the Society of Authors an official appeal to its members to write poems or other copy on the subject. Anyone who can make up a readable poem on the War Loan must possess remarkable talents!

Windham Club   *30th January, 1917*

I have come to town to attend the Dominions Royal Commission, our last sitting I suppose after five years of them. I hear that Lord Tennyson is to be the Chairman of the new Emigration Commission or Committee. I do not think that he is a strong personality, though an agreeable gentleman. He will have a difficult hand to play. I am to be one of the members. Harding, much against his will, is to be Secretary. He says the terms of reference are very vague.

31st January, 1917

Today I received my appointment to the new Empire Emigration Committee. I have accepted, though of course I should have liked the Chairmanship.

Budleigh Salterton   *2nd February, 1917*

I left London in a black fog — the weather there is truly awful and obliged me to cancel my appointment to meet ex-King Manuel.[1]

                                              3rd February, 1917

I have to pay the first instalment of my Income Tax today. It is a tremendous proportion of one's earnings.

Windham Club   *16th February, 1917*

Today we signed our report and the Dominions Royal Commission is practically dissolved. It was rather a sad function after five years of corporate work. Tonight we all dined with Bowring at Claridge's Hotel. So ends the Dominions Royal Commission. Peace to its ashes and may its labours prove fruitful! They have not been light. I know that personally I have worked very hard at the business.

Budleigh Salterton   *17th February, 1917*

I have received a letter from Sir Sydney Olivier asking me to write articles on behalf of the Board of Agriculture and its measures. I have replied that I cannot do so without the necessary knowledge and suggested that if they want my services in the matter they had better put me on one of their Advisory Committees so that I may know what is going on. Whether they take the hint or not is a matter of indifference to me, but I think from their own point of view that they would be wise to do so.

                                              1st March, 1917

Today I have received an advance copy of our Dominions Commission Report which was sent to the King on the 27th February. Our remarks about the Imperial Institute seem likely to excite comment. It is an interesting document and will, I hope, advantage the Empire.

                                              5th March, 1917

The weather continues very bad with heavy snow in the north and makes agricultural operations difficult. Never do I remember such a winter.

                                              8th March, 1917

I see that *The Times* announces the election of Sir John Cockburn, General Sir Edward Hutton, and myself as Vice-Presidents of the Royal Colonial Institute.

[1]He became King of Portugal in 1908, but was forced to abdicate on 3rd October, 1910.

This is a very nice compliment which has been paid to me, especially coming so soon after the conferring of the Honorary Fellowship.

10th March, 1917

Today I finished a romance that I have been writing, called *Yva*.[1] I am rather proud of having been able to do this work in the midst of so many distractions and anxieties, especially as I think it good of its sort. However this may be, it has served to take my mind off all the troubles among which we live, at any rate for an hour or two each day. My stay here is coming to an end, and I go to town on Monday. The weather continues awful.

Windham Club   *12th March, 1917*

Today, with some regret, I left Budleigh Salterton where I have been since last autumn. The weather there this winter has been as vile as everywhere else, but the place suited me and is pretty. Without work to do, however, I should not have cared for it, as it is 'quiet' to the verge of exasperation. As I departed, the sun shone out a little after two days of steady downpour. I managed to bring with me a good deal of luggage which I saw the Inspector regarding with a malevolent eye!

Norfolk Hotel, North Kensington   *15th March, 1917*

Conan Doyle, whom I met at the Athenaeum, told me that yesterday he was breakfasting with Mr Lloyd George who informed him that there is a revolution in progress in Russia, which I have been expecting for some time. It appears that amongst other events the Guards broke out and shot all their officers except one subaltern. This revolution, he said, however is not anti-war, but if anything is pro-war, a rebellion of the Army against bureaucrats and corruption. Thus when the revolted troops rushed into the armoury they found there an English Delegate and instead of killing him gave him an ovation and escorted him to his hotel. Doyle said that Lloyd George did not seem to be depressed about the business.

Today I met D'Abernon. When I asked him how he thought things were, he answered 'bad' and added that there was a revolution in Russia, thereby confirming my previous intelligence.

17th March, 1917

Today I went to see General Smuts[2] and had a long and interesting talk with him.

[1] *When the World Shook.*
[2] Jan Christian Smuts was the Minister of Finance and Defence, South Africa. He first became Prime Minister in 1919. As Botha was unable to attend he was representing his country at the Imperial Conference of the Dominion Prime Ministers.

He says that in East Africa the Germans are practically finished; their only hope being to retreat into Portuguese territory — those who are left of them. I have never met Smuts before, having always missed him. He strikes me as a most alert and able man, as indeed he has always proved himself. I was much impressed with him. He appeared to be very glad to see me and thanked me for coming.

Also today I left D'Abernon's and my own cards on all the Prime Ministers. We are thinking of entertaining them to dinner at the Athenaeum.

At luncheon I saw Kipling and we went together to Brown's Hotel where they are staying. Mrs Kipling is, he says, very unwell, but she was out. Kipling himself I thought looked far from well. He complains of his stomach, indigestion he calls it — as I remember he did two years ago — and looks thin and aged.[1] He is writing a history of the Irish Guards to which poor John belonged. They have heard nothing further as to his fate, but are trying to win news from the Germans by means of messages dropped from aeroplanes. The truth is that business has knocked them both out and when I said so he did not deny it. Since it happened he has changed greatly and I fancy that I am one of the few with whom he cares to keep up associations. As he said, after a certain age friends are not many. He is deeply interested in my *Yva* story and I have promised to take it to him to read.

20th March, 1917

Kipling and I lunched together at the Athenaeum and had a very pleasant talk. Afterwards I attended the meeting of the Council of the Royal Colonial Institute, sitting as a Vice-President for the first time. Louie has gone to Ditchingham for a few days, taking Jeekie with her.

21st March, 1917

Dined with Kiplings at Brown's Hotel. Very pleasant. I read them the 'Gyroscope' theme in *Yva*.

23rd March, 1917

Today I went down to Hampstead to listen to a reading of Sir Ronald Ross's[2] poems in the beautiful house of Sir William Lever — the soap magnate. The pictures there are wonderful and I was delighted to meet Ross after efforts extending over many years. He is an able and many-sided man, and once he wrote

[1] In 1933 a Parisian doctor discovered that for many years Kipling had been suffering from undiagnosed duodenal ulcers.
[2] He was the discoverer of the malaria parasite, winner of the Nobel Prize for medicine in 1902, and Professor of Tropical Medicine at Liverpool. He and Rider Haggard became close friends.

an admirable romance, now out of print, called *Child of Ocean*. I wrote to congratulate him upon it and that is how our epistolary connection came about.

The weather continues to be awful, indeed almost unparalleled.

24th March, 1917

I met Oliver Lodge[1] at the Club and had a talk with him about his spiritualistic propaganda; I rather taking the other side. He agrees that these researches should be conducted by scientists.

26th March, 1917

I called on Dean Inge[2] today at St Paul's Deanery. This great and acute thinker is a withered little man and rather deaf — also somewhat shy. I was very glad to make his personal acquaintance as he is an interesting personage. He informed me that he had learned on good authority that America considers herself at war with Germany.

27th March, 1917

I believe that the sovereignty of the world must ultimately pass to America, with her enormous wealth and natural resources. Perhaps it is as well that this should be so, especially as America is our child, but thank God I shall not live to see all these changes. At least Britain has played a gallant part in the history of the world.

Our Dominions Report was published today. It is, I think, a great State paper but no one, if a judgement may be formed from the Press, takes, or is likely to take, much notice of it. At any rate we have worked hard, gratuitously and disinterestedly, for five long years on behalf of the Empire.

28th March, 1917

Today at the Athenaeum Sir George Goldie[3], whom I consider one of the really big men of my generation, and I lunched together. We have not met since we travelled as far as Aden and I went on to India before joining the Dominions Royal Commission on its first tour through Australasia. He is growing old and short-sighted now, as he said, something of a 'back-number' like myself, but still manages to control the finances of the London County Council, though he has given up his Imperial

[1] Although an eminent physicist (and first Principal of Birmingham University), he gave much time to psychical research.
[2] From 1911 to 1934 he was the Dean of St Paul's. Because of his pessimistic pronouncements he was called 'the Gloomy Dean'.
[3] He was called 'the founder of Nigeria'. At the time he was President of the National Defence Association.

work. Had it not been for him much of Africa which we hold today would have passed from us, and I well remember his account to me of his struggles with official stupidity and 'don't-care-less' at home and of the series of chances by which he was in the end able to save it to the Empire.

This afternoon I attended a meeting of the Executive of the Relief of Allies Committee of the Royal Agricultural Society. We debated the question of supplying Scotch fir seeds to reafforest devastated areas in France.

30th March, 1917

I said to Kipling at the Athenaeum today that I trusted that we should not be expected to inhabit that region in the next world which was occupied by Germans. He replied that he was quite convinced that we should find none in any hell that he and I might land in. I think so too; whatever our sins we have not deserved that! Rudyard Kipling and Martin Conway[1] were lunching together. Afterwards Conway came into the billiard room downstairs and informed me that Rudyard Kipling had been talking with admiration and amazement of the MS. of the story *Yva*, which I had given to him to read, saying that it was as full of go and imagination as though I had been sixteen instead of sixty.

Later Rudyard turned up and repeated this and more. He said to me that he had read the whole thing at a sitting 'interlineations and all', really read it, and that its grip and 'freshness' astonished him. He lay upon a sofa with those slippery sheets before him, unable to leave it, and thought it a remarkable work of imagination — really a new thing. I asked him if he had any criticisms to make. He said that he would not venture to offer any — there was the work — in a way outside of criticism — as good as anything I had ever done — or words to that effect. Evidently too, he meant all he said. This from such a man is complimentary, especially as he is not prodigal of compliments, but I am sure that when it appears the public — or rather the critics — will not discover these virtues in the book. It is not their fashion to praise my work. However, I am glad that the tale pleases its first reader so completely. The truth is that he (Kipling) has imagination, vision and can *understand*, amongst other things that Romance may be the vehicle of much that does not appear to the casual reader.

31st March, 1917

I lunched with Charles Longman and his wife, rather a sad couple now, I fear. Then I went to West Kensington to see the Hildyards in their new house. While there I walked to 69 Gunterstone Road, a house I have not seen for thirty years or more, and stared at the outside of the ground-floor room which was my study. In

[1]He was a mountaineer, art critic and, from 1918 to 1931, M.P. for the English Universities.

its window stood my desk, now at Ditchingham, on which I wrote *She* in 6 weeks.[1] That stuccoed, suburban residence was a queer birthplace for Ayesha, the immortal. My earnest gaze brought out a servant who evidently thought I contemplated burglary and regarded me and Cecil Hildyard with much suspicion. In that room also I had the experience with the mummy, which is now in the Norfolk Museum at Norwich.[2] More heavy snow this morning making the streets a river. Indeed the weather is awful beyond words.

2nd April, 1917

The ferocity of the weather continues. This morning there was a fall of several inches of snow in London, turning the streets into pools and rivers of icy slush. Longrigg writes that he cannot get in the barley. This endless winter is nothing short of a disaster, but I suppose it afflicts the Germans as well as ourselves.

3rd April, 1917

Kipling has returned *Yva* and writes: 'Dear old man, Here's your MS. back again and a thousand thanks for the privilege. As I told you yesterday it's as fresh and as convincing as the work of a boy of 25 and it held me like a drug. That's your d---d gift!' Then follows a small criticism about the description of one of the characters and of the spelling of biretta, which has been typed baretta. Just like him to notice this slip!

6th April, 1917 (Good Friday)

D'Abernon and I are in a mess about our dinner to the Colonial Premiers etc. at the Athenaeum on 12th April. Yesterday I saw in *The Times* that the Pilgrims, of which I am a member, had fixed that night for a great national entertainment to the American Ambassador, with Balfour, who was to dine with us, presiding. Negotiations followed and to cut a long story short it is now arranged that our party should dine (for the most part at one table) at the Savoy at the Pilgrims feast. I think this is a good way out of the trouble, but heavens! what a worry it has been.

7th April, 1917

The United States of America has declared war upon Germany. The event is of stupendous importance in the history of the world and to what it may lead none can say, possibly to an alliance between the English-speaking peoples and a league to enforce peace on the world. Let us hope so.

[1]The manuscript was finished on 18th March, 1886.
[2]Unfortunately Rider Haggard does not say what the experience was.

This afternoon I went to see the Epstein sculptures about which everyone is talking. An inspection of them suggests to me that I must be sadly deficient in taste and artistic insight since in them I can find nothing to admire. The head of Lord Fisher is recognizable but unpleasing and of those of the ladies I can say nothing, as for aught I know they may all be as ugly as the artist makes them. But what of the Venus? A great block of shapeless marble with a head like a comma or a query, on which the female attributes are rudely and unpleasantly indicated — such is Aphrodite according to Epstein. Well, I prefer the Greek conception of that goddess. I suppose it all means something ultra-futurist and wonderful, but the only objects the work reminds me of are the vulture-headed poles on the walls of Zimbabwe, also emblems of a goddess of love — to which it has some superficial resemblance. As for the 'Mother and Child' (unfinished according to the catalogue), it might have been hacked from a granite boulder by a mad Aztec or Bushman. There is no 'Mother' visible and the child is a flat-headed Hottentot doll in relief.

I have just received a letter from Roosevelt dated March 14. He writes: 'Dear Haggard, your letter of Feb. 23rd. has just come, and of course it pleased me very much. Indeed, I shall be delighted to have the Allan Quatermain book dedicated to me.[1] I eagerly look forward to seeing it. Well, friend, what you did on the staff of Sir Theophilus Shepstone was only one of the incidents in your honourable career of lifelong service to your country.' Then he continues about some books I sent him and a letter he wrote to me which I never received and continues: 'As you say nowadays one does not know who will read one's private letters. Yet I cannot forbear saying that I am sick at heart, and burnt up with fiery indignation, at Wilson's timid shuffling and hesitancy. He is as baneful to this country as an overdose of morphine to an invalid. We should have been in the war six weeks ago. He has not even been preparing. He seems impervious to every consideration of national honour and right; and he has behind him the solid alliance of the utterly base materialists, the utterly silly sentimentalists, and all that portion of the population which is at heart treacherous' etc., etc. Is not this interesting reaching me (censored) three days after the States have declared war? What, I wonder, was the real cause of Wilson's change of attitude? I will write and ask T. Roosevelt.

Today I lunched with Lady Allendale.[2] Sitting next to her there at table, I could not help remembering another meal I ate, also as her guest, at Maritzburg in Natal

---

[1]The book was *Finished*. It was published by Ward, Lock & Co. on 10th August, 1917.
[2]In 1891 she had become the second wife of Wentworth Blackett Beaumont (as he then was). He had died on 13th February, 1907.

in 1882 — thirty-five years ago when we both were young, on that fateful night before Sir George Colley, her husband of those days, started up country to disaster for his country and himself. Of that dinner of, I think, thirteen she, my wife and I now alone survive!

12th April, 1917

Yesterday morning our Empire Settlement Committee, which is the result of my journey round the world on behalf of the Royal Colonial Institute, held its first meeting. It is a huge body of thirty-five, so unwieldy indeed that it was found necessary to appoint a General Purposes Committee of about twelve, of whom I am one, and an Agricultural and Industrial Problems Committee of about seven, of whom I am also one. These two committees will take evidence and indeed do everything, only reporting at intervals to the main committee.

13th April, 1917

The Pilgrims dinner last night was a very interesting function — more interesting than the food which was distinctly of a 'war' order and not too plentiful — indeed we were almost starved, except for speeches. All or nearly all our Athenaeum dinner party, which it knocked out, turned up — Sir R. Ross, Sir Joseph Ward, Lord Burnham, Mr Walter Long, D'Abernon, myself, Mr H. G. Wells, Mr Massey, General Smuts, Dean Inge, Will and Sir A. Bateman. (I think that they must have regretted the oxtail soup, roast turkey, plum pudding I had proposed for them!) We all sat at one big table next to that of the guest, Mr Page. I was between Smuts and Massey with Wells on the other side of Massey. The former aired his republican views on the latter and Massey, being of a rather conservative type and a great believer in monarchy, was rather horrified, seeing which I fanned the flame for fun. At the beginning Massey inquired of me in a whisper whether Wells was not a Socialist and I replied that I believed he had leanings that way. However, Wells was amusing, especially when he declared that Roosevelt was not a real man but one of *my* 'creations' come to life. Undoubtedly he is a brilliant man.

16th April, 1917

I had a talk with Lord Milner[1] at the Athenaeum yesterday. He is disturbed about the submarine menace and not happy as to the Russian situation which, having just returned from that country, he should understand. He is not sure where the revolutionary movement will end. Undoubtedly the hatred of kings is growing, in Russia and elsewhere, and I hear that our own George R. is very anxious about the Czar and 'much upset'.

[1]Alfred Milner, 1st Viscount, was, as Minister without Portfolio, a member of the War Cabinet.

19th April, 1917

Last night I addressed the 'Rainbow Circle' on matters connected with the land, commenting on a paper that was read by Mr Percy Alden, M.P.[1] It was an interesting little gathering of advanced 'intellectuals' at 33 Bloomsbury Square. One of those present expressed strong Socialistic views which others, although most of them appeared to be Radical in their views, by no means endorsed. One cannot improve the conditions of English Land by imposing death duties of 20/- in the pound!

Ditchingham   *20th April, 1917*

I have returned here after an absence of six months.

Today I attended the 'solemn service to Almighty God on the occasion of the entry of the United States of America into the great war for Freedom' at St Paul's. I had a seat which Inge gave me in the Dean's Closet, a queer little box of a place above the Chancel, over where the Bishops sat, whence I had an excellent view of everything, especially as there was plenty of room in the 'closet'. It was a most impressive historical ceremony and one that touched the imagination. Of course the mise-en-scène was splendid: the mighty fane filled with thousands that yet somehow gave no impression of crowding (I suppose because of the vastness of the place), the great reverent audience, the military band, the full trained choir, the pealing organ, the rows of robed dignitaries of the Church, Archbishops, Bishops, Clergy of high degree — representatives of the Hierarchy of Heaven on earth — and the rest. Then there were the King and Queen and other Royalties, the Lord Mayor with his mace and sword bearers and the scarlet-robed Sheriffs and Corporation, the vergers bearing crosses and croziers and I know not what beside. The service was what it is named, solemn, extremely so indeed, and yet simple. The preacher was Bishop Brent, an American, Bishop of the Philippines.

I do not think that ever before I realised how small the King is. Beside the Queen, who after all is not so very large, he looked tiny and unimpressive, though perhaps the tall feather in her hat accentuated the difference in height. (Were I His Majesty I should ask her to dispense with lofty plumes on public occasions.) To be frank he did not look half an inch a King, notwithstanding his Field Marshal's uniform.

Windham Club   *1st May, 1917*

I have come up to Town today to attend my Empire Settlement Committee, also to see about the Flat at 26 Ashley Gardens where I had a tumultuous hour this afternoon with builders, electrical people etc.

[1] He was a Christian Socialist who at the time was the member for the Tottenham division of Middlesex.

At the Athenaeum I met the Bishop of St Asaph whom I have not seen for over a year, during which time he has grown appreciably older — as I daresay I have also. He had just been seeing his friend Lloyd George (who is off to France again). From the Bishop (or rather from Lloyd George) I hear that we can hope for little effective help from Russia during the remainder of this war. It seems that the other day two divisions calmly walked out of the trenches saying that they would fight no more.

I attended a meeting at Burlington House this afternoon about Proportional Representation and sat next to H. G. Wells who made a good speech. I came out converted to the plan. Anything that would help us to get rid of our thrice accursed party system is to be welcomed.

Gt Eastern Hotel   *8th May, 1917*

I am up on my Committee of which I attended a meeting this afternoon. It seems likely to be an indistinct business since everything depends on future developments which, not being prophets, we cannot foresee.

I have just returned from dining with Sir Owen Phillips[1], one of the 'Merchant Princes' whom I suppose the war has benefited. It was a party of very distinguished people, among them Carson, Admiral Meux[2] (who said he had just been reading one of my stories, *The Holy Flower*, with delight and introduced himself to me), Long and many others.

Smuts was the guest of the evening. I asked him if it were true that he was going to stop here in some command but he appeared to be very doubtful on the point, and said that he wished to get back to S. Africa.[3]

Ditchingham   *10th May, 1917*

Today I went to the Royal Academy where I met the Duke of Portland, the President of the Royal Agricultural Society. I suggested to him that it would be a good business if it could be arranged, when conditions are favourable, for me to visit the devastated areas on behalf of our Allies Help Committee, on which we both serve, and write a little book about it with the object of exciting interest in our cause. He appeared to be struck with the idea and said that he would write to Lord Northbrook, the Chairman of the Committee, about it.

Windham Club   *15th May, 1917*

On arrival in London I went to the flat at 26 Ashley Gardens and found that good progress is being made there. Also I ordered a safe for the place, as in these days it

[1]He was Chairman of the Union Castle Line.
[2]Sir Hedworth Meux (formerly Lambton) had recently resigned as Commander-in-Chief, Portsmouth. He was returned unopposed as Conservative M.P. for that city.
[3]Smuts was in Britain as a member of the Imperial War Cabinet.

is desirable to lock up manuscripts etc. The price of the thing has gone up 50 per cent! All the afternoon I spent in giving evidence and being examined before my Committee, which seemed interested in what I had to say. I dined at the Athenaeum and employed my time at dinner and after it in reading Wells' book on God — a large subject.[1]

Ditchingham   *17th May, 1917*

Sugar is giving out. At my club, the Windham, I am only furnished with one tiny lump for my morning tea.

24th May, 1917

It is Empire Day when everybody is supposed to wear a purple badge to show that he or she is keeping the 'King's pledge' about food restrictions. Neither in London[2] or on the way down here have I seen a single purple badge!

2nd June, 1917

During the afternoon I heard the guns thundering on the French Front.

3rd June, 1917

The bombardment at the Front today is of a fearful character. I have been in the garden listening to it (3.40 p.m.). One continuous thudding roar of guns. I should think that it must herald some attack. It is strange to stand amidst the blooming mays and hearken to the thunderous matter that tells of the death of men!
   The weather remains terribly dry.

4th June, 1917

There is a lengthy list of Birthday Honours. D'Abernon, the Chairman of the Dominions Royal Commission, becomes a G.C.M.G. and Harding, the Secretary who has worked hard, a C.M.G. The five-year-long labours and journeyings of the rest of us are not acknowledged.

26 Ashley Gardens   *5th June, 1917*

We have made a beginning of getting into this flat. I think it will be comfortable when arranged.

[1] *God: The Invisible King.*
[2] Rider Haggard had gone up to town the previous day for a meeting of his Empire Settlement Committee.

I met Alwin Fellowes in Victoria Street. He promised (as Vice-Chairman of the Great Eastern Railway Board) to see about the reserving of carriages for ladies on the railway. At present women travelling are invaded by numberless soldiers who smoke them into kippers.

6th June, 1917

I lunched with Reggie Cheyne and Dolly. Reggie is off to France tomorrow morning to take command of his regiment after leave. He has been engaged in very heavy fighting, most successfully on the whole. Although so keen a soldier he seems weary of the war like everyone else.

7th June, 1917

D'Abernon writes to me that he had no idea that a G.C.M.G. was being conferred upon him and that his list of our names, which he was given to understand would be passed, was simply 'shelved' without his knowledge. He is much disturbed about the business, but I suppose the fact is that we unpaid Empire-toilers were turned down to make room for more 'political' promotions. It is a rather shameless affair. He still hopes that 'justice will be done', especially to some of our number who, after all their years of hard work, may never have another chance of earning public recognition. The joke of it is that all these things should happen in the name of the King!

Ditchingham   *8th June, 1917*

Yesterday I received the bill for the rent of the telephone at 26 Ashley Gardens. I have already paid a £4 fine for the installation of this telephone and now, in addition to this and to ordinary rent, I am charged an entire pound for contingencies and expenses. I wonder if it is all legal.

No rain yet, the drought is becoming serious but the weather is beautiful for every purpose except farming.

9th June, 1917

Again on this perfect June night I hear the heavy guns booming ceaselessly at the Front. I noticed them first about 6 p.m. This may herald some fresh onslaught or be but the usual bombardment. What a horrible and wonderful thing is a modern battle. The preliminary furious cannonade, levelling the woods, rending the earth and turning all natural things into an abomination of desolation, spotted with bursts of flame and reeking with poisonous gases, stench and smoke. Then the attack of ant-like helmeted men crawling in and out of the shell-craters, accompanied by monstrous machines resembling prehistoric animals, with one rain of fire bursting on them, that of the enemy, and another rain of fire preceding them by a few score of paces. Also thousands of feet above them the air-machines struggling against each other and now and again crashing to the ground in flaming ruins. And all around death, death, nothing but death and wounds and the misery of men.

13th June, 1917

The weather continues scorchingly hot and the drought is very bad indeed. Certainly, except from a farming and, therefore, a National point of view, so far the summer is lovely. Only sitting on the lawn beneath the green of the trees everything is spoiled by the booming of the distant guns in France. Not for a single hour will those guns allow us to forget. Nature may sleep at peace but man wallows in a hell of war.

14th June, 1917

The drought continues and for the time of year the weather is extremely hot. We have fallen on very evil days! The bombardment at the Front is tremendous this evening (7.30 p.m.).

17th June, 1917

There were more excitements here last night. About 10.30 Mason came with the intelligence that a Zepp raid was on. The others went to bed. I sat up, from time to time talking to Mason out of the window. About 2 (summer time) I laid down in my clothes. I heard a bomb or two, then some violent anti-aircraft firing from the direction of the coast. (This was after it had grown light.)

26 Ashley Gardens   *18th June, 1917*

At Liverpool Street today I found it impossible to get a taxi and had to ask the porter at the hotel to send my things by messenger. I don't know what has become of the cabs, but there are few to be found in the streets. At the hotel I thought all my friends the employees there looked very solemn. I think those bombs within a few yards have shaken them, and no wonder. London is *very* oppressive notwithstanding the thunderstorms which so persistently miss us in Norfolk. At the luncheon to Mr Holman, the Premier of New South Wales, given at the Savoy Hotel I thought the bombs were falling. However, it was only thunder. Holman spoke well, but at too great length, I thought. I appreciate the comfort of this flat and having a place of our own to come to.

19th June, 1917

The weather is a little less hot, but still extraordinarily close. Such rain as has fallen is very partial and where it comes so violent that it does almost as much harm as good.

20th June, 1917

We have been considering our Empire Emigration Report all day.

22nd June, 1917

My birthday! I am now old but I should be thankful for such health and strength as remain to me and so indeed I am. Having begun active life so young I seem already to have made a long journey in the world. Well I hope it has not been altogether useless.

28th June, 1917

Yesterday I was taken to tea at Brooks' in St James' Street, a club that, as it happens, I had never entered before. I was much interested in the old horseshoe gaming table with its seat for the banker which still stands in the room, itself practically unchanged, as an old drawing shows, where the gambling went on over 100 years ago. On the wall of the stairway is a case with counters or tokens, some of them marked as high as 500 guineas, which were used in the play, such as I speak of in my tale *Finished*. What excitements and tragedies must that room have seen, what beating of hearts and trembling of hands must have taken place around that table! And the players — where are they?

29th June, 1917

I have received another interesting letter from Roosevelt dated 1st June. He writes: 'My dear Rider Haggard, I thank you for your letter, and for the copy of the dedication. It pleases me very much. I shall re-read the end of your *Rural England* at once, although I well remember the general drift of those conclusions. I felt you were speaking the truth at the time. The 'miserable party politicians' mocked you, of course, as they mock all others. On this side, in the smallest spirit of party and personal politics Wilson has refused to allow me to raise and take abroad the divisions. However, I did force him into sending some troops abroad. He represents a common type in politics of democracies; the purely selfish rhetorician who has no thought except for his own advancement, who has no sensitiveness about either his own or the country's honour, and who has been trained in the dreadful school that treats words as substitutes for deeds. However, I am enormously grateful that we have gone to war. Under Wilson we shall not accomplish one tenth of what we would accomplish if there was a genuine man in the White House, but still we shall do something and we are on the right side. Theodore Roosevelt.'

110

30th June, 1917

Today I went down to Southend to open a new Salvation Army home for children. The function went off very successfully. Among the audience which I addressed was Sergeant Coward, of the old 13th Regiment, whom I was delighted to see again, as I thought he was dead. He is a very old man now. Coward was an orderly to Sir T. Shepstone when we annexed the Transvaal in 1877 and still has the flag which I hoisted at Pretoria on the Queen's birthday in that year. Brooks lifted the Union Jack from the ground and *I* ran it up. Sergeant Coward, who was present, is emphatic on the point, remembering everything clearly.

1st July, 1917

This is Sunday morning and in the street beneath a military band is playing and soldiers are marching by companies; perhaps they are going to attend service at the Roman Catholic Cathedral opposite. On the pavements other soldiers off duty are standing at attention. The scene is very martial. We are a wonderful people. Three years ago we were a nation of trading civilians, who screamed at the very word conscription. Now, behold! an armed camp or rather a nation in arms and everyone (practically) content to have it so.

I went to dine with Julia and there to my surprise found Tom[1] just arrived from France on thirteen days' leave. He seemed well, though he has had several turns of trench fever. He is a captain now, which he says is as high as a temporary Medical Officer goes.

Ditchingham   *3rd July, 1917*

Sir Herbert Tree, the actor, has died suddenly of a heart attack after a slight operation on his knee. I think that the last time I met him was in Dublin and before that at a Colchester oyster feast. I cannot remember if I have ever told the story anywhere, but he was amusing on this occasion. When the time came to go in, marshalled by the Mayor, Tree was nowhere to be found. At last an agitated secretary appeared and said to that dignitary, 'If you please, your worship, Mr Tree is in the lavatory with a typist.' Enquiry revealed that he was dictating his speech! We sat next to each other and I said that I wondered at one who had faced the public nightly for years finding it necessary to read a speech, whereas I did not. He replied, 'I can assure you that it is a very different thing repeating the words of others to improvising your own!' I had to leave the festival immediately after I finished my speech in order to catch my train. As I departed I heard Tree, who followed me on the toast list, saying in his deep voice with a tragic wave of the hand, 'Exit Literature; enter the Drama!'

[1]Thomas Barber Amyard Haggard was the second son of Baggett Haggard, Rider's elder brother. He had married his cousin, Agnes Angela Rider Haggard, Rider's eldest daughter, in 1907. Julia was his mother.

111

6th July, 1917

I have been sitting all yesterday and this morning on the Empire Settlement Committee considering our report. It is a difficult job with a score of people all starting new suggestions at once; indeed I do not know a more impossible way of correcting a proof! Result: we have not got through and must meet again next week.

9th July, 1917

9.30 p.m. The bombardment at the front tonight surpasses anything I have yet heard and this although the wind is northerly and blows half a gale. It is, or was, absolutely continuous, as though a thousand great guns were being fired as fast as they could be served. I say 'or was' because, oddly enough, as I write I cease to hear it though the window is open. I wonder whether it heralds some attack.

26 Ashley Gardens   *11th July, 1917*

Today we finished our discussion on the Empire Settlement Committee and signed the Report. So there is an end of my public work — at any rate for the present. I wonder whether the Government will take the business up, and, if so, when.

Ditchingham   *20th July, 1917*

The firing last night, especially about 7.15, was something tremendous, shaking all the windows of this house. It went on through the darkness though less continuously, and is going on at this moment. I suppose that it heralds some attack of ours on the Flanders front.

24th July, 1917

Today I have accepted an offer from John Murray, who has acquired Smith Elder's business, under which a story of mine is to be published in the *Cornhill*[1] and I am to get back a half interest in *Jess*, the copyright of which I sold for a small sum thirty years ago.[2] For sentimental reasons I am much pleased at this arrangement, although Murray's offer for *Moon of Israel* is at 'times' prices, as the auctioneers say. I have always bitterly regretted having parted with *Jess*, but truly everything comes to him who waits — if only he can live long enough!

[1] The story was *Moon of Israel* which appeared serially between January and October, 1918.
[2] The copyright was sold for £450.

Longrigg, my steward, a man of over military age who has been totally exempted, now informs me that the military authorities are appealing against his exemption, and this although it has been again and again announced that under no circumstances are more men to be taken from agriculture. Yet here an appeal is entered against a man who is looking after 700 acres of ground and who, within three months, is taking over a considerable proportion of that land as its tenant. What is one to say as to the foolishness and insincerity of the military authorities?

11th August, 1917

A curious circumstance of the time is the prevalence of theft. For instance, groceries coming to this house from the Junior Army and Navy Stores have on several occasions been opened and portions of the contents abstracted. Apparently this is done on the railways, but those in authority there say that they are quite unable to stop the practice. The tradesmen at Bungay all tell the same story, saying that hardly a package reaches them which has not been robbed. Louie, who has been in town, saw some of the head men at the Stores upon the matter. They allege that the evil is universal and that the goods which they send out by van are constantly plundered before delivery. Such conduct can scarcely be due to poverty, as even allowing for the high prices wages are higher than they ever were before. To what then is it due? A wave of moral corruption, I suppose, resulting from the loosening of every sort of accustomed restraint.

Our Empire Settlement Committee has issued its Report and I see passages that I wrote approvingly quoted in the papers. *The Times* has a sensible and sympathetic article upon the subject.

21st August, 1917

The harvest in Norfolk and most of Suffolk this year is said to be one of the worst ever known owing to the bitter winter and the spring drought. Wheat is especially poor, while beans and peas for the most part are not.

There have been more air-raids. Last night at 11.30 Mason whistled outside the window to attract our attention and informed us that the warnings were out. Result: I did not get my clothes off till 4.30 a.m. However, we heard nothing of the raid and at present do not know where it occurred.

This morning when I reached the bench at Loddon I was informed by the superintendent that warnings were out stating that another raid was in progress. These were given at 10.20 a.m. and not until 1.50 p.m. was it announced in the official telegram to the police that the raiders had left this country. One would have preferred that they had stopped here — 6 feet beneath its surface.

1st September, 1917

The weather continues awful for the harvest, showers, gales and thunderstorms. I was in Norwich to lunch and never before have I seen the market place so bare of cattle on a Saturday.

3rd September, 1917

I have just had a note from Kipling in which he says he is back from Scotland and adds: 'I have been seeing ships — and ships — and ships at Edinburgh, whereby I am a little cheered and happy. So buck up and believe me ever yours, Rudyard.'

8th September, 1917

Mr Burch, a gentleman connected with the Cape Sunday River Settlements, came down here yesterday to ask me whether I would be inclined to go out and write a report upon these settlements. I answered — yes, all being well, on certain terms immediately after the war. He seemed to think that these terms would be acceptable, and there the matter stands. I confess that I should like to have a house there in which to spend the winter since, as I grow old, the longing for South Africa where I spent my youth has become very strong with me. Also the climate of this country at that season of the year no longer suits me with my bronchial tendencies.

10th September, 1917

Today, Mr F. Leney, Curator of the Castle Museum, Norwich, has been here and has departed with a motor-car full of gifts. I have presented to the Corporation all my bound-up manuscripts, with two exceptions — *Allan Quatermain*, which I gave to Charles Longman, and *Mr Meeson's Will*, which I think I gave to my late friend, Mr A. P. Watt.[1] These MSS. run from about 1882 to 1892, after which date I was obliged to give up writing long books with my own hand, as the constant leaning over a desk affected my health. Bound up with them are certain letters of considerable historical interest: one, for instance, from Sir Theophilus Shepstone, written just before his death and treating of all his policy which resulted in the annexation of the Transvaal, and others from the late Empress Frederick of Germany as to the Dedication of *Eric Brighteyes* to the memory of the Emperor Frederick. I have felt for a long time in view of the risks of one sort and another to such documents both on the book shelves of an ordinary house and after the death of their writer and owner, that they would be better in the comparative safety of a museum. Therefore, since Norfolk has been the home of my family for several generations and I am Norfolk born, I have presented them to the castle collection, as I said in my covering letter — 'the gift of a Norfolk man to Norfolk'. Otherwise, within a very short period of a man's decease, there would be no one left who

---

[1]He did. The MS., originally entitled *Meeson v. Addison & Another*, consists of 174 foolscap pages. (A.P. Watt died in 1914. His son, H. Watt, took over the firm.)

would take the slightest interest in them, and probably in the end they would find their way, unless they were destroyed by accident, to the counter of a sale room. Still it makes me rather sad to part with them.

Our harvest is not yet up though, thank heaven, the weather has turned fine. In all my farming experience of about thirty years, I have never known the men work so badly as this season. Although their harvest money is very large, about £11 a head, and their labours are very light, as even the barley is cut with reapers and binders, they are slower and less efficient than they have ever been. Indeed it exasperates one to watch them dawdling about their business. Even when rain is coming up and but a little piece of a field remains to be carted, they will stop off for a lengthy tea, leaving the crop to take its chance, instead of postponing the tea for an hour or even thirty minutes and getting it safe under cover before the rain falls. This morning too, in a year when beans are so scarce and precious, I found four or five heaps of these that had been hand pulled grown through with grass and rotting, because the carters have not taken the trouble to collect them, and so on. Both Mr Simpson, my agent, and Longrigg, my steward, say that the fact is that the more money the East Anglian labourer makes, the less will he do. When they were badly paid owing to the poverty-stricken condition of farming, on the whole they worked fairly well, that is by comparison; now that they are better paid they work ill, and what will happen after the war in all the labour troubles ahead, I am sure I do not know. I am glad that I am giving up farming in England. It is altogether too anxious a business, although we are receiving better prizes for our produce than has been the case since I entered thereon.

Yesterday my gift of manuscripts etc. was reported to the Town Council of Norwich. There are columns about the matter in the *Eastern Daily Press*, and I observe that one of the speakers at the Town Council remarked that it was fitting that I should make this gift, to be exhibited in the Norwich Museum, in view of the great interest which my father, a very old Chairman of Quarter Sessions for the County, took in securing the utilisation of the castle for the purposes of a museum. In short, everyone seems to be highly pleased with what I have done, as I am myself, since whatever they may be worth the manuscripts etc. are now in safety.

Today I held my sale of stock as I am giving up farming. We were favoured with fine weather and on the whole it was successful. The stock realised between seven thousand and eight thousand pounds and I think that I may consider myself lucky to get this amount back into my pocket, plus the valuation and the value of the corn which are to come, although, as I told them at the luncheon today, during the thirty years that I have been farming never have I had out of it a five pound note to spend. I have farmed that I might know, as I consider that no man who does not know ought to write about the great agricultural industry as I have done in *Rural England* etc. Now, when I grow old and the responsibilities and worries are so many, the time has come for me to stop. Farming is a tricky business and who can tell what will happen to it in the future. Indeed I am glad to be on the right side of this sale, since some alarm or a couple of German aeroplanes passing over the ground might have cost me thousands of pounds, for whatever happened the auction must have gone on, even in the absence of the company.

I observed that the best animals, especially the high-bred Shire mares, sold the worst. It does not pay to have really excellent stock in Norfolk, unless it is *all* pedigree and enough in quantity to draw buyers from all parts of the kingdom. The average Norfolk tenant farmer does not care to buy, and indeed cannot afford to pay for, really good animals. Thus a tip-top pedigree bull purchased in the North a little while ago fetched less than its cost, whereas much of the rubbish fetched more.

However, on the whole the sale was successful and I consider that I am well out of the business. I have made nothing, if return on capital is taken into account, but I have gained a vast amount of experience, without which I could not have written my books on agriculture, which will, I trust humbly, prove of permanent value and interest in time to come. It has been a tiring and an anxious day, and I am glad that it is over.

25th September, 1917

It was fortunate that we had our sale yesterday, since the evening and night were disturbed. Just after it was over, explosions were heard, and we now hear that the south-east coast was being attacked by aeroplanes. If this had happened on Sunday night, it is probable that there would have been a small company at the sale. I am very glad to be rid of the responsibility of all these animals, most of which will have departed by tonight.

I've received a letter from John Murray *a propos* of my gift of manuscripts to the Norwich Museum, which he thinks wise. In it he says: 'Early in 1914 the German Government borrowed from us some very valuable Byron manuscripts and volumes of special editions for their Leipzig Exhibition. I lent them, all unsuspecting, and they insured them for nine thousand pounds. Shall I ever see them again? I doubt it.' So do I. Another argument for museums. Also I have heard on the same subject from Charles Longman, who highly approves what I have done. In his letter, which I have sent on to Norwich, he says that he considers *Colonel*

Quaritch[1] the best description of English country life in the nineteenth century extant; the only word-pictures of the sort comparable to it being those of Anthony Trollope.

24th September, 1917

Particulars of the new National War Bonds have been issued. These seem liberal, and include a four per cent Income-Tax-free issue, into which I think I shall put some of the money I have realised from the farm sale.

Havercroft, Ledbury   *29th September, 1917*

I came here yesterday *via* London, which struck me as very empty. The luggage porter at Paddington told me that vast numbers are leaving town. 'And I don't blame them if they can afford it,' he added grimly.

26 Ashley Gardens   *8th October, 1917*

Today I came up to town from Ledbury. As we drew near London the train became very crowded with refugees returning thither after the air raids, which now that the moon has gone down they *hope* are over for a while.

11th October, 1917

Today ends my thirty years career as an English farmer. Vale!

12th October, 1917

Today I lunched with Mr Spurgeon, the manager of Cassell's, and the head editor of the firm, Mr Flower. It was an interesting meal, at which I gave them my recollections of Cassell's before their time there, not altogether complimentary all of them, for in those days the firm treated authors like the dirt beneath their feet. I met too the recent chairman of their board, whose name I forgot, who remarked to me laughing, alluding of course to *Mr Meeson's Will*[2], 'They used to call us "the Hutches", didn't they?' I made various suggestions to Mr Spurgeon as to a collected edition of my works, which seemed to impress him a good deal. Indeed he appeared to wish to take the matter up.

Mr Flower produced out of his pocket-book a letter-card in my handwriting written in the nineties to himself as a boy in answer to some epistle evidently expressing pleasure in my work and announcing the writer's intention of adopting

[1]The book was published in three volumes on 3rd December, 1888.
[2]It was first published by the *Illustrated London News* in 1888.

a literary career — just a kindly note of mine wishing him success in his aims, that is all. I said that it had got very dirty in the last two decades, and he explained that for years he had kept it pinned over his desk as a reminder and encouragement to exertion. Well he has succeeded. I told them both how the success of *King Solomon's Mines* had ruined my prospects at the Bar. They seemed to think that the 'fame' more than made up for this. Perhaps!

15th October, 1917

This morning I heard that Reggie was leaving Charing Cross by the seven o'clock train, so I went to try and find him. For half an hour I hunted in the crowd without success; but at last, as I was giving the business up, I saw him. He had come up by the night train from Budleigh Salterton, and been much hustled, so much that he had left all the purchases he had made in the 'bus. We had a few minutes' talk.

Charing Cross is a curious and a melancholy spectacle when such a train is departing. Dozens of officers, from Generals down, with their kit, and a certain number of men of inferior rank of both Services. Also their womenkind come to say them goodbye. They are wonderfully brave, these women — mothers, wives, sweethearts, daughters! A quiver of the lip, a breaking of the voice — that is all! though occasionally as I walked up and down seeking for Reggie, I saw a pair in each other's arms in a compartment of the train. How many farewells have this station and Waterloo witnessed during the past three years — farewells, hundreds of them, for the last time on earth! The thing is terrible; if there is haunted ground anywhere it should be at this prosaic railway station.

I lunched with Julia who got caught out in two of the recent raids. In the excitement of one of these, at a club, I think a highly respectable lady burst out, she said, into the most profane and obscene language. I have heard of the same thing happening to the most virginal persons in the delirium of fever. But why in terror, or any unbalanced state, does Nature express itself in such terms? Is it because the impulses which dictate them are in fact nearest to our secret selves and cloaked over only by convention or religious restrain? Is it another instance of *in vino veritas?* Also, why are these stories generally told of women? Because they have less self-control, I suppose, not because they are worse than men at heart. Or perhaps it is because as a general rule, although not in this particular instance, the stories are told by men.

20th October, 1917

Last night Zeppelins visited London. A man from the Junior Army and Navy Store who has come to put draught-excluders on the doors says that there is a bad smash by Piccadilly Circus. This seems to have happened about half past eight, but he never heard the bomb. At a little after twelve I looked out of the window and saw people gathered in the doorway of the Westminster Cathedral, which I thought suspicious. At half past two we were roused from bed by fire engines and motor-bicycles rushing about furiously, blowing blasts on sirens. Then we got up and prepared for raids, but it seems quite doubtful whether this was not meant for the 'all clear' signal, which it was said would be given by bugle. Nett result: midnight vigils for several hours and precious little sleep. The odd thing is that no guns were fired, which suggests that the Zeppelins got here unobserved, also that they are now noiseless! The confusion as to 'warnings' and 'all clears' seems to be complete.

Since writing the above I have walked down Piccadilly and seen some of last night's damage. A single bomb was dropped near the Circus, opposite Swan and Edgar's shop. The damage done is great; Swan and Edgar's windows and those of many other establishments are wrecked. (In Swan and Edgar's case I observed that even the windows on the Regent Street side are blown out.) The roadway has a huge hole in it and is blocked, so that the buses must go round by other routes; the whole place is thickly strewn with fragments of glass. I was told in the Athenaeum that six or more people had been killed here, but I do not know if this is true.

Rose Mullion Hotel, Budleigh Salterton   *23rd October, 1917*

It is curious to come to this peaceful place after the strain of London. For that there is a strain in these times none can question: to say nothing of the actual air-raids, the anticipation of them, the hurrying home after dark lest a barrage of which one has missed the warning should suddenly begin and catch one in the streets, even the constant flow of news — good, bad and indifferent — all induce nervous strain. Therefore, the quiet and repose of such a place as this charming Budleigh Salterton is particularly welcome in this year and month of grace, especially when one's daughters are here.

The train coming down was very crowded, especially the first and third class, which made me glad I was travelling second, although it received the overflow from both.

27th October, 1917

Louie writes that she has taken a flat for us at St Leonards. I hope it will be more peaceful than London, where really it is impossible to do work under the present conditions, at any rate of the sort by which I earn my bread.

29th October, 1917

I have had a letter from Roosevelt (censored as usual) acknowledging the copy of *Finished* with my dedication to himself of which he says, 'I am very proud.' He adds, 'I shall not forget your visit here. It was one of the most enjoyable afternoons

I have spent with any friend. I wish I were to see you again.' He tells me that three of his sons are in France under General Pershing, and the fourth (Kermit, I suppose) is with our forces in Mesopotamia. Also one of his two sons-in-law is sailing for France. A fine record!

5th November, 1917

5 p.m. I have just heard from my brother Arthur that my nephew and godson, Lance, an Acting Major in the Princess Patricia's Canadian Regiment, which he joined as a private at the beginning of the war, is reported 'Missing; believed killed'. Indeed he seems to have no doubt as to his death, together with eleven other officers of the regiment, in an attack on a farm-house on the dreadful Ridge on the thirtieth of October. It is a terrible business. He was a most gallant young man, a very type of the 'Happy Warrior', for he loved his soldiering, and had nerves of iron. Another of these endless tragedies — Geoff, a prisoner in Turkey, and Lance killed, on the threshold of his days. Oh, when will God lift this cloud of death and blood from the face of our tortured world?

26 Ashley Gardens   *6th November, 1917*

The train from Budleigh was very crowded, and there was great difficulty in getting a taxi.

7th November, 1917

Poor Lance's death is in *The Times*. It seems that he was killed by a shell at the beginning of a charge within two hundred yards of the trench. Soon there will be few young men of the upper classes left in England.

Today Lord Kitchener of Khartoum, brother of 'K. of K.' — to whom he has a curious and rather distorted physical resemblance — came to see me about a scheme he has (on which he has written a book, whereof, alas!, he has left me the MS. to read) for the establishment of a great African Commonwealth, including German South West Africa, British East Africa, and German East Africa. In the course of our long conversation he told me a curious thing, which may be true or may be a morbid fancy of his own. He declares that his late brother's memory and everything to do with him is in the greatest disfavour with both the military and naval authorities, so much so, he says, that as a result of this prejudice both he and his son, to whom K. left all his property, have been extremely badly treated.

8th November, 1917

I had a long talk with my agent, A. P. Watt, this morning, as to the value of my copyrights, etc. He said that in his opinion, as an expert, it is impossible to estimate what this may be. He stated decidedly that in his judgement a number of my books will certainly live, and gave his reasons, which appear to be sound — among them that he finds that the new generation is reading them as much as ours did. I hope that he is right. At any rate I find that I can still command a market even in this time of war and misery. Thus I have just disposed of the English serials of *The Ancient Allan* and *Yva*, to Cassell's at a fair price[1], not so much, of course, as one used to get in pre-war days, but still a good sum, with the usual advance on the books. This is something at my age, and after publishing books for so long, and I am thankful for it.

15th November, 1917

This afternoon I attended the Memorial Service at Brompton Parish Church to the Officers and Men of The Princess Patricia's Regiment who fell in the recent attacks, of whom one was my dead godson and nephew Lance. It was a beautiful and moving service, and the address by the vicar was extremely good. The Duke of Connaught and the Princess Patricia were present. She is a nice-looking lady. The church was crowded and among the congregation were many of our family.

Alas! I have to give up my proposed 'She' story. It will not do. My hands are too tied by the contents of *She* and *Ayesha*. Also it is impossible to keep up interest in a tale laid beyond the confines of our Earth, since before it the average human imagination fails. So there's an end of She! I was reading *Ayesha* last night. It has weaknesses, but I must say I think that it contains some fine things — the transformation of Ayesha, for instance, and all that it symbolises. If that is not good of its sort, I do not know what is. On the whole I am glad I attempted the sequel, dangerous as it was. But there I think the venture had better end, although I had thought of some celestial — or infernal — scenes.[2]

I have been to the Stores to order some winter clothes and find that a suit which used to cost me five guineas now costs eight! I am informed, moreover (the steward at the Athenaeum had it from his tailor), that presently seventy-five per cent of the output of 'civilian' cloth is to be stopped, so that practically there will be no clothes at all or the prices will become quite impossible. A pleasant prospect!

17th November, 1917

I have got my bronchial catarrh. The fact is that I cannot stand the climate of London in winter.

---

[1]For each of the books Rider Haggard was paid £400 for the serial rights on receipt of the MS. and £750 advance on publication.

[2]She was not, however, to be buried quite so easily. Rider Haggard wrote about her again in *She and Allan* (1921) and *Wisdom's Daughter: The Life and Love Story of She-Who-Must-Be-Obeyed* (1923). For each of the books Hutchinson paid him £900 on receipt of the MS., for the serial rights, and a £1,000 advance on publication — far more than he was given for any other post-war book.

18th November, 1917

Today I met General Maurice[1], who is General Robertson's Deputy and right-hand man at the War Office. He seemed to think that in some way I might be of assistance through Roosevelt. I am to see him tomorrow afternoon at the War Office and go into matters.

19th November, 1917

I have been to see General Maurice, who propounded to me a whole set of questions to put to Roosevelt of a somewhat important nature. I have written the letter and posted it to General Maurice to send on, as I will not do this myself until he has approved it. The whole proceeding strikes me as rather curious[2] and I do not quite understand what it means. However, I have been very careful to do nothing that I was not asked to do and the responsibility is that of the War Office. I am not sure that Roosevelt will answer the letter.

I went to Cassell's also about the books of mine that they are going to publish and at the request of Mr Flower, the Editor, identified the room in which I had my famous interview of thirty-two or three years ago with the Editor, when inspired by a clerk in the corner I suddenly changed my mind and took the royalty agreement of *King Solomon's Mines* instead of the sum down. They were much interested and suggested that the place should be labelled 'Room Where Sir Rider Haggard Saved His Bacon'. It is remarkable that all this while afterwards I should still be disposing of books to Cassell & Co.

28 Grand Parade, St Leonards   *21st November, 1917*

The letter has come back from General Maurice, who, after consulting the Foreign Office, has concluded that we had better hold our hand a little to see if Wilson will move in these matters of his own accord on official reports. If he won't, he now thinks it will be time to invoke the Rooseveltian Jove. So do I, since if he got to work on my letter there might be trouble. Meanwhile I am to rewrite the letter with a few unimportant additions and send it to Maurice with a blank date so that this can be filled in and the epistle despatched if necessary. I have written to say that I quite agree with his amended view and will do whatever is required.

[1]General Frederick Maurice was the Director of Military Operations of the Imperial General Staff.
[2]The letter asked for help because of 'the Russian smash and the Italian trouble'. One of the questions was, 'Could the United States in your opinion send over aeroplanes in the largest number possible by April next?'

Today I have signed the contract for the purchase of a quaint little house in this town, known as North Lodge, in which, all being well, we hope to spend the winters in future, for the sake of the climate, which I find helpful to my chest. It was once the pay-gate of St Leonards and is about the oldest house in the place. A feature of it is that the public roadway runs under the stone arch that in its upper part forms the long room which I hope to take as a study. It stands high, and yet is singularly sheltered from the rough winds. Miss Rhodes, whom I used to know, a sister of Cecil, once owned it, or at any rate lived there.

26 Ashley Gardens   *13th December, 1917*

We came up to town today.

Louie today was in the Junior Army and Navy Stores, which were hung with meat, that many had come to buy. They went away disappointed for suddenly the Government commandeered it all!

10.45 p.m. We have just had some food after a raid, if indeed it is not still going on, for we have heard no 'All Clear'. The warning of police whistles came about 7 p.m. and the guns began a minute or two later. We retired to General Moore's flat in the basement, where we were hospitably received and spent a couple of hours there. The bombardment was heavy; we heard a good many bombs burst, and there appeared to be several waves of attacks. That is all we know, such is life in London in the winter of 1917. (We now learn that the 'All Clear!' was sounded twenty minutes ago; but we never heard it.)

A dense fog in London today, to add to the general depression. About midday there was an air-raid warning, for we were in a shop at Islington buying some second-hand furniture for the house at St Leonards when suddenly they began to put up the shutters all along the street. Soon, however, specials gave the 'All Clear!' and they were taken down again.

Greeba Hotel, St Leonards   *21st December, 1917*

The fog has been too much for me. I have had to fly from London and as our rooms here were not available owing to lack of servants have come to this little private hotel where Louie stayed. It seems very comfortable. In London I choked and began to feel my heart, and indeed still feel it, being very short of breath.

26th December, 1917

Yesterday was Christmas Day. It was, I think, the most melancholy Christmas that England has spent for many a long year. Certainly I felt it so, perhaps to some extent because I was quite alone.

31st December, 1917

So farewell to 1917! It has been a bad year on the whole, yet in it much has happened for which we may be thankful. May God send us a better in that which begins in two hours' time, and at the end of it may Peace once more rule on Earth!

Vale 1917. Salve 1918. And, oh, be kind to us!

1918

Although his friendship with Rudyard Kipling became even closer, it was not a happy year for Rider Haggard. He was asked to be an investigator for the Agricultural Wages Board, but ill-health forced him to resign. William, his elder brother, could no longer afford to keep the family home, Bradenham Hall, and so in August it was sold. Rider Haggard's popularity as a writer continued to decline and he dismissed himself as 'the deadest of dead letters'. His book Moon of Israel, *a story of the Exodus, which was published in the autumn, was but scantily reviewed.*

In November the war ended, but Rider Haggard felt uneasy about the peace. He was concerned that German militarism had not been defeated and would eventually rise again. But perhaps what saddened him most was the knowledge that 'it has not been my lot to stand at the front of high affairs'. He began to feel old and the future ceased to hold for him either promise or pleasure.

Thank goodness there is something to laugh at in the papers today, namely the comedy of Mr Galsworthy, the clever writer of fiction. Mr Galsworthy is, I am informed, a Socialist, or at any rate a very advanced person, and, being undoubtedly able, doubtlesss it was thought wise to 'rope him in', to muzzle him before he developed formidable powers of attack upon the Powers that be. So he was knighted in the sure and certain hope that henceforth there would be naught to fear from him. But Mr Galsworthy was not 'taking any' and declined the honour. Unfortunately his letter of refusal was received too late and willy-nilly it was thrust upon him. Now it has to be cancelled and whatever happens it is certain that Mr Galsworthy will not be offered another knighthood. It is all very funny!

I have received a letter from Sir Henry Rew, the head of the Agricultural Wages Board, asking me if I will be one of their investigators for some district. I have answered that I should have been delighted at any other time of the year, but now I am not sure. Also I have asked certain questions. I doubt if my health would bear prowling about the country in winter on such a job. Doubtless I shall hear more, but probably nothing will come of it. He says, 'I recognize it would be asking a favour of you to undertake such a job.' I am not proud and would gladly help, but will my 'pipes' stand it? Alas, I grow old and am no longer as strong as I was. Every afternoon I want a nap!

7th January, 1918

Yesterday was the day appointed for the service of national prayer and thanksgiving. I cannot pretend that it was very effectively celebrated at the church which I attended at St Leonards.

8th January, 1918

Today I have been to town to see Sir Aylwyn Fellowes and Sir Henry Rew. It is practically arranged that I am to undertake the investigation of Cornwall, Devon, and Somerset in order to report on the matter of agricultural wages, starting on the 28th instant. They put it at a three months' job, but I hope to do it in two, given health and strength. Arthur Cochrane is to accompany me. I have been wrestling to get a motor-car to travel in as my chest will not stand these draughty stations, also travelling expenses for Cochrane. They wish to help me in every way they can, being anxious for my services, but they are up against the Treasury. No doubt the end of it will be that I shall find myself considerably out of pocket. However, I undertake it as part of my war work, knowing that it is a task which I can execute as well or better than most, so I must put up with that.

28 Grand Parade, St Leonards   *9th January, 1918*

The weather seems to have put a stop to important fighting for the present. It is unprecedently bitter. Here at St Leonards half the cisterns and pipes are frozen; there is not a drop of water in this flat whither we have returned today.

28th January, 1918

Tomorrow I expect to start on my investigations for the Agricultural Wages Board.

New London Hotel, Exeter   *29th January, 1918*

I went to the Agricultural Wages Board, after which I lunched with Sir Henry Rew at the National Club, where I met Alfred Bateman and Edmund Gosse, the latter of whom I had not seen for some time. He wears wonderfully well, although he is nearly seventy. He seemed pleased to see me and informed me that I looked 'very picturesque'. Well if one can't look anything else, one may as well be 'picturesque'. His talk was of Andrew Lang, also of Kipling who, he says, associates with no one except myself, though I have not seen anything of him latterly. I suppose it is thirty-three years since I first met Gosse and it is strange how little he has changed.

The Treasury has agreed to pay Cochrane's travelling expenses and sustenance allowance, which is satisfactory as now I shall not be so much out of pocket. It seems very quiet down here, far from war's alarms.

30th January, 1918

Have been working all day interviewing people as to the objects of my mission.

Red Lion Hotel, Truro   *31st January, 1918*

Last night at 10.15 Reggie Cheyne turned up at the New London Hotel at Exeter on his way back to the front to take command of his regiment. Partings on these occasions are somewhat melancholy, especially when, as in the present instance, they involve requests and directions as to what is to be done in the not improbable event of a 'casualty'.

Today we came here to commence our investigations in Cornwall. It is curious to Arthur Cochrane and myself to find ourselves together at this business of agricultural research again after a lapse of nearly twenty years. Many of those whom we saw when we were in Devonshire before seem to be dead. Their place knows them no more and soon, perhaps, what is written of them in *Rural England*[1] will be their only record. Food does not seem to be too plentiful in this hotel under the new regulations.

[1]The book, dedicated to Cochrane, records the investigations of the state of the English coutryside carried out by Rider Haggard in 1901 and 1902. The work was commissioned by the *Daily Express* in which about a quarter of the book appeared serially.

2nd February, 1918

I have been working all day, chiefly at interviewing school masters. I am rather afraid that I may have to give up this work as I have contracted a bad cold which may or may not be influenza. If it is anything of the sort, I dare not attempt motor driving in this weather. Perhaps I shall know tomorrow.

4th February, 1918

My fears have materialized and my career as an investigator has come to an end. Yesterday Dr Sharp of this town arrived and examined me with the result that he put a stopper on my travelling activities which he certified could only be carried on at 'grave risk'. I have not got influenza at present, but I have got 'emphysema', whatever that may be, and bronchial catarrh. He adds: 'I consider Sir Rider Haggard is running grave risk in going about the country in a motor-car and stopping at casual inns. I have told him definitely that in my opinion he ought to give up his investigations and stop at home at St Leonards.' Of course that finished it and I sent in my resignation which has just been accepted by telegram. The fact is that I should never have taken on the job in winter; I ought to have known that I should break down with my constitutional delicacy, but in a sense my eyes were bigger than my stomach. I mean that I wanted to bear a hand and do the work which was so kindly pressed upon me and hoped that I should stand it. But I can't and there's an end. I have still a very bad cold and aches, but I hope nothing more. So tomorrow, all being well, I return to St Leonards. I attribute my troubles (and so does the doctor) to a damp bed. I trust that Cochrane will be appointed in my place and think from Rew's telegram that this will be so. Then perhaps I can help him with the report.

28 Grand Parade, St Leonards   *6th February, 1918*

I was travelling all day on my return from Truro to St Leonards, which I only reached about ten last night.

14th February, 1918

I had an interesting letter from Rudyard Kipling this morning about the war. As his views are always able and singularly clear-sighted I copy it here for reference. Once letters are put away I never seem to find them.

Batemans, 7th February, 1918

Dear old man,
    I was very glad to see your handwriting again and to learn that you are so near

to us, though in these days of no motors, 18 miles are as bad as 100! I think you're wise in what you've done — for every reason. The less one has to bother about these days the better. We are still stuck with the farms, the cattle etc. and all the Government Departments make us their sport with regulations after regulations. It's a mad world. I fancy, however, that the Russian debacle is by no means smooth going for Germany.[1] One can't do much with a thousand mile front of raving lunatic asylum and — as one sees behind all the German papers — there is always the fear of political infection. Again remember that the Hun knows what the United States is capable of doing and he has a very fair idea that now the United States is launched it will be very difficult to stop the blow. That is a point we do not consider as much as the Hun does. My own notion is that the second there is any sort of armistice to discuss peace, the minute the thoughts of the German army are turned to their own land — then the real trouble will begin for Germany. Up to the present the external pressure has kept her solid. Once this is removed we may see developments.

But these are strenuous days all the same, I am sure our national unimaginativeness is going to be our salvation in the long run and, between ourselves, I look for peace by the end of the year — a bad peace for Germany too. I would say that I am coming down to see you except there seems no means of turning a wheel in that, or any other, direction: so I'll e'en have to take my chance of it and send you a wire if by any happy accident it is possible. I hope to goodness the milder air is keeping your bronchitis under. I have a small collection of petty diseases in my interior but nothing that makes one ill. You know the difference. The wife is *very* nervy and very tired, the daughter is well and we all send you our love and blessings. Affectionately ever, Rudyard.

I have no doubt but that he is right as to the external pressure keeping the Germans quiet, also, as I have written to him, I too feel that the war will end this year, one way or another. My views about America I have often expressed in these pages. Their appearance on the field will win the war — and *the Germans know it*, or at any rate their leaders do. Hence their anxiety for Peace before the American strength develops, especially their air strength. My fear, as I have also written to Rudyard, is that our food position may be profoundly unsatisfactory, and that our people may refuse to bear the privation and discomfort which it will entail! But, at bottom, I cannot believe that; surely we are made of better stuff.

15th February, 1918

In another note I have just received from Kipling he talks amusingly of my 'damnable gift' of prophecy. I shan't see him at present as he is off to Bath for Mrs K's annual treatment.

---

[1]These were the negotiations that led eventually to the Treaty of Brest-Litovsk between Germany and Russia.

16th February, 1918

Kipling made a good speech at Folkestone yesterday in which he pointed out what a German victory would mean — slavery, no less. I wonder whether the English people really understand this even now.

18th February, 1918

I hear from Lilias today that the food supplied at breakfast at the Dover Street Hotel where she and her mother are staying was so insufficient that they had to retire to their rooms and eat potted meat and biscuits! What will it be a month hence — and six months hence?

21st February, 1918

The butcher with whom we deal here told Louie today that the meat position is going to be even worse than it is.

Meanwhile there is still a great deal of waste, especially in connection with the Army. An officer who is attached to a home mess for a course of instruction told Lilias the other day that food is *lavish* and that every kind of cold meats appear upon the sideboard, exactly as though it were peace time.

27th February, 1918

This afternoon I attended the Memorial Service to Lord Brassey at Hastings. The church was not full; I suppose that he had lived so long that Hastings which he had greatly benefited has begun to forget him.

6th March, 1918

I went today to town to sit on my Agricultural Relief of Allies Committee, where we dealt with sundry business. I met Aylwyn Fellowes who told me that his investigators, of whom I was one, are doing very good work.

8th March, 1918

I am delighted to hear that Reggie Cheyne is home for six months under some rule which gives commanding officers who have been more than two years at the front a change of employment to rest them. I trust that before this period has elapsed the end of the war may be in sight.

12th March, 1918

Yesterday we were startled here by a series of tremendous explosions spread over several hours which evidently were caused by bombs. So loud were they that they shook this house and indeed broke some windows in the neighbourhood.

23rd March, 1918

I hear from the Hartcups who have come down here that Mr Bezant, the Russian merchant who has a house in our neighbourhood at home, believes that the Czar and Czarina and possibly their children have been murdered. It may be so since nothing seems to have been heard of them for a long while.

4th April, 1918

Love Eternal appeared today and there is a very good and sympathetic review of it in *The Times*, which says that it should prove a comfort to many and is especially suitable to these days of ours. As usual, however, it falls foul of my writing and tells me that I am not a 'literary artist', though it is good enough to add that I make what I want to say very clearly understood. This, to my view, doubtless a quite inartistic one, is the real point of all writing! But such is the fashionable way to talk of my work so I must not complain. It is a part of the Stevensonian, Meredithian and Henry Jamesian tradition to decry simple, straightforward English. Meanwhile if what I have said in my own humble fashion does bring any comfort to bruised and sorrowing hearts, well, I have my reward. As a matter of fact the book was rather hurriedly written, and I should have liked to see another set of proofs but there was no time.

8th April, 1918

Today I have received a letter from Roosevelt dated March 12. He writes: — 'My dear Haggard, I value your letter. I am now on the high road to recovery. I feel that in my case, as you say is the case with you, age will hereafter forbid my doing certain things that I have done in the past, but there yet remains very much work of a less exposed type that I can do rather better than even before. I don't wonder at what you say about the effect of the prolonged strain of this hideous war upon you. I am of course devoutly thankful that America is in the war and I bitterly regret that she did not go into the war two years previously, in which case it would be over now. We are doing much slower work than I like. That was a very extraordinary prophecy of yours. I am very glad you showed it to me,' etc., etc. 'One of my sons has been badly wounded.'

Well, it is no fault of Roosevelt's that America did not come in earlier. The prophecy he alludes to is that from *A Farmer's Year* where I wrote twenty years ago that a time would come when the British Empire and America would fight together for the freedom of the world.

I hear that my brother Will has sold Bradenham where the family has lived for over a century and where we were all born — a place of a thousand memories for every one of us. Could he know of it, it would break my father's heart, especially as I have a strong suspicion that the estate has gone to one of those speculators who are roving about the country buying up properties and, after cutting down every stick of timber, peddling them out in lots for what they will fetch. It is terribly sad but Will is not to be blamed. He gets nothing out of the estate; indeed I believe that it costs him money and there is no prospect of his son being able to live there, in short he is freeing himself from an intolerable burden. Moreover the remoter parts of Norfolk are no longer desirable as places of residence, except for the rich who can keep their houses filled with guests. I remember my father telling me that when he was a lad, scarcely an afternoon went by on which a carriage and pair could not be seen on the drive of Bradenham Hall, but now I wonder how many visitors there are in a month. Save for the country clergy the district is depopulated, although even in my own youth it was gay enough. To an old ex-diplomat accustomed to mix with the world, existence in such a rural retreat in days when motors are not allowed, is scarcely congenial. So it is not wonderful that he has made up his mind to be rid of the worry of it all, since now-a-days the ownership of land is nothing but one constant worry and expense, especially if it be burdened and repairs are needed, while he is loaded with abuse, pelted with 'orders' and hunted by perpetual demands for money. Also he is threatened continually with all sorts of vague but oppressive legislation. Still all these considerations scarcely lessen the sadness of the break. To me, it is true, Bradenham Hall for many years has been a haunted house, in which ever since I saw my beloved mother die there, I have not cared to stay. Yet it was her home for nearly fifty years, and there was spent most of my childhood. Myself I was not born at the Hall, since at the time of my appearance it was let and my mother was lodging at the Wood Farm, half a mile away, but with it are connected all my youthful memories. Now it has gone and doubtless soon the axe will bring down all its familiar woods and even the great copper beech on which every one of us cut his name, while probably the Hall itself will become a farmstead or a ruin.

Well, so everything must go. Vale Bradenham. Its fate after all is typical of that of many hundreds of the homes of past generations of the gentlemen of England. For one thing I am sorry. The cottagers in the village are still the children of those with whom our family has been connected for several generations. Now the old links are severed and they must look to themselves.

Mrs Tuck, a friend of ours here, told me today an interesting story about Cecil Rhodes. It appears that it was at the house of her late husband, a clergyman whom

I also knew, that he made up his mind to go to South Africa years ago. He and some other young fellows had come over from Oxford to play a cricket match and talk arose in the Rectory as to what they were eventually going to do in after life. When Cecil was asked by one of the company, he replied that he thought he should go to South Africa as he believed there was something to be done there. Thereon one of his companions said with a friend's frankness — 'To hang about as usual, I suppose.' She added that he was not an attractive youth with his curious face and long nose. Also that he was very silent. Of course, however, what really took Rhodes to S. Africa was his chest weakness. Our conversation today arose owing to Miss Rhodes, his sister, having lived in North Lodge, the house which we have bought here. Cecil used to stay with her and made a habit of sleeping on the *roof!*

29th April, 1918

Poor Mr Oxley, the architect whom I am employing about the little alterations at North Lodge, silently handed me a telegram today which he had just received from the War Office announcing the death of his son and only child, a Lieutenant in the Sussex Regiment, in action. It was a painful business, since the unhappy man burst into tears and then went on talking about pipes and painting. Such is the experience of thousands in these hellish times in which our lot is cast. And there may be worse to come.

From our window we have been watching a torpedoed or mined steamer with destroyers cruising round her. She has now sunk till only her masts are visible. Probably she is on a sandbank.

Greeba Hotel[1]   *1st May, 1918*

The Times has a remarkable appreciation of Kipling as 'The poet-prophet of the Empire', written by an Oxford correspondent. It is all true. He is a great writer and a great man and we should be thankful for him. Personally too I value his friendship very much indeed. He is now one of the few old friends who are left to me who in this respect grow lonely in my old age.

3rd May, 1918

In a letter I have received from Rudyard Kipling he says *a propos* of the appreciation of his work in *The Times* a couple of days ago: 'That was a glowing review in *The Times* but — if they'd only listened in the years before instead of jawing about it *now* one would have been more content.' I have answered that if one rose from the dead our politicians of both parties would not have listened in the past, unless by doing so they could catch votes. What chance then had the common or garden prophet? Rudyard is very amusing also about the practical

[1]Louie went on ahead to London and then, on 20th May, to Ditchingham.

134

seizure of his land by 'Dora'[1]: 'Hun prisoners are ploughing up our pastures and the estate is apparently being administered by a committee composed of "agriculturalists". I look on in wonder and stupefaction at their performance. All I've got to do is pay out money and watch the circus. It's all part of the variegated lunacy of these days which we shall survive and put behind us.' He thinks that, 'The Hun is meant to kill himself and — awful though these days are — he is dying much and often and will die more later on.'

16th May, 1918

I was in London today. The place is strangely crowded and yet strangely empty — that is the streets are curiously devoid of wheeled traffic but the pavements are full. I had to order a suit of summer clothes; these have gone up very much in price. The object of my visit to London was to interview the Pelman Institute people who offered me a good fee to write something about them. I replied that I would prefer to investigate first. I have investigated and I am much impressed.[2]

22nd May, 1918

The heat has been very great; I do not remember anything like it in May, but tonight thunder is growing. Most of the day I spent with the Kiplings at Batemans. Rudyard is not well. I thought him looking better when I arrived, but when he came to see me off at the gate I noticed how thin and aged and worn he is. Elsie says that he varies much. He suffers from fits of pain in his inside but he told me that although there is 'something' there, X-ray examinations show that there is no cancer or tumour or anything of that sort. I hope and pray that this is so. Seated together in his study in the old house at Batemans, we had a most interesting few hours together while he fiddled about with fishing tackle with which he tries to catch trout in the brook. There are two men left living in the world with whom I am in supreme sympathy, Theodore Roosevelt, and Rudyard Kipling. The rest, such as Theophilus Shepstone and Andrew Lang, have gone.

What did we talk of? So many things that it is difficult to summarise them. Chiefly they had to do with the soul and the fate of man. Rudyard, apparently, cannot make up his mind about these things. On one point, however, he is perfectly clear. I happened to remark that I thought that this world was one of the hells. He replied that he did not *think*, he was *certain* of it. He went on to show that it had every attribute of a hell, doubt, fear, pain, struggle, bereavement, almost irresistible temptations springing from the nature with which we are clothed, physical and mental suffering, etc., etc., ending in the worst fate that man can

[1]The measures contained in the Defence of the Realm Acts.
[2]The article was published in *The Sphere* on 3rd August, 1918.

devise for man, Execution! As for the future he is inclined to let the matter drift. He said what he has often said to me before, that what he wants is a 'good long rest'. I asked him if he wished for extinction and could contemplate without dismay separation eternal from all he loved — John for instance. He replied that he was never happier than when he knew that as a child his boy was asleep in the next room — why therefore should he mind it in the grave, or words to that effect. I pushed the subject and found that he does not really want to go out, only to *rest*. I pointed out that his notion was futile since if he rested for a million years or for a minute, it would make no difference to him in a state of unconsciousness, should he awake after all. Here he agreed. The upshot of it is that he is no unbeliever, only like the rest of us, one who knows nothing and therefore cannot understand.

Like myself he has an active faith in the existence of a personal devil and thinks (I gathered) that much which is set down to God is really attributable to that personality who at present cannot be controlled *even* by God, at least not altogether. He holds that the story of Pharaoh is being repeated in the case of the Germans. God is 'hardening' their heart, to their ultimate destruction. His humility is very striking. We were talking of our failings. I said that what grew on me from day to day was a sense of my own utter insufficiency, of complete humiliation both in the case of those things that I had done and left undone, and of the knowledge of sin ingrained in my nature which became more and more apparent to me as I approached the end of my days. He answered that it was absolutely the same with himself in every sense and detail and proceeded to speak very strongly on the matter, pointing out how we were subject to different weaknesses and temptations at the various periods of life. I commented on the fact that he had wide fame and was known as 'the great Mr Kipling', which should be a consolation to him. He thrust the idea aside with a gesture of disgust. 'What is it worth — what *is* it all worth?' he answered. Moreover he went on to show that anything which any of us did *well* was no credit to us: that it came from somewhere else: 'We are only telephone wires.' As an example he instanced (I think) 'Recessional' in his own case, and *She* in mine. '*You* didn't write *She*, you know,' he said. 'Something wrote it through you!' or some such words.

On general matters he was caustic about President Wilson to whom he thinks the world owes much tribulation because he delayed so long in coming into the war — as I do. As for the Irish he thinks that they should have been conscripted long ago, but now he would leave them severely alone that they may suffer the undying scorn of the rest of the Empire and the Allies. He repeated to me a really remarkable and most bitter poem he has written on the conduct of the Pope, called, I think, 'When the Cock Crew'.[1] Of course he compares him to Peter, to Peter's infinite advantage. He says he means to publish it as he has nothing to gain or lose from anyone. I hope he may for it will certainly make a hubbub. I trust that the Pope will enjoy its perusal. Also he read me a quaint story about Death and St

---

[1]'A Song at Cockcrow' appeared in *The Years Between* and in *Rudyard Kipling's Verse, Inclusive Edition*, both of which were published in 1919.

Peter written in modern language, almost in slang, which his wife would not let him publish.[1] It would have been 'caviare to the general' if he had, but the keynote of it is infinite mercy, extended even to the case of Judas. He opines in his amusing way that, if the present taxation, etc., goes on much further, he and I shall be seen on opposite sides of the Strand selling 'Recessional' and *She* for our daily bread.

How interesting it would be to have a shorthand report of such a three hours' conversation as ours, especially upon the nature of the Divinity, the destiny of man, the quality and consequences of sin, etc., etc., of which I can only recall a point here and there, especially as I who write them down am very tired after a long, hot day. I believe honestly that outside of his own family, there is no one living to whom Rudyard opens his heart except to myself. Practically he lacks intimate friends; it is not in his nature to make them; he said he could count those he had cared for 'on my fingers', although all mankind interested him.

I remarked that now-a-days, although with the exception of himself and one or two others all my friends were gone, I still made acquaintances. '*I don't,*' he replied grimly. He parted from me with much affection and said how delighted he was to have had the opportunity of a good mental and spiritual clean out. So was I. How he hates politicians! Worse than I do, even.

P.S. Rudyard asked me how much older I was than himself exactly. I told him, ten years. 'Then you have the less time left in which to suffer,' he answered, or words to that effect. I think he was alluding chiefly to the great loss which has overtaken both of us in life.

23rd May, 1918

I write this in bed before rising for my journey. I have slept well and it has been a blessing for a night to go by without the sounds of bursting bombs or mines or other hellish explosions. Last night there was only thunder and lightning which seemed quite innocent by comparison. Wherever one goes, St Leonards, or London, or Ditchingham where the distant guns growl continually, one is pursued by these voices of war and death. What then must it be at the front?

The more I think of that poem of Rudyard's, 'When the Cock Crew', the more I feel the terrible nature of the indictment it conveys. When he had repeated it to me, amongst other things, with that marvellous memory which he has, I said what a great gift was his of being able to express in terse rhyme exactly what other men like myself are thinking. He answered that this was the great object and power of verse, to put things in a form in which people would not only read but *remember* them. Doubtless what most of us lack is the power of *expression*. For instance there is not a thought in the poem which has not been in my own mind, only alas! I could never clothe them as he can.

[1]"On the Gate: A Tale of '16' was not published until 1926, when it appeared in *McCall's Magazine* and *Debits and Credits*.

He is convinced that Rome is working all she knows to regain the temporal Power — that this is to be her fate if Germany wins, in reward for her support throughout the world and her condonation of the frightful crimes of the Kaiser and his armies. Also he is convinced that if she regained her coveted power, soon the Inquisition and other religious methods supposed to be obsolete would be at work again in the world.

Also we discussed the possibility (and probability) of reincarnation and agreed that every year which passes draws back a curtain as it were, and shows us to ourselves in yet completer nakedness. He was of the opinion, however, that there are many to whom this did not happen: 'little' men who are increasingly pleased with themselves. It is so: the small man is the vain, the larger he grows the more clearly does he see what a *Thing* he is. Thus of all the men I know I think that Roosevelt and Kipling are the humblest.

Rudyard tells me that when first the Americans came under the fire of high explosives they retired with more rapidity than grace. We agreed that this occurrence has no particular meaning. The same thing has happened to sundry of our own divisions under pressure of the first fearful experience. Doubtless the Americans will fight like heroes when they come to understand the horrible game. The only fear about them is not whether they will stand high explosives but whether they can bear a Flanders winter. It is true that they have severe cold in their own country, but their winter is 'steamheated'. They all live in very warm houses.

Ditchingham   *24th May, 1918*

I returned here from St Leonards yesterday and found the place looking beautiful, notwithstanding 'war conditions'. The pink mays on the lawn which I planted about thirty years ago are lovely and so are the copper beeches and indeed all the trees. The garden too flourishes though vegetables are growing in the flower beds and most of my orchids, the collection of many years, has been thrown away to make room for tomatoes and beans. Well I had rather they went than see them perish from neglect. We have kept one house of Cypripediums, but these do not look too well from lack of potting etc. Jeekie, our black Cocker, had been told by Louie that I was coming and literally the dear beast understood. He got onto the drawing-room window-seat and watched and when he heard the trap went into the porch. When he saw, or rather smelt, me who had vanished from his view for more than six months he went on in a remarkable way, talking in his own fashion, leaping up and licking my face (which he only does on these grand occasions after long separation) and generally showing a marvellous exhibition of abandoned joy, after which he was obliged to refresh himself with large quantities of water. Poor little beast, he has not had too much to eat in his winter quarters for his bones stick out in his black skin. I fancy there is little nutriment in war dog-biscuits. What a dear creature is a loving dog.

27th May, 1918

Day and night here at Ditchingham we listen to the sickening thuds of the distant guns, firing, firing eternally at the front and reflect that each of those explosions probably is followed by the death or the mangling of men. They are going on at this moment, spoiling the peace of the perfect day. Oh! Kaiser William! great War Lord, let us hope for your sake that there is no hell!

3rd June, 1918

After discussion, we are ringing the church bells as usual here on the King's Birthday, but, in view of what is passing and to the drumming of big guns at the front that accompany them, it sounds rather like beating an accompaniment to cheerful music on a coffin! However, we think it will keep up the people's spirits.

4th June, 1918

Last night there was a great deal of firing or bombing or both within twenty or thirty miles of here. It lasted from 11 to 1.30 this morning but what it all was about no one knows. The strain of this long war tells upon one's nerves. When those bombs explode I confess that my heart jumps and flutters. I do not think that I ever quite recovered from the shock of the double bombing of this house just after I returned from my long, risky and anxious journey round the world. Also one grows no younger and does grow a great deal *thinner*. My clothes almost slip off me now as do the rings off my fingers. The drought still continues.

17th June, 1918

This war produces strange developments. Yesterday there was lunching here a gentleman named MacWhirter, a son of the artist[1], whom I used to know, who is a private in some regiment at Flixton, having come from America to join up and not being very strong having never been sent abroad. Today in the kitchen with his father, the gardener, and his mother is Lieutenant Mason, who used to work as a boy in the garden here. He also has never been abroad but has been promoted because of his ingenuity in matters to do with mechanics. The thing is awkward, and I am glad that the two did not meet.

18th June, 1918

The drought has broken at last, but as yet there has been but little rain of a thunder nature. The trees are suffering much from a pest of caterpillars which has stripped many oaks bare, as happened in the year 1830.

[1]The artist John MacWhirter (1872-1911) painted many oft-reproduced paintings such as 'Crabbed Age and Youth' and 'Lord of the Glen'.

19th June, 1918

Today I received a letter from John Murray about my book *Moon of Israel*.[1] In it he says: 'The other day I had to reprint from plates 2000 copies of a very popular novel which sells at 6/- nett, and I find that if all are sold there will be a loss! This of course is unprecedented!' He encloses a circular which he is sending out to authors in excuse for declining to publish their books. In it he says: 'Ever since 1906 Government has made successive concessions and capitulations to "Labour", and there is now practically no control over the rising wages ... We are now paying from three to four times as much for every item in book production as we paid three years ago, and prices continue to rise. A few weeks ago, in making estimates for reprints which used to cost £830, we found that they now cost between £2,400 and £2,500 ... It is obviously impossible to raise the prices of books proportionately to the rise in cost of production ... e.g. to offer a book which normally would be 5/- at 15/-. No one would buy it. In these circumstances I am almost daily compelled to decline books which in ordinary circumstances I would readily undertake to publish.' It is obvious that this is a very serious state of affairs for all connected with literature. Indeed, if it continues I do not know how we are going to live.

20th June, 1918

Today, after the rising of the Bench I went to Sturgess, the bootmaker, with a view of obtaining a pair of boots. When I found, however, that some of moderate quality would cost me 55/- I said I would see him somewhere before I bought them. He replied that he did not wonder at it. I added that there must be profiteering somewhere. 'Yes Sir,' he answered, 'and do you know who the Profiteer is — the Government.' I hear this on all sides. The Government supplies all the leather at its own price, and often enough very bad leather into the bargain.

22nd June, 1918

I am 62 today.

24th June, 1918

My brother Will has been here, telling melancholy tales about the sale of Bradenham which has depressed me very much. Also he had brought me a bundle of old letters which he has found, some of them written by me as long as forty-three years ago — one is that of farewell to my mother, which I wrote when I sailed for

[1]The book, after serialisation in *The Cornhill Magazine,* was published on 31st October, 1918. In his biography of Rider Haggard, Morton Cohen records, 'When he sent his manuscript of *Moon of Israel* to John Murray, he sent along a note from Kipling praising the tale, and then, after Murray had agreed to publish it, he wrote urging him to put the book on sale for six shillings instead of five.'

S. Africa with Sir Henry Bulwer in 1875. One of these letters written by me from Mexico City on Feb. 10, 1891, is *very* sad reading, even today. Its perusal affected me much.[1]

28th June, 1918

The weather has been most unnatural everywhere, so bitterly cold that I have been wearing all my winter clothes and the furnace has been lit in the house, also on some nights a fire as well in the study.

29th June, 1918

I went to Norwich today. The city is very crowded and it is almost impossible to find a place in the trains. Travelling there by train has become difficult, every possible inconvenience being placed in the passenger's path. No doubt the war necessitates much, but scarcely so much as people are asked to put up with. For instance, although our afternoon letters arrive at Bungay and elsewhere as usual, the postmen are not allowed to take them out, with the result that it often takes two days to receive communications from London. Nor are we allowed to collect them at the post office except sometimes at a charge of 3d.

5th July, 1918

The influenza outbreak, or the Spanish sickness as it is called is growing very bad indeed. Tom, who himself is a sufferer at the front, writes that he has seen men fall down with it suddenly as though they were shot, and one hears much the same in other quarters. It seems rather hard that in addition to all our other troubles, a pest of this sort should be inflicted upon us in the height of summer. Perhaps it is the precursor of another outbreak of the plague of the Middle Ages.

Coke here is now 45/- a ton, which means that the rest of my orchids will have to go. This is rather sad when they have taken twenty-five years and a considerable expenditure of money to collect, as the hobby of a hard-working man. Still it must be so. There is something queer about this cost of coke, seeing that only today the Bristol merchants offered to deliver good coal at Ditchingham Station at a price of over 10/- a ton less. Profiteering no doubt. I suppose that no price has been fixed for coke.

15th July, 1918

I thank God that I have lived to see the downfall of the Victorian idea and ideal.

[1]On 8th February, 1891, the Haggards, who were with the Jebbs in Mexico, received a telegram to say that their only son Jock had 'passed away peacefully'. He had been left in the care of Edmund Gosse and his wife.

Personally I always knew, that is ever since I began to think, that the whole business was an elaborate show and sham, but so far as I am concerned that knowledge made things worse rather than better. And what a sham. it was! The pretence that war has gone by and that thenceforward the nations lived only to make money, honestly or dishonestly, it did not matter which. That Free Trade and its consequences created a very fair copy of Heaven upon earth, even when no one else would adopt its sacred doctrines. That the foreigners should be encouraged in our midst especially the German foreigner who could put down hard cash in exchange for titles and social consideration, which was taken greedily by the politicians although they knew well that he and his kind were spies and touts sent forth to ruin the Country of their adoption. That the Land did not matter except as a place for sport and week-end parties that were furnished by the rich who owned it, since food could always be brought in in cheap plenty from abroad. That the real aims of life were not Patriotism and Duty (the former indeed was much deprecated as a survival of primeval barbarism) but pleasure and money. That no lady of consideration could possibly spoil her figure by extensive child-bearing which also prevented her from dancing and other delights. That the one thing to be discouraged, indeed, was the growth of population, since it meant a decrease in the amount to be divided. The population was only useful in the event of war, and war was done with, human nature having totally changed at the approach of the Victorian top-hat. That the Empire was a nuisance and that every possible opportunity should be taken to lessen our responsibilities in this direction and above all to oppress and 'give away' those pests who showed loyalty to their King and country — such as the English in the Transvaal, or the inhabitants of Ulster in Ireland. That it was better to take the risk of having practically no army than to incur the certainty of the loss of votes at an election: such are a few samples of the Victorian ideal, evolved from decades of greasy plenty by men whose gods were Wealth and Place, men without imaginations or a spiritual side, however often they attended church because it was the proper thing to do.

And now look whither their great ideal has led us! Save for the Empire which they, or some of them, tried to stamp out, where should we be? And were it not for the unquenchable spirit of Englishmen, and their high and ancient courage which of malice prepense they did their best to debauch and destroy, what would have happened to us in this hour of our winnowing on the threshing-floor of God? The fine, superior folk, for instance, who for years set me down and proclaimed me a barbarian because I wrote of fighting — horrid, vulgar fighting — when only the sweet-smelling problems of high civilisation were worthy of treatment, are glad enough today of the virile fighting spirit which I believe I helped to evoke in many of the young men who are all that stand between us and dishonour, the yoke of slavery and ultimate destruction.

22nd July, 1918

I was interested and amused this morning in watching two German prisoners who are engaged or supposed to be engaged in cutting the weeds in the River Waveney. To me, and I looked at them for quite a long while, they seemed to do nothing except stare at the water while the armed guard walked up and down wearily and stared at them. I imagine that the British prisoners in Germany find it expedient and indeed necessary to work in a very different fashion.

30th July, 1918

At this moment, 12.55, the guns are going so heavily on the Western Front that the constant drumming of them interferes with my work here at Ditchingham.

Today I have received from Bradenham another great bundle of my own letters. The earliest of them was written fifty-five or six years ago, and evidently kept because it was my first, and the last not long after my mother's death when I was corresponding with my father as to the Memoir I wrote of her.[1] Among these, so far as I have had time to go through them, I have found one or two interesting documents. For instance that in which I describe the arrival of the news of Isandhlwana and the attempts made by Lagden and myself to raise a mounted corps, which afterwards resulted in the Pretoria Horse. Unhappily all my letters concerning the Annexation seem to have been lost, or not found, whereas every scrap that has to do with business in any form has been carefully preserved. There is something extremely melancholy in such old letters, rather terrible also, with a suggestion of recording angels, and Judgement Day about it, for there, preserved for always, suddenly leaps to the eye so much that time has buried beneath the forgotten debris of our lives.

5th August, 1918

We have much for which we should thank Providence at the beginning of this fifth year of war, more indeed than we could have hoped in March and April, while the Germans must read with terror of the endless supplies of war material that are being turned out by the factories of the United States.

6th August, 1918

In the local paper are advertised particulars of the sale of furniture at Bradenham. To me who have known these articles from childhood they are sad and very depressing.

10th August, 1918

Today I received a circular from a magazine in America which has published

---

[1]Rider Haggard wrote a preface 'In Memoriam' to an edition of his mother's poem 'Life and Its Author' that he had published in February, 1890, shortly after her death.

stories of mine, asking for more stories. It contains the following paragraph. 'There is one limitation, at least during the war; it is more than a century since America and England were at war, but, since any reminder of even a distant time when a present Ally was arrayed against us, would doubtless appeal to the Hun as German propaganda, we will avoid stories of 1776 and 1812 until those periods can have no other significance than closed chapters to anyone.' This extract from the office of a magazine of the sort strikes me as hopeful for a really good understanding between the English and Americans for the future, especially as the pestilent lesson books which were used in their schools with their distorted representation of historical facts are now suppressed.

15th August, 1918

The position is really growing serious for authors. Today I received an account of the sale of cheap editions of my books which are published by Hodder & Stoughton. Every one of them is out of print. This may be necessary owing to the cost of paper, bindings and labour, but I cannot help wondering what would happen to me if I broke my agreements even on such grounds without explanation or apology. I think that in such a case an author would hear a good deal of the matter, but the boot being on the other foot, he is expected to shrug his shoulders and say nothing.

20th August, 1918

Today I have paid a heart-breaking visit to that abomination of desolation, an ancient home that is being broken up. Perhaps destroyed would be a better word, since the timber is to be felled by the speculative purchaser, the farms are to be sold to whoever will buy them for whatever they will fetch and the house will, I presume, become a ruin, for who will care to occupy a place of that size when all the estate is gone? It was rather an awful experience — but then life is full of awful experiences, and such in its sum it is itself. Yet to one who was born and bred at Bradenham, it is somewhat terrible to see the half-empty rooms filled with the debris of the auctioneer; to be shown by the caretaker the ancient clock whereof the chimings which were the first and last sounds that one's fore-fathers heard for generations that, she said, had 'stopped last night', appropriately enough at midnight; to find lying on the floor drawings and likenesses of sisters now departed, to see the articles familiar as only those we have known in youth can be scattered about and labelled with the tickets of the sale; to visit the rooms where we have seen our begetters die — and so forth. But such is the lot of man and such the fate of all earthly things. We ate the food we had brought with us in the garden under the great beech tree where my father always sat in summer, and having visited his and my mother's grave, I bade farewell to Bradenham where, if I can help it, I shall never go again. I notice that the oak planted by my mother in 1845, now a good-sized tree, is dying at the top, at which I do not wonder. If only houses could talk what a story they would have to tell. Such places should be burnt after the African fashion, when a death has occurred. But enough of these mordid obsequies of a county family.

21st August, 1918

I have been trying food cases at Loddon this morning in which the persons prosecuted have violated the maximum prices order. Of course there is a great deal of this going on but the offenders are rarely caught. We inflicted moderate fines.

28th August, 1918

All my cheap editions have gone out of print and I have been communicating with Charles Longman on the subject, to see if anything can be done. Today he writes to me: 'The whole position is very difficult owing to the monstrous price at which paper stands. This is a matter which Government could rectify if they would. I suppose there is no article which has arisen to anything like the extent paper has; it is between five and six times the normal price and it is the raw material of literature. The amount of paper used in book production is not a very large amount in tonnage compared with many articles, and if the intellectual side of life made the slightest appeal to the Government I believe it would be possible for them to bring the price down with a run. But that would bring down paper makers' Excess Profits which are very large and which bring in a good deal to Bonar Law!' This, from one of the leading and most experienced men in the publishing business, speaks for itself. As is the case in many other trades, the Government is deliberately crippling us in order to put more money into its own pocket.

29th August, 1918

The Bradenham sale is over and the effects there fetched enormous prices. Bullen, the dealer, who was bidding for me, informs me over the telephone that my name had something to do with this, as the auctioneer announced to the company that it was the home of my childhood and that, therefore, all these articles would be of great value in the future! He added that the effect on the dealers was very marked indeed. I am flattered even by this exaggeration, but the result is that the kid was seethed in its mother's milk, since the lots I wanted went for the most part beyond my means. Thus the two old clocks for which I bid fetched respectively over £100 and £200 guineas, while my mother's inkstand went for £17.10. However, I did secure some things, for instance the table at which my father wrote so many thousands of letters and the old three-cornered chair in which he sat to do so, though even for these I had to pay highly. Also the old bed (in which I slept as a boy with the pin in the pillar that I drove into a worm hole) and my butterfly cabinet. But where are the butterflies of fifty years ago? But one remains, a dilapidated moth, I think. I also got the remains of my mother's favourite blue Copeland breakfast service. It is a melancholy business and like the rest of my family I find it hard to forgive my brother for having ordered the sale of these relics. However, he has done well out of the transaction.

Mason, my gardener, informed me with a long face this morning that he has been ordered to attend for medical examination with a view to his being called up. On investigation I find that he is six clear months over the age fixed by the Military Service Act, being all but fifty-two. I have written to point this out and hope that no more will be heard of the matter. I suppose the answer will be 'a mistake' — but it is curious that such mistakes like those of tradesmen who send in their bills twice over are nearly always on the wrong side. Admitting that the need for men is great, and leaving the age facts out of consideration, it seems foolish to call up a gardener no longer young, who is already producing a great deal of food, much of which is sold, and who is also a special constable and the machine-gun sergeant of the local volunteers, especially when one knows that a number of younger men are left untroubled.

30th August, 1918

I hear that there is great activity in the village as to the calling up of elderly men; for instance Hunting, the village blacksmith, is summoned for examination, and if he is taken I know not who is to shoe the horses or to do other necessary jobs.

4th September, 1918

The war has changed all our habits of courtesy that used to prevail. Few now among what are known as the working classes, unless they are very old friends, and this especially applies to the children and young folk, will condescend to take the slightest notice if one meets them on the road or elsewhere; indeed it is not too much to say that often they give what is known as the cut direct. Now I have never been one of those who cared for the bowing and scraping habit, still there are degrees in haughtiness, as in undue familiarity at the other end of the scale. A little courtesy, especially when it is known that it will be reciprocated, harms no one and oils the wheels of life. I observe further that when these lofty ones come to sickness or any other trouble they are willing enough to waive their pride and to fall back on older methods.

14th September, 1918

It is quite extraordinary how the value of everything seems to be increasing in this time of war. Having had my eyes opened by the Bradenham sale, I, on advice, have caused the furniture in this house to be revalued for insurance, with the result that the figure reached is almost double that which it was a few years ago. Moreover, I am assured by the valuer, a most reliable man, that if the articles were put up for sale they would fetch more than he had set them at. I suppose the fact is that money to a certain extent has become demonetised. Also there seems to have arisen a sudden appreciation of the value of old things, of which the stock is limited. Also there must be a great deal of cash in circulation. Anyhow the results are somewhat astonishing.

I asked Lord Curzon the other day whether he would care to have my romance *When the World Shook* dedicated to him in acknowledgment of the great kindness he showed me many years ago, thirty indeed, in trying to protect me from a most outrageous charge of plagiarism, and in proving by elaborate analysis its complete falsity.[1] Before he made up his mind I requested him to read the story. This he has now done, and writes back, 'I shall be only too proud to have my name, however indirectly, associated with it.'

23rd September, 1918

The year has been a cold one; today for the first time I have seen a Red Admiral butterfly on the wing, and it looked unhappy.

28th September, 1918

In Norwich I attended a meeting of persons connected with East Norfolk, in which constituency Ditchingham is now situated, as to the choice of a Unionist candidate. The chairman, in some hole in the corner kind of way, had already practically asked a young gentleman, the son of his own land agent, to stand, although he is now serving in Palestine — the chief argument in his favour being that he is a nice fellow and a good cricketer. In short we were asked to buy a pig in a poke, and this has been done practically without consultation with others except as to the *fait accompli*. Indeed I had not been consulted at all, although I am the person who has fought East Norfolk and the only one who has gone near to winning that most difficult seat. At the meeting I objected to all this and was supported in so doing by Willie Carr, with the result that now the young gentleman is to be asked to state his views.

It was obvious to me that we are by no means out of the old party rut, and all the old party humbug and wire-pulling. What is wanted at this juncture are *men*, not persons who are recommended on the ground that they are good cricketers and supposed to be able to pay. Carr is anxious that I should stand again. But really I

[1]In April 1887 Curzon wrote to the editor of the *Pall Mall Gazette* defending Rider Haggard against an accusation of having plagiarised *She* from Moore's *Epicurean*. When the editor refused to publish it, Curzon sent the letter on to Rider Haggard whom at that time he had not met.

cannot see my way to it. Putting aside all the question of money, I am not now strong enough to attempt canvassing and speech-making over a large constituency in winter. Also I doubt whether I could bear the climate of London and attendance at the House of Commons throughout most of the year. Fifteen or even ten years ago it might have been different, but one must face things as they are.

Ledbury   *7th October, 1918*

I came here to visit Ella from Norfolk today. Travelling now is very tedious and crowded, and also I observe an unpleasant tone in many of the railway servants. Cabs are hard to get in London.

Pembroke   *14th October, 1918*

On my long journey from Ledbury here to see Reggie[1] and Dolly, I observed that a great deal of corn, mostly oats, is still out in the fields, spoiled and sprouting, while I even saw some uncut. It appears that it has been raining in these parts since the end of August, almost without a break! Reggie is ordered back to India to train some of the new troops, he thinks. Nearly all the Indian officers at the front have been or are being sent off for this purpose.

15th October, 1918

This is the land of plenty; here in Wales it is evident that the writ of the Food Controller does not run. Last night in this hotel I was given a chop such as I have not seen for years; this morning I feasted on kidneys and bacon, and generally there is no difficulty about food and very little as to coal. I suppose that the authorities are afraid of the miners, and therefore turn a blind eye to the breaches of regulations which the English must obey.

North Lodge, St Leonards   *21st October, 1918*

My first night in this house. In London today I saw Watt. The position about paper for books is growing desperate. Most of my works are out of print, and on all such as remain the royalties are cut down because the publishers can make no profit even at greatly enhanced prices. But, as Watt pointed out, books only take five per cent of the paper consumed; most of the rest goes in newspapers and Government forms. The truth is, of course, that the authorities are afraid to stint the newspapers which would attack them if they did, however unnecessary many of them may be. As for authors and all their tribe — they may go hang! Longman

---

[1]In March, Reggie Cheyne was appointed to the command of the Shropshire Light Infantry at Pembroke Dock for the period of his home service.

told me today that even to export a single copy of a book they have often to fill up a form in triplicate. What waste of paper is there where officials are concerned!

28th October, 1918

There is a certain something in the air which seems to suggest that the end of the war is not far off. I do not know, no one knows; but the feeling is there like that of spring while winter still endures.

6th November, 1918

I have been to London today to attend a meeting of my Agricultural Relief of Allies Executive Committee. We voted fifty thousand pounds to France and a like sum to Belgium and Serbia. The total amounts of the agricultural losses by German devastation were put before us. They are enormous, and must run into tens, if not hundreds, of millions. The streets struck me as very empty. I see a new poster on the walls to encourage the buying of War Bonds which strikes me as more horrible and in worse taste than most of them. It represents a British soldier realistically driving a bayonet into the stomach of a German, and the legend underneath is 'The Last Blow Tells', or something of that sort. Its coarse brutality made me feel sick.

8th November, 1918

Today I have received a very charming letter from Kipling about my new book *Moon of Israel*, which I did not send to him, fearing lest it might bore him. He says, 'Dear old man .... Meantime I've been reading *Moon of Israel*. What is your secret, old man? It goes and it grips and it moves with all the first freshness of youth and — I got into a row with the wife because I had to finish it with the electrics turned on. It's ripping good, and I'm damned jealous. You've got a new type in Ana, which you know as well as I do. Also you've developed what Scripture made plain, but which no one else dwells on, the essential turbulence and unaccommodativeness of the Israelites in the captivity. I don't know what to think of these annoying days. We're back in the eighth century after the Holy Roman Empire turned in its hand ... and there was only a welter of small Powers left. Next time you come along, bring your diary with you. I want to see how it struck you day by day.' etc. etc.

This opinion is worth a ton of professional criticism, because it comes from a great writer who knows what creation is and its difficulties. But, as I wrote to Rudyard today, it makes me laugh to hear him say that he is jealous of *me* who am written down as the deadest of dead letters. Also I wish that I could rise to his high opinion of my own work.

10th November, 1918

The Kaiser and his son, the Crown Prince, have abdicated. The 'All-Highest' is in the dust, and the 'glittering armour' rusts upon Time's muck-heap; the mailed fist smites no more; the 'destructive sword' ceases to rattle in its Imperial scabbard, the 'good old German God' is no longer exhibited to the world ventriloquising and nodding his head like an ancient Egyptian deity in a temple! In short, the curtain has rung down upon the Imperial Cinema Show, and all the tinsel and pinchbeck trappings, filled-gold sceptres, gilded crowns, and the rest are cast to moulder in the bin of discarded footlight properties. Never more will the ex-Kaiser, never more will any monarch, as I believe, be able to arrogate to himself a flesh different to that of the herd of men, or to flaunt the banner of a Right Divine in the faces of the struggling peoples.

11th November, 1918

There is Peace. To this city, flags hanging flaccid in the November damps, a few bells rung out of time (for lack of ringers), some cheering from recruits of the Essex, Norfolk, and Suffolk regiments, who now will never be called upon to feel a wound or crawl down a ditch of Flanders mud, and the explosion of certain bombs which can be spared proclaim that there is Peace.

I am thankful that I began to keep this diary, imperfect and full of mistakes and misjudgments as without doubt it is, and have been able to continue it through the weary years, with scarcely a day missed up to the present hour. At any rate it is a record of what an average not unobservant man, whose lot it has been to endure those years, thought and experienced in the course of them, and therefore perhaps of some value, at any rate for future time.

It is true that I have not been in the actual fighting, though I have known what it is to have the great shells exploding round me, and what is worse round my women folk, and on more than one occasion. Also I have passed many perils on the seas. But if I were a younger man and had been called to take my place in the trenches, an opportunity that I could wish had come to me, it is probably that my outlook would have been more limited, as I should only have known what was passing within my immediate ken. Again it has not been my lot to stand at the front of high affairs, but then those who did probably have kept no record of all that happened about them or at any rate no impartial record. Also it chanced that at the outbreak of the struggle I was in Canada and that during its continuance I have travelled round the Empire and come in touch with the most of its leaders, also from time to time with some of importance at home. I trust too that my work for the Empire, although at present it is in suspense, will bear fruit, direct or indirect. So perhaps on the whole I have no cause to complain of my occasions.

And — there is the diary of the four and a half years, and as I write the guns or maroons are firing and I hear the cheers of Victory!

150

15th November, 1918

I have been spending the day at Batemans with the Kiplings. Rudyard is much better than when I last saw him, at the beginning of April, I think, fatter also; he puts it down to the war news. So I think is Mrs Kipling. Elsie has had influenza and is a bit peaky, but recovering and in good spirits.

As usual, we discussed all things in heaven and earth, especially the great danger we have escaped. I took this diary over, as R. had asked me to do, and read him passages out of it till I was tired. These interested him greatly. He thinks that it must be a very important work some day; of much value indeed to the generations that are to come. His chief anxiety is as to its preservation, concerning which he made various suggestions — that I should hand it over to the British Museum in a packet not to be opened for fifty years (which is the time he thinks should go by before its publication); that I should deposit it with one of the 'Safe Deposit' Companies; that I should put it in an iron box enclosed in a lump of concrete and bury it, and so forth. I told him what I am doing, namely, depositing one typed copy with Longman's and keeping the other, also the original, myself in different places.[1] Of course, I recognise the danger, i.e., that when I have been gone a few years someone may get hold of it and publish a highly-Bowdlerised version of it as the whole 'War Diary'. Well, it must take its chance.

After the reading I happened to say to him that I wished I were a poet, as so many things occurred to me of which I should like to make poems. R. answered in these words, as nearly as I can remember them: 'Don't you see, Rider, that much of what you write, in your reflections, etc., is poetry, and very fine poetry? Only the rhyme is lacking; the fall of the sentences and the essentials of poetry are all there, also the poetic imagination. You do not chance to have the gift of rhyme as I have it. I'm glad of it, as I should not like your competition.' (This he said jokingly.) 'The foolish critics,' he went on, 'and the ordinary readers think that poetry consists of rhyme, but it is not so. The matter is or is not poetry.' Also much more of the same sort, that I cannot recollect well enough to write down. He and the others were full of *Moon of Israel,* which they seem to know much better than I do myself; no single point in the tale has escaped R.'s piercing attention. I asked him if he really thought it a great piece of fiction? He replied 'What does one understand by "great"? *I* call a book which can hold a man in a vice in the midst of such times as we are passing through, with his daughter in a high fever in the next room, so that he forgets everything else, and is lost in the characters and the story "great"!' 'All the same,' I answered, 'seeing how poorly many of the critics seem to rate me, you would not dare to say over your name that you thought me a great writer?' '*Wouldn't I just,* if it came my way to do so!' he exclaimed. Well, it is pleasant to have one competent admirer left now that Andrew Lang is dead. He described to me a dinner to which he had recently been bidden at Buckingham Palace and its appalling dullness, the being shepherded up to speak to Royalty, and the rest. It was a most amusing

---

[1] The original is now in the Norfolk Record Office. The two typed copies are both in the possession of Commander Cheyne, Rider Haggard's grandson.

account. Altogether I had a very pleasant afternoon. A long talk with Kipling is now one of the greatest pleasures I have left in life, but I don't think he talks like that with any one else, indeed he said as much to me. He is a very shy bird, and as he remarked, has no friends, except I think myself, for whom he has always entertained affection, and no acquaintance with literary people. 'But then,' he added, 'I don't think I am really "literary", nor are you either.' I suggested that our literary sides were 'bye-products'. 'Yes,' he repeated, 'bye-products.'

In one way R. is a very curious man; when he talks he always likes to be doing something with his hands. 'I must occupy my hands,' he said, and went to fetch a holly-wood stick he had been drying, and peeled and sandpapered it, continually asking my advice as to the process and subsequent treatment of the stick, which I told him to hang up the chimney like a ham. Last time we talked in this fashion he employed himself with a fishing-rod and line.

Poor old boy! John's death has hit him very hard. He said today that I was lucky to have lost my son early when I still had youth to help me to bear up against the shock and time in which to recover from it, at any rate to some extent (which I never have done really). 'If he had lived to see this war,' he added, 'he would now have been dead or mutilated, perhaps leaving a family behind him.' Mayhap he is right; often I think so myself. I pointed out that this love of ours for our lost sons was a case of what is called 'inordinate affection' in the Prayer book which somehow is always bereaved. 'Perhaps,' he answered, 'but I don't care for ordinate affection, nor do you.' He thinks that imagination, such as mine, is the sign of expression of unusual virility. A queer theory, that may have something in it.

Rudyard told me that he had been approached during the war and asked to give his active support to and identify himself with the interests of certain political persons — as to whom, although he mentioned no names, one can hazard a guess — to write them up (in short, to give them the weight of his name, which is, of course, considerable). In return, he was informed, he could get 'anything he wanted'. His answer, practically, was 'Go to Hell!' He added that his experiences during the war had not raised his opinion of the Press! He rejoices over the Republican victory in the States, which he thinks will save us trouble with President Wilson over such matters as the 'Freedom of the Seas'. (Of President Wilson he is no admirer, remembering those two long years of inaction, as I do.) He has been writing to Roosevelt to congratulate him[1], and says I should do the same. I think I will.

17th November, 1918

I attended the club Peace dinner here last night, and made a speech on the Navy and Army.

[1]On a speech attacking Wilson.

1918

21st November, 1918

I made another speech last night at a Masonic dinner, in which I dwelt on the atrocities of the Germans.

Reggie Cheyne has been dining here to say goodbye before starting for India. He has grown deaf from ailments contracted in the trenches, but after all he is fortunate to have come out of these years of hard fighting with nothing worse than deafness. He means to give up the army, as soon as he can, having wearied of it like thousands of others. But what is to become of them all?

6th December, 1918

Today a woman in a shop where I was buying some trifle said she had hoped that I would stand for Hastings 'instead of a man like this Mr Lyon'. Then she added that she did wish that I would come out as a Labour candidate, as the man who was putting up was a Socialist whom they did not like. Still they must vote for him because he was 'Labour'. 'All right, Mam,' I answered, 'but at that rate let me tell you that soon you will have no shop left!'

It is a joy to see the streets lighted again, if insufficiently. After more than four years of an abysmal darkness with the knowledge that often enough Death was floating overhead, I feel as though I should like to pass the rest of my days in a lake of light — as though night and day I could never be satisfied with brilliance.

9th December, 1918

Today I have presented the prizes to the boys at the Hastings Grammar School, and made an address to a large audience. It was quite successful, but I think that boys are the most difficult of all audiences. One never knows what to say and what to leave unsaid. Everyone seemed pleased, however, and there was a deal of cheering.

10th December, 1918

I have had a busy day. This afternoon I attended a drawing-room meeting on behalf of the Coalition candidate, Mr J. Lyons, where I made a speech. He is just an ordinary sort of a candidate, not deeply versed in affairs, I should say, but I believe that he has plenty of money. His opponent is a Socialist who, they say, has a good chance of winning the seat.

On my return I found a telegram which had been forwarded from Ditchingham by post asking me to 'write five hundred words in support of Coalition and the New England and enclose your account. Request emanates from official sources,' signed Dennis Crane, 50 Parliament Street. I don't know who Mr Crane is. Yes I do, he is a gentleman who runs Government propaganda, but I wrote what was asked in fearful haste for the post and told him that I wanted no money in payment for support of the Coalition Government. Hope the thing is not a newspaper fake and that my view may be useful.

14th December, 1918

This is the day of the General Election, as grey and dreary in its hue as has been the confused and misty conflict from first to last. I have not gone to Norfolk to vote as Louie has done. I am afraid of the journey in this horrible damp, as it would probably bring back my bronchitis. I confess that I feel somewhat 'out of it'. It is galling when, whatever may be the case with the physical, one's mental qualities are as good or better than ever to feel that one is a 'dead letter' of no account. Yet doubtless it is better so at my age and in my present state of health. If I could have gone into Parliament young, I dare say that I might have made a fine career there; but I was a Unionist, and from Unionists too much *money* is expected. Also how could I have done the public work and earned my living as well?

18th December, 1918

I have been to London to attend a meeting of the Empire Land Settlement Committee of the Royal Colonial Institute. With reference to the Empire side of the business, I suggested that the Institute should attempt to take the matter up privately and send me or some other person to the Dominions to see what can be done. The matter is to come up for discussion at a subsequent meeting.

25th December, 1918

This morning was typical Christmas weather, a white frost and a brilliant sky. I have been to a children's party at Dolly's where we played games. It was happy and yet sad to an old man. One remembers so many Christmas parties as far back as fifty years and more ago and oh! where are the children that played at them? There is a tall oak clock ticking away at the end of this room; the man who cleaned it the other day said it was the oldest he had ever handled. It has seen many more Christmasses than I have, four or five times the number, and still it ticks unconcernedly, marking the passage of the hours and the years. Doubtless it sounded the moment of my birth as it will do that of my death. Remorselessly it ticks on, counting the tale of the fleeting moments from Yule to Yule. Yes, Christmas is a sad feast for the old, and yet — thanks be to God who giveth us the victory — one is full of hope.

27th December, 1918

Today I have received a letter from Roosevelt, dated 6th December, 1918. Here it is: 'My dear Rider Haggard, In a moment of pessimism the other day I said I never wished to hear from an Englishman excepting Arthur Lee[1] and Rudyard Kipling. But that was because I had forgotten you. I doubt if I ever again go back into public place. Like you, I am not at all sure about the future. I hope that Germany will suffer a change of heart, but I am anything but certain. I don't put much faith in the League of Nations, or any corresponding cure-all! Yours ever, T. Roosevelt.'

Today I received a letter, forwarded from Ditchingham, from the Home Secretary, who mysteriously signs himself 'Cave'[2] as though he were a peer (I find that he *is*; new peerages are so many that I had forgotten it), informing me that it is proposed to submit my name to the King for the purpose of conferring on me by His Majesty the rank of a 'Knight-Commander of the Most Excellent Order of the British Empire'. Of course I am gratified, though what I have always wished to become is a Privy Councillor, which however I suppose is now beyond my reach. Or I would rather have belonged to the Order of St Michael or St George than to this one, which is new, mixed and large, though it is finely named. However, one must not look a gift-horse in the mouth, and it is a recognition of my work for the Empire — which I hope has been extended to my colleagues on the Dominions Commission. I hope sincerely too that it may lead to my being offered more honorary work to do before I grow too old for it, but this of course is doubtful. I suppose that I must owe this compliment to Curzon. Anyway it shows that my work is not altogether forgotten, as I feared was the case.

31st December, 1918

I remember on this day last year ending my entry with an invocation to that which was being born, 'Oh! be good to us!' Well, on the whole it has been very good, though at first its frowns were rather terrible. We have got through the war and come out victorious, and a Parliament has been returned which I hope may be trusted not to 'monkey' with the Empire's interests.[3] What gifts will 31st December, 1919 have for us I wonder?

[1]Arthur Hamilton Lee, 1st Viscount Lee of Fareham, had served as military attaché to the American Army during the Spanish-American War.
[2]George Cave, 1st Viscount Cave, was Home Secretary between 1916 and 1919.
[3]The General Election, which had taken place on 14th December, resulted in the Coalition, led by Lloyd George, being returned with a great majority.

1919

Although at the beginning of the year Rider Haggard was awarded the K.B.E., the news that affected him most was the death of his friend, Theodore Roosevelt. The rest of the year was full of anxieties and disappointments. He was not asked to serve, as he had hoped to do, on the Royal Commission on Agriculture. His home at Kessingland was handed back after its war-time occupation in a terrible state. His books were not reprinted. The national strike in September he saw as an act of tyranny. He and Rudyard Kipling were even more disturbed by developments in Russia and both men became convinced anti-Bolshevists.

1919

The weather has turned horrible — dark, cold, with pouring rain.

Theodore Roosevelt is dead! He passed away in his sleep at four o'clock yesterday morning of pulmonary embolism, which means a clot of blood upon the lungs, no one being present in his room except his attendant. It was a merciful, if a lonely end, supervening on six weeks illness from inflammatory rheumatism. I can only say that I am desolated, since although we actually met but seldom, he was one of my few remaining friends.

The more I think of Roosevelt's death, the more distressed I am, both for myself, who have lost a friend, and for the world's sake.

Today my name is announced as one of the Knights of 'The Most Excellent Order of the British Empire'. Without being anything very wonderful this is better than nothing at all, especially as the honour is conferred for war service, or rather for public service during the war. Personally I am not particularly keen on the system of honours, especially of hereditary honours, while purchased honours — of which, directly or indirectly, there are so many — I abhor. But under our system honours are useful to any man, except perhaps the very foremost, who wish to do work in the world.

Today I went to town to attend the Pilgrims' luncheon to Mr Davis, the new American Ambassador. It proved an interesting function, and at it I met a good many people, including the Duke of Connaught, who, with the faculty peculiar to the Royal Family, remembered my small promotion and congratulated me.

I have a nice note of congratulation from Kipling today in which he says, 'Dear old man, I am glad to see you took it, because if ever any one was Knight of the Empire — by land and sea and shipwreck — you're it! Like you, I am awfully heavy-hearted about Roosevelt. He was the best friend we had out there, and I can't see who takes his place. I noticed you suppressed the two names.[1] He sent me

---

[1]After Roosevelt's death, Rider Haggard wrote a letter to *The Times* (published 8th January) in which he quoted the letter he had received on 27th December, 1918, but omitting the two names of Roosevelt's friends.

a long and sad (I don't wonder) letter the week before. It is curious the papers don't seem to realise that it was the wound when the crazy fool Socialist shot him, at a public meeting[1], which was the deferred cause of his death.' I did not know this either, who thought that it resulted from the fever he caught on his South American expedition. I have written to Rudyard and told him that his was one of the names, which I think will please him.

The weather continues to be of an unparalleled awfulness, and London is simply beastly.

13th January, 1919

Yesterday we attended a lecture in Hastings given by Sir A. Conan Doyle in furtherance of his spiritualistic propaganda, and afterwards Doyle and his wife came to supper here. What he told us, both at the lecture and privately, was interesting; but I cannot say that it carried conviction to my mind. It may be all true, but 'the spirits' seem to be singularly reticent upon many important points. However, he believes in them most earnestly and preaches a most comfortable doctrine, so earnestly indeed that he travels all over England giving these lectures in order to make converts to this creed.

16th January, 1919

This morning I went to a local wine-merchant to buy a dozen of wine for our humble after-dinner glass of sherry (port being altogether too expensive). I found that the price of this wine since the last purchase had been put up two shillings a dozen. This I simply refused to pay, saying I would go without, with the result that the merchant discovered that he had a little left from a former shipment at the old price! He informed me that the enormous cost of port is due to the stock in the country having been drunk up by the munition workers who, male and female, have taken to port *en bloc*.

20th January, 1919

Some American soldiers came here today and cinematographed me for the benefit of their troops, who have developed a desire to look upon my antique countenance. It appears that they are great readers of my books and want to see a picture of their author.

23rd January, 1919

Today in London, whither I went to attend a meeting at the Royal Colonial Insti-

[1]On 14th October, 1912, Roosevelt was shot and wounded in Milwaukee. He made a scheduled speech before going to hospital.

tute, I visited the Canadian War Pictures Exhibition at Burlington House. They are very large, very impressionistic and, I imagine, not great works of art. But they do give a wonderful idea of the muddy and bloody horrors of this war, and as such I am glad to have seen them.

31st January, 1919

I have received a letter from Lord Milner asking me to come to town to see Colonel Amery at the Colonial Office and himself, if he has not gone to Paris for the peace talks. It sounds as though it is intended to make use of my services in connection with emigration. Otherwise I scarcely think that Lord Milner would have written.

5th February, 1919

I went to town today to see Colonel Amery, the new Under Secretary for Colonial affairs, and discussed the whole problem of emigration with him. I am glad to say he seems to be quite alive to its importance. Also, apparently, they want to make use of me in some capacity in connection therewith, but in what way they do not yet know. Probably it will all boil down to a seat on the advisory council — or to nothing at all. Unfortunately I missed Lord Milner, as like everyone else he is in Paris, for which he left this morning.

6th February, 1919

Farmers cannot be doing so badly notwithstanding their loud and constant complaints. About eighteen months ago I lent my steward £900 to enable him to take the farm. Today I hear from him that he has repaid £600 of this money. Of course, however, he is an able man, and a good farmer, but making all allowances, his prosperity must be considerable. The weather is, thank Heaven, better today.

7th February, 1919

Today I have been going into the question of the insurance of the furniture in this house with Mr Oxley the architect, who is the agent for the Insurance Office. I find I have to pay 1/6% to safeguard myself against fire, but if I wish to do the same against civil tumult and revolution, I should have to pay 2/6% more, i.e.. nearly double the fire insurance. In the case of premises and goods in London this charge according to a letter from the office in London which Mr Oxley showed me, rises as high as 5/-%. These figures show how little confidence this particular office has in our national outlook at the present time. As I do not think we are likely to have tumult of the sort at St Leonards, whatever may be the case in the big manufacturing cities, I propose to take the risk and remain uninsured on this head.

10th February, 1919

After all, owing to the cold, the weather and the transport conditions, I was unable to attend the Memorial Service for Roosevelt at Westminster Abbey. However, I thought of him which perhaps he would appreciate as much.

19th February, 1919

Yesterday and today some of us have been amusing ourselves by watching from the Hastings Club windows a German mine that has dragged its anchor and is bobbing about within a few yards of the shore. It is said in the Club that the Dover authorities have been communicated with and have replied that they have no mine sweeping boat to spare to deal with the article. So I suppose it will be left until it comes ashore and either does or does not explode.

Windham Club   *25th February, 1919*

Today I attended the Investiture at Buckingham Palace and was formally created a K.B.E. It was rather an amusing ceremony. We were separated up like sheep and goats, the Knights and Ladies being placed in one room and the rest somewhere else. Then Lord Cromer appeared and told us what to do. Afterwards a band played 'God Save the King', and the march began in a long line. There was much confusion about gloves. We were told to put a glove on the left hand (luckily I had a new pair!) and not on the right. Then we were told to put them on both hands — then to take off the right glove again. Lastly a disturbed official informed us that for some reason or other which he could not understand, we were to replace the glove on the right hand. (Somebody told me that he believed it was because the King had a sore or something on his hand and feared lest we should catch it; if so it was very considerate of him.) I observed Sir C. Kinlock Cooke in front of me fidgeting and trying to hide his hands. On my asking what was the matter he said, 'I haven't got any gloves!'

Ultimately we marched into the Throne Room where His Majesty stood upon a dais looking, I thought, ill and worried, and played our parts to the best of our ability, trying to bow at the right times etc. The King, after hanging the ribbon with the crown and cross over our heads as we appeared before the Presence one by one, shook hands with us and conversed a little with each. To me he remarked upon my living in Norfolk and congratulated me. The knight before me he tackled about the strike — that gentleman said to me afterwards he could not conceive why as he knew nothing about the matter! After this we bowed ourselves out and I fled, glad to have the ceremony over.

The crown and cross are pretty, with a figure of Britannia and 'For God and the Empire' engraved on red enamel, but I think they would be more effective if they were somewhat larger.

North Lodge, St Leonards   *17th March, 1919*

I have been to London today. I went to my bank and had an interview with the manager as to the selling and re-investment of certain government securities, if anything connected with government can be called a 'security' in these times. He spoke about the rumours of an increase in the income tax and said that it would spell ruin.

29th March, 1919

Superstitions of every sort are rampant now-a-days. Here is an instance which I take from the *Daily News* of 26th March. It seems that whenever a certain battery were sent any of my books, the S.O.S. signal was immediately received, three of them coming when one of the battery was reading *Allan Quatermain*. So poor Allan and the rest were always burned upon arrival, with the result that the S.O.S. calls declined. As the *Daily News* remarks, 'The story might not be so surprising if the books had not been Sir Rider Haggard's and the battery itself had appealed for help.' Also I may point out that the prodigy might be read otherwise. Allan was always a helpful person and his spirit on these occasions obviously indicated when and where help was needed! In the twentieth century can anything be more childish and ridiculous than this burning of books for such a reason? It does not raise one's opinion of the average modern man. But perhaps it is not true.

Windham Club   *7th April, 1919*

Today I left St Leonards with regret, although the weather there this winter has been horrible, and came to town where we are going to the flat at 26 Ashley Gardens a while before departing to Ditchingham. By an irony of fate, this morning at St Leonards was the only one that has been really fine and warm since we went there last year! Also my Glory of Leyden daffodils were just beginning to come out. I went to look at the first of them in full bloom before I had to leave for the train.

I had to pay 3/- for a taxi from Charing Cross to St James' Square!

26 Ashley Gardens, London   *8th April, 1919*

I saw Colonel Amery at the Colonial Office today who explained to me the situation of all the Emigration business. He informed me that if an Advisory Committee is appointed I shall be asked to serve. I also saw Admiral Sir Reginald Hall, M.P.[1] and arranged to be interviewed of behalf of his movement to explain the real meaning of Bolshevism etc. Saw Glaisher[2] also, who told me that my

---

[1] He was M.P. for the West Derby Division of Liverpool. During the war he had been the Director of the Intelligence Division of the Admiralty War Staff. His movement was called 'National Propaganda'.

[2] He worked for A. P. Watt, Rider Haggard's literary agent.

books are selling well. I spent a happy afternoon at the British Museum and had a long talk with Budge[3] about Primitive and Modern Religion. He told me that at a celebration of a kind of All Souls Day in Egypt when the Egyptians pray to the souls of their ancestors he had on several occasions, I think he said four, heard the souls arriving through a certain gap in the hills! The sound they made, he declared, was like to that of a deep note upon the organ. He has often tried to hear it at other times and failed. Cross-examination quite failed to shake his belief upon this point, the statement of which he prefaced with the remark, 'I am not mad.' Very curious!

The Mummy Room is occupied by the lady clerks of some Government Department (Friendly Societies I think). It is rather appalling that these dreadful girls should chatter and fill up their forms in the midst of these priceless mummies which lie higgledy-piggledy upon the floor.

11.45 p.m. I have just returned from the dinner of the Cecil Club held at the St Stephen's Club, presided over by the Marquis of Salisbury, at which Curzon was the principal guest. He (Curzon) made an excellent and open speech in the absence of reporters of which, as I have just written to him in a note from the Athenaeum, the general effect was very depressing.

10th April, 1919

Today I lunched with the Rev. Mr Marchant to talk over a proposal made to me about the contemplated *Mayflower* film.[2]

12th April, 1919

I have been engaged all day as to Admiral Sir R. Hall's proposals to combat Bolshevism in this country in which it is wished that I should take a prominent part and in bringing him and Sydenham together etc. It is a very large business of which it is useless to write until something definite occurs. At the best I fear it would take up much of my time but, if only I can manage to live somehow, I would not grudge that if thereby I could help my country in this hour of its peril.

16th April, 1919

Today, having read a statement in *The Times* that a Royal Commission on the lines of the recent coal commission was to be appointed to consider the present crisis in

---

[1]Sir Ernest A. Willis Budge was the Keeper of Egyptian and Assyrian Antiquities, British Museum. His advice and his writings contributed to many of Rider Haggard's books.
[2]The film was never made. (See the entry for 7th September, 1920.)

agricultural matters, I went to see Lord Ernle, the President of the Board of Agriculture, and told him that I would serve, if wanted. He said that my name was one of the first that had occurred to him and generally was very pleasant to me (he is a most courteous old gentleman). He remarked that what they wanted was someone who could cross-examine, pointing out that the coal owners on the Commission suffered for this reason as they lacked the ability. I replied that I thought I could fill *that* bill. I don't know if anything will result, but when I asked him if he thought it necessary that I should apply to the Prime Minister he answered No, as he presumed that his nominations would be accepted. Whether I shall be nominated I cannot say, nor do I greatly care. At best the job would be anxious and responsible.

Afterwards I went with Captain Kelly to see Bramwell Booth[1] about Admiral Hall's anti-Bolshevist campaign in which we want the Salvation Army to join. The General was really pleased to see me and is left considering. I pointed out to him all that is involved in this business, further that he was a saint and I was a sinner but that in this our aims were identical. He replied that I was 'a very promising sinner'. These arguments I reinforced in a note written from the Athenaeum. He informed me that my book, *Regeneration*[2], was still doing them a lot of good and that he was thinking of bringing out a new edition. I am glad. As I said to him, my work is not 'flashy' but it wears. He looked well. Captain Kelly was much impressed with the business-like atmosphere of the Army Headquarters and with the interview generally.

After lunch I attended the Annual Meeting of the Royal Colonial Institute and made a speech on Oversea Land Settlement.

21st April, 1919

There is nothing much to chronicle in these empty hours of waiting for a peace that may or may not come within a week, especially during the long procession of Sundays which make up an Easter holiday in London. The streets are, by comparison, vacuous, and at the Athenaeum everyone is out of town (almost) except the Club Bore who as ever pervades it and ought to be charged five subscriptions!

28th April, 1919

I had a long talk this morning with Captain Kelly, Admiral Hall's assistant, as to our anti-revolutionary propaganda and the way in which it should be managed. He showed to me a most poisonous leaflet issued by nobody knows who, which is

[1]W. Bramwell Booth was from 1912 to 1929 General of the Salvation Army, which his father, General William Booth, had founded.
[2]In this book, which was published on 16th December, 1910, Rider Haggard gives an account of the social work of the Salvation Army in Great Britain. The copyright of the book was presented to the Salvation Army.

being circulated, probably with German or Bolshevist money, by being left in lavatories in seaports. It is aimed at the seduction of the Royal Navy and, as he says, found its way on to battleships. It points out that the Russian Revolution was begun upon the Fleet and suggests that the English revolution would also commence there very nicely. Then follow all the usual arguments about the equality of men and statements about the wonderful things that Bolshevism has done for the British sailor and others in these islands. In short it is a most infamous and disloyal document and a very good specimen of the secret venom which is being injected into the honest blood of Britain by foreign anarchists. I hope that the common sense of our race will neutralise this dangerous filth.

We are preparing a counter leaflet which also is to be left about in lavatories — as I understand, but personally I should like to see some of these villains seized and tried. Unfortunately, however, now-a-days nobody seems to dare to stand up for anything — least of all does the Government dare.

This afternoon for the first time I have been sitting on the Birth-rate Commission[1] where interesting evidence was given by experts upon the effects of alcoholism, the natural as against artificial feeding of infants etc. It is interesting to hear ladies still young putting questions to witnesses which would have caused their mothers' very hair not only to stand up on end but to fall off their heads. Truly we advance.

The awful weather of this awful winter culminated yesterday in a violent blizzard which buried the London streets in snow.

2nd May, 1919

I have been to the private view of the Royal Academy, a crowded function where figuratively speaking there was almost as much paint on the women's faces as on the pictures that adorned the walls. It is quite curious that even old ladies should think it worth while to decorate themselves in this fashion. Some of the costumes were truly marvellous; one of them reminded me of an Indian squaw in her feathered best. On the whole, although there is not very much of it, I thought the sculpture better than the painting. Indeed I was so attracted by one little bust, called 'The Crown of Victory', by F. J. Halnon[2] that as it was not costly I purchased it. But I don't quite know why it is so named, unless it be because the sweet-faced lady who seems to be mourning for someone wears a wreath of laurel leaves. Kipling, whom I met there, thought she was a very good likeness of 'Yva' in *When the World Shook*.

[1] Rider Haggard appears to have been appointed because of Lord Curzon's involvement in the matter.
[2] Frederick James Halnon was a lecturer at Goldsmiths' College. London. His work was regularly exhibited at the Royal Academy.

6th May, 1919

Last night I was the guest at the Royal Academy at a dinner of the Academy Club at which Sir T. Brock[1], the sculptor, was in the chair and the President and most of the other Academicians were present — a large company with their friends. I was called on to respond for the visitors. I spoke on 'The Mission, Consolations, and Aspirations of Art'. We got the lights turned on in the Sculpture Rooms and I showed Greiffenhagen (my host) and others Mr Halnon's bust which I had bought. They all thought it a beautiful work.

Lord Sydenham writes to me this morning: 'I have heard from Ernle[2], and I gather that he has put forward your name (for the Agricultural Royal Commission) but does not trust the Prime Minister to accept his recommendations. Of course he is not strong, and the Prime Minister is surrounded by wire-pullers who view everything from the political and not the national standpoint. I find people here in despair about the future of the land' etc., etc. This letter exactly confirms my own impressions and I shall view the issue with amusement and interest. I doubt my being put on this Commission but if I am I don't think that the fact of my fitness for the work will have much to do with it!

12th May, 1919

I have just returned from seeing what is called the Trade View of the film of *King Solomon's Mines*.[3] The Alhambra was crowded, and Mr Nesse, who is managing the affair, has just told me over the telephone that it was the most successful trade show that had ever been held in London. He said that during the whole performance only two people went out, which is the great criterion, and they had told him before that they must do so owing to an engagement. Nearly thirty-five years have gone by since this story was written by me and it is remarkable that it should still have so great a hold upon the imagination of the world. My belief is that it will live.

13th May, 1919

I have received this morning a dozen closely typed sheets of dilapidations resulting from the occupation of my house, Kessingland Grange, by the military. The place seems to be so wrecked that unless adequate compensation can be recovered, which seems doubtful, I am inclined to believe that it might be better to knock it

---

[1]Sir Thomas Brock was a designer and sculptor. The Queen Victoria Memorial outside Buckingham Palace is one of his works.
[2]Rowland Edmund Prothero, Lord Ernle, was President of the Board of Agriculture and Fisheries.
[3]It was made by African Film Productions Ltd. under the direction of H. Lisle Lucoque. It starred Albert Lawrence, H. J. Hamlin and Ray Brown.

down. Even the taps and brass hooks have been stolen, and the blinds etc. have, I suppose, been burned.

15th May, 1919

This day I attended the funeral service of Edith Cavell[1] at Westminster Abbey. By a stroke of fortune Louie and I were moved up into the lantern and given seats within a few feet of where the coffin rested on its bier. It was a wonderful ceremony.

Anything more beautiful and solemn than the reveille I never heard. I suppose the drums were stationed in the apse where they remained unseen. First of all they began in the tiniest and most distant whisper of sound that by slow degrees grew greater and nearer till at last it thundered in the ears, then again began to recede and, by infinite gradations, became no more than the breath of an evening wind in far-off trees, and died away.

The rest of the music also was soul-stirring, especially the clarion cry of the Last Post. What a great fortune was that of this noble woman who in death has found immortality on earth, as well as I believe in heaven. Others have suffered also, but she is chosen out of many. The Abbey was crowded, the nave and lantern to the last seat, and so were the roads with reverent crowds from Victoria to Liverpool Street, as she was borne to her rest within the precincts of the Cathedral at Norwich.

This service is one of those things that I am glad to have seen in my life.

19th May, 1919

A film-proprietor, with whom I was discussing the sale of the cinema rights in one of my books today, told me that he had lost a great deal of money over one or two films that he had produced containing pictures of some of our Royalties, in which British audiences could not be persuaded to take any interest. I think he said that he had invested £5000 and had only got £1000 back. The incident is suggestive but may bear various interpretations.

22nd May, 1919

This morning I went to the Board of Agriculture to try to find out whether I am or am not to serve on the Agricultural Commission as I want to make my plans. I saw Edward Strutt[2] who apparently did not know. I gathered indeed that the whole thing is hung up waiting for the Premier's decision.

[1]Rider Haggard was so moved by the service that he wrote a letter to *The Times* about it while sitting in the Abbey. It was published the next day.
[2]The Hon. Edward Gerald Strutt, a very successful land agent, was an unpaid agricultural adviser to the Board of Agriculture.

23rd May, 1919

I have heard from Lord Ernle that my being asked to serve on the forthcoming Commission will depend upon what terms of reference are ultimately decided on. These at present are not available as he says he can get no reply from the Prime Minister. If they are very narrow and deal only with the future (as he is anxious that they should, lest the true facts of the profits made by farmers should be revealed), I shall not be wanted as the Commission will consist of farmers, labourers and statisticians and will not include general men like myself. In short the names of the members will not be considered until the scope of the inquiry is settled.

26th May, 1919

I have been spending the afternoon cross-examining Mr Harold Cox[1] at the Birth-rate Commission. He rejoices at the drop in our population and takes the serious responsibility of advocating every kind of birth-control. I cannot go into all his arguments with which I totally disagree, holding as I do that if there are too many people here, they should be redistributed in the empty lands of the Empire. It was a case of 'when Greek meets Greek' and we had a serious set-to, of course of a most friendly order. I think that on the whole I had rather the best of it, although Mr Cox is one of the cleverest of men and a very tough nut to crack. But probably he is of a different opinion.

Ditchingham   *29th May, 1919*

I came to Ditchingham today after many months of absence. The place is looking beautiful as it always does at this time of year and just the same. Some of the old inhabitants are dead however, for thus do the generations glide into each other, amongst them old Johnson, who was gardener here for a full generation of time. God rest him. It must be getting on for a score of years since he left my service, incapacitated by age, and became a pensioner in a cottage at the gate where he died. Of him I have written in my book *A Gardener's Year*. He was a quaint old man and faithful.

Many people are travelling on the railway 'spending their gratuities perhaps', as Lambert the motor driver suggested, and the train-service has much deteriorated. At Beccles indeed I found it simplest to drag my own luggage to the motor that had come to meet me. Some of the guards and ticket collectors at Liverpool Street, however, were very glad to see me again. Also I found myself in a carriage with two Essex gentlemen who are great admirers of my books which was pleasant, espe-

[1] He was a successful journalist, being from 1912 to 1929 the editor of the *Edinburgh Review*. From 1906 to 1909 he was M.P. for Preston.

cially as one of them who got out at Colchester rushed and brought me a present of a cup of tea!

31st May, 1919

Last night at twelve o'clock I heard a tremendous noise as of railway trains running in the sky — a most familiar noise — and looked out to see a great Zeppelin hanging over this house where it remained for about twenty minutes. I suppose that a British air-ship was manoeuvring, but by a kind of instinct I at once put out the lights. This shows how deeply our experiences of the past four years have cut into us. There was the Zeppelin, large and ominous and at once one expected the bombs as before. (By the way, on cleaning the skylight in this room of the black paint with which it was coated, many of the panes are found to have been cracked by the air-rush from the explosions near the garden and it is now too late to recover their cost from the insurance office.) This house seems to have a natural attraction for air-ships, hostile and friendly.

I went to Norwich today. The town was so crowded that people had to walk in the middle of the streets. Some of my tradesmen friends told me that they are doing record business as people are spending the great profits they made during the war. They do not anticipate, however, that it will last. The buyers, they say, belong to a new class. At the Museum I was told that the extra wages absorb all their resources from the halfpenny rate so that they have no money to buy cases in which to exhibit the manuscripts etc. that I have given them.

4th June, 1919

The domestic servant question is becoming most difficult in England. The women will not go into service, and when they make an engagement often do not keep it. A parlour maid who was coming to this house simpiy did not arrive. Nor did any explanation.

7th June, 1919

It is hot for June. The thermometer in this room stands at 80 degrees and the drought holds.

14th June, 1919

In Norwich today I saw Mr Morgan who made the valuation at Kessingland. It appears that the government valuers reach their estimate by supposing the houses were in a bad state when occupied. In the case of The Grange this opinion was arrived at on the strength of an *ex parte* inspection made by representatives of the military authorities six weeks after the house had been occupied by mobs of soldiers! The whole business is most dishonest — shameful indeed, seeing that the house was in good tenantable condition when seized.

18th June, 1919

The posts are all wrong: one rarely receives a letter posted in London for the 5.30 mail until the afternoon and the telephone in big centres seems almost to have broken down.

The drought continues and grows more devastating. Unless it breaks before the 21st according to our local lore it will be too late to plant swedes and there are few mangolds up. On the light lands also the barleys are dying.

20th June, 1919

I have received a great batch of reviews of my books from America. On the whole, with exceptions, they are very favourable but the interesting thing about them is their variety and the divergence of opinion which they express. Some, as Andrew Lang used to say, are clearly written by the newspaper 'Office Boy', others are very careful and thorough, much more so than the vast majority of those published in this country. The States being so large, their literary lights do not follow a 'fashion' in reviewing as ours do, where almost every critic tries to copy what other critics say so as to be 'in the movement'. The individual scribe in America thinks for himself and says what he thinks, which is as it should be.

26 Ashley Gardens   *23rd June, 1919*

I see the Army and Navy Stores hung with hundreds of lamps for peace decorations and signs of the same sort everywhere. I do not feel at all like decorations and bonfires and shoutings and orgies, and think that a day of thought and solitude would be more appropriate to the occasion. It is useless to cry 'Peace, Peace' when there is no peace, but merely an armistice, for it looks as though it would be that and nothing more.

26th June, 1919

Yesterday I went to Hastings to meet Lord Leconfield, the Lord Lieutenant of Sussex, at a luncheon to forward the fund for rebuilding the Hastings hospital as a war memorial. I was amused to see the trams placarded with a passage from the last speech I made at Hastings about this hospital memorial and to hear the Mayor (or the Lord Lieutenant, I forget which) most erroneously attribute the whole scheme to me.

Last night I went to the Royal Society Conversazione and came away filled with reflections upon the marvellous advances of science, even since I have been in the world. For instance there was an exhibit by Dr A. O. Rankine[1] of the transmission of speech by light. I omit the details but I myself went to the further end of the building, say 300 feet away, and put the receiver to my ear and above the roar of the conversation of the hundreds in the place myself distinctly heard Dr Rankine talking along a beam of light. He says that his invention or discovery will operate to the horizon, that is as far as the beam can be thrown.

Ditchingham   *27th June, 1919*

I have just returned from the funeral of my old friend of forty years' standing, Captain Percy Meade of Earsham Hall. It was a sad function. He was laid by his daughter Dosia whom the influenza carried off at the age of eighteen a few months ago and whose grave still lacks a headstone. The son who was killed lies where he fell. Percy Meade was one of the best men, a country squire of the old sort of whom few are left such as I knew in my youth, in my father's time. He was a good friend, a good sportsman and a perfect gentleman. God rest him!

7th July, 1919

Yesterday — Peace Thanksgiving Sunday — was celebrated throughout the Empire in special and appropriate services, the King and Queen attending that at St Paul's. Here the occasion did not appreciably increase our congregation either in the morning or in the evening. Doubtless, however, the attendance will be better at the parish feast.

We sold our remaining two farms at North Walsham on Saturday and made £600 more than the reserve on them — about £20 an acre. This is not a great price, but more than Simpson expected. Indeed neither he nor I can understand why farmers are buying properties everywhere. I suppose it is in the belief of the coming of high protective duties. But, as I have said, I believe that the women voters will see to that! Anyway I am glad to be rid of them as all property has become a burden nowadays. The net income from this land is increased by 60% by turning it into cash.

8th July, 1919

The list of those appointed to serve on the Royal Commission on Agriculture has been published. The names are not those of persons generally known and the terms of reference are strictly limited. I offered to serve on this commission, but on the whole I daresay that I am well out of it.

[1]Alexander Oliver Rankine (1881-1956) was from 1919 to 1937 Professor of Physics at the Imperial College of Science and Technology.

12th July, 1919

I have spent all day writing a memorandum on matters connected with the birth-rate for the commission on that subject. It is a depressing topic, but no more so than any others just at present. Of its vital importance, however, there can be no doubt since in it are concerned the safety and indeed the continuance of our Empire.

21st July, 1919

The Peace Celebrations are over, of which everybody is glad, except some festive people who wanted them prolonged for a week. On the whole they went off very well in London, where the enthusiasm for shows is so great that thousands, notwithstanding the rain, stood all Saturday night in the parks, as they had stood all Friday night waiting for the celebrations to begin. All through the Empire there were similar rejoicings; we even rejoiced at Ditchingham where there were sports, fireworks in the evening and a tea was given to about 700 people who were addressed by Carr and myself. Here we were fortunate in having no rain.

We have an outbreak of small-pox down here. At present I know of about a dozen cases, all from one man in whom the disease was unrecognised by the clever specialists who examined him. It is being kept very dark in the Press, doubtless for fear lest visitors should be scared away from the East coast, which is prudent but not honest. Dr Ransome has been here to vaccinate us.

29th July, 1919

For the frightful damage which the officers and gentlemen and those under their command caused to Kessingland Grange — damage of a nature in some particulars more like the acts of apes than of men — which was valued at £492. 8. 8., about half was offered by the Government. I wrote to the member, Sir Edward Beauchamp[1], and told him all the iniquitous story, after the government valuers had firmly refused to increase their offer. This letter Sir E. Beauchamp gave to Lord Peel, the Under Secretary for War. Probably because it contained an intimation that I thought of publishing my moving tale in *The Times*, negotiations were mysteriously reopened and to save further trouble and worry I have been advised to accept an offer of £429.15.11, in satisfaction of all claims, which is to include £40 on account of rent for the time during which the house has lain derelict. This amount will still leave me out of pocket, but on the whole I think myself fortunate to have got so much.

5th August, 1919

I made a speech at the Harleston Agricultural Show yesterday. There was a great

[1] He was the M.P. for Lowestoft (Northern Division of Suffolk) in which Kessingland was situated.

crowd, but I observed that those at the luncheon seemed to be of a different class to the people who used to attend such functions before the war. Then they were farmers pure and simple in their Sunday-best farming costume. Now they look to me more like tradesfolk and among them was a very large proportion of women. All the usual fair side-shows were in evidence, but I noticed that the prices charged were enormously increased. In the same way the luncheon was 5/- instead of half a crown.

12th August, 1919

Andrew Carnegie is dead. I saw him in 1905 when I was a Commissioner in America, wishing if possible to interest him in the settlement of the poor on the land. I failed totally, the impression left upon my mind being that he did not care two pence about the poor. However, he was so engaged in discoursing of himself that it was not easy for me to set out my public aims and objects. I remember that I left wondering how a man with such a second class mind had managed to make so much money.

13th August, 1919

The weather has turned fine and warm of late which is good for the harvest. Something like starvation is promised for this country next winter, and already there is very little coal to be had, at any rate in these parts. I have secured a ton as a favour, but my neighbour Carr has only got 10 cwts.

Yesterday I plucked up courage and went to Kessingland. The sight is lamentable, especially perhaps the garden which was handed over to these soldiers free of charge that they might grow their vegetables. Really one might think that the place had been occupied not by men, but by a colony of apes!

25th August, 1919

In a note I have just had from Rudyard he says, 'But it is a perfectly crazy world and, like you, I don't see the end of it — or rather I see the end a little too clearly to comfort me.' In my answer I have said this — 'You say you see the end — I don't quite. I am not sure whether it will be of the comparatively painless boa-constrictor kind — by absorption of all accumulations, property, savings, bequests etc., or of the Russian back against the wall kind with suitable accessories. As we are a "constitutional people", possibly the former. Meanwhile I have insured this place and contents against "Riot". I am much struck by the change in the demeanour of the local inhabitants. People whom one has known from their childhood now twist their heads away or whistle when one passes them on the road — their return for sundry good turns! The manners of the adolescent are particularly charming.'

1st September, 1919

Yesterday I went to visit Mrs Meade at Earsham Hall, the widow of my old friend, Percy Meade, who died a few weeks ago. On a table I saw poor Percy's gloves all laid out as though waiting for him to use them, and on the pegs above were his hats and over-coats. Nothing for a long while has brought home to me more acutely the sadness and mutability of our temporal existence. What I have heard from her about the Death Duties she and her son will have to pay, has caused me to try and insure against this awful tax which falls with peculiar weight upon families who lose their source of income with the bread-winner. As a preliminary step I have just been medically examined, but at my time of life the premium I shall have to pay must at best be very heavy.

26 Ashley Gardens   *13th September, 1919*

I travelled here today from Ditchingham. The train was terribly crowded and even on a Saturday afternoon Liverpool Street station a seething sea of people among which porters were hard to find. I cannot imagine where they come from; I remember nothing like it.

15th September, 1919

Angie has been trying today to buy some fixed basins from Dolby to be used at Kessingland. Those which were priced at 50/- a little while ago are now marked £6!

23rd September, 1919

Both Watt and Sir E. Hodder Williams were complaining to me today of the enormous increase in the costs of their offices. The figures they gave are remarkable. So authors must get less![1]

I have received from America an infuriated letter, evidently written by a German, enclosing certain pages from *When the World Shook* torn across. These pages give a few simple atrocities (all of which happened) that are supposed to be witnessed by Ozo, the superman of the story who has come to life again after a sleep of 250,000 years. My correspondent suggests that I might have found better ones, which no doubt I could have done as there are plenty to choose from.

Also I have received what amused me very much, namely the account of the excellent Tauchnitz for certain books of mine, on which he pays a royalty, sold in Germany during the period of the war, which he sends as though nothing of the sort had happened. War or no war these seem to have commanded quite a decent market which increased towards its end. Whether they were purchased by Germans or by prisoners I do not know.

[1]Rider Haggard had just received a letter from A. P. Watt stating that he would have to increase his commission rate from 5% to 10% on all new agreements.

27th September, 1919

The strike[1] is on in good earnest. All the railway men are out from one end of Britain to the other. The London tubes have ceased to run. I had to go to the city to Cannon Street this morning to see my lawyers. On my way up I managed to get a seat in a bus, but coming back this was impossible and I was obliged to walk the whole way. At Young, Jones & Co's office I think only one clerk was in attendance and the streets presented an extraordinary sight with thousands of pedestrians thronging the roadway and making dashes for every passing bus off which they were pushed again by the conductors. In Trafalgar Square opposite the National Gallery there was a queue of more than a hundred yards in length formed by thousands of people waiting on the chance of getting into a bus.

Tonight the strikers are parading Victoria Street and doubtless elsewhere. As they come they cheer, to keep up their spirits I suppose, but nobody cheers them, not even the rough-looking men who march alongside of them. I have great hopes that the women will intervene with good effect in this business, since they and the children will be among the first to suffer. I suppose that even a striker's wife objects to starvation in place of plenty. The hardship and inconvenience that must have been inflicted already are incalculable and I believe will turn the country against the strikers. England only learns in one way — by experience, and now it is getting the experience. So long as one class paid for everything, the masses did not mind, but when directly or indirectly they have to bear their share of the trouble and contribute their quota of the blackmail, it may be a different story.

29th September, 1919

The strike goes on, and notwithstanding some reports as to its 'weakening' that are not very well substantiated, seems likely to go on.

As yet there is no shortage of food owing to the motor transport which is well organised. Hyde Park is a sight with hundreds of motor vans and thousands of milk cans standing about. As yet there has been no disorder, but a vast amount of inconvenience and even hardship to thousands. In some cases trains were left standing between stations, while the guards and drivers departed in motor-cars. Special constables are being enrolled and military guards placed in certain spots. Endless numbers of people are offering their services to the government; my daughter, Angie, went on this errand this morning, but could not get near the place of enrolment. I think that nothing which has happened so far will do these strikers more harm with the general public than their cold-blooded decision to leave all the railway horses unfed and unwatered. We are a humanitarian nation and this kind of example goes home to the simplest intelligence. Up to the present

[1]When Lloyd George's Government tried to force wage reductions on the railwaymen, a national strike was called.

the strike seems intensely unpopular and I think the whole nation is determined to see it through, as this tyranny cannot be borne much longer.

1st October, 1919

At the Athenaeum today there was no sign of food shortage. I have not seen such joints of cold beef and other meats upon the sideboard since the beginning of the war. I expect, however, that these will be the last for a long while.

3rd October, 1919

I went to the British Museum today to try to see Budge, who is marooned in Scotland, and found that the Friendly Society flappers are still in occupation of the Egyptian rooms which are shut to the public. Really, eleven months after the Armistice, this is disgraceful! I asked the old commissionaire when they were going out. He replied with heavy sarcasm, 'I think, sir, about this time next year.'

6th October, 1919

Yesterday afternoon it was suddenly announced that the strike was at an end on terms which neither side can claim as an actual victory. The relief of the country at the settlement was well shown by the joy-peal of the bells of Westminster Abbey[1], to which I stood and listened for some time at about 6 o'clock.

7th October, 1919

London yesterday was more uncomfortable than it has been at any time during the strike. All the crowds reappeared, among them hundreds of thousands of women coming up to shop or amuse themselves, with the result that the trains, trams and buses were absolutely choked as were the streets, and travelling was a misery. This state of affairs seems to grow worse instead of better. So does the pressure upon housing accommodation for which the rich appear to be willing to pay anything. Here is an example. A relative of mine has taken a seven year lease of a tiny flat in a fashionable block of Knightsbridge. Now a lady appears who offers her £1200 premium to surrender the lease of these three rooms to her; or alternatively she can obtain an enormous rental — I think she said up to eighteen guineas a week. There must still be people with plenty of money to throw away in England.

8th October, 1919

Today I was in the chair at a meeting of the Empire Land Settlement of the Royal

[1]This is a mistake. Canon Westlake told me afterwards that the ringing of the bells had nothing to do with the termination of the strike. H.R.H.

Commonwealth Institute. There I asked Commissioner Lamb what the Salvation Army thought about the strike and the way it was concluded. He told me privately that although they were peace-loving, in their opinion (including that of the General) it should not have been ended thus but ought to have been fought out while the opinion of the country was so greatly against the strikers who had done a wicked thing in trying to starve and hold it up. As it was, he feared that the real issue would be postponed.

North Lodge, St Leornards   *13th October, 1919*

I am back here for the winter, I hope, and thankful to get out of London which is very overcrowded and unpleasant, having let the flat for the winter to an old lady who is afraid to come in today because it is the thirteenth, disturbed also because as she points out its number, 26, is double thirteen! St Leonards seems much the same as usual except that there is hardly any electric light in the streets owing to strikes and coal shortage. Also coal is 50 or more per cent up in price. Everything is up, including the rates; only the conveniences of life are down.

29th October, 1919

The unemployment dole is rotting this country to the bone. Parnell, the ex-soldier I engaged nine months ago, suddenly left without notice the other morning and returned to ask for his wages and say that the work was 'too hard for him'. (There are three people in this small house and three servants to wait on them, hardly any fires, no entertainment and every labour-saving contrivance!) Doubtless soon he will again be in receipt of the dole. The man who used to come in the morning cannot return because he 'has signed on with the Unemployment Office'. So it goes on.

31st October, 1919

I have been to town today to see the private view of the film of *Allan Quatermain*.[1] It is not at all bad, but it might be a great deal better. I wonder if the cinema business will ever be adequately handled in this country. It has great possibilities but it ought to be in the hands of artists and strictly upright men.

4th November, 1919

I had a shock this morning when I opened *The Times*. My dear friend from whom I have received more spiritual help and comfort than from anyone else in my life-

---

[1]On 3rd November, Rider Haggard wrote to *The Times* asking, 'Cannot better arrangements be made as to the release of films? Is it really necessary that these should be kept in cold storage for a solid year, as I understand will happen in the case of *Allan Quatermain*?'

time, the Rev. Philip Bainbrigge, Vicar of St Thomas, Regent Street, which church I have attended for many years when in London, is suddenly no more. We parted after the communion service at St Thomas on Sunday, 5th October. He told me in a chat we had at the church door that he was much worried about many things, financial and others, and that it seemed to him that he 'could do nothing right'. I offered such assistance as lay in my power and we agreed to lunch together at the Athenaeum on the following Thursday. Afterwards I received a note from him in which he said that he was 'much touched' by my suggestion of help and that he would remember it at a pinch, also that he could not lunch as his doctor had ordered him away at once. Now I see that he is dead 'after a short illness' of which no doubt this break-up was the beginning, as indeed I feared it might be. Last year I dedicated *Love Eternal* to him, speaking of him as one 'whose privilege it is by instruction and example to strengthen the weak hands and confirm the feeble knees of many', as indeed it has been.

7th November, 1919

A new 'Theory of the Universe', discovered by a German, Einstein, has been proclaimed. I have read several accounts of it in the train on my way to and from London, but confess that my limited intelligence cannot understand it at all, though it is said to be a revolution in science and to overturn the theories of Newton. It appears to be something to do with the 'warping' of space, whatever that may mean, or the bending of light deflected by the attraction of the sun. But if light does bend or space does 'warp', I cannot see that it matters much to us who for so long have remained ignorant of the fact without inconvenience.

10th November, 1919

I had a compliment paid to me this morning. The traffic superintendent from one of the St Leonards stations came to make a proposal of settlement as regards certain Persian tiles that were broken in transit. I offered him a cigarette, which he declined to light. When I asked him why, he answered because he meant to keep it 'always'. It turned out that he is an ardent admirer of my humble works — especially those that have to do with history like *Fair Margaret*.[1] I was so touched that I gave him a book with which he went away quite delighted. So far as he was concerned, I think I might have asked any compensation I liked for the tiles!

19th November, 1919

In a note I had from Kipling today he says: 'There are no words this side of Hell to describe what the vanity of man can work of evil upon earth. And now — not a soul

[1]The book was published on 9th September, 1907, after appearing serially in *The Lady's Realm*.

dare laugh since the U.S.A. holds the mortgage on us all! I would like to hear your language.' He wouldn't hear much, for I have given things up and just content myself with recording events as they pass my bewildered eyes. In truth now-a-days, we have to take things as we find them.

4th December, 1919

Kipling, who has been lunching here today, is of opinion that we owe all our Russian troubles, and many others, to the machinations of the Jews. I do not know, I am sure, but personally I am inclined to think that one can insist too much on the Jew motive — the truth being that there are Jews and Jews. If, however, they are as mischievous as he believes, the evil that they do is likely to recoil on their own heads, since in extremity the world has a rough way of dealing with Jews. For my own part, I should be inclined to read Trade Unions instead of Jews, for surely they are the root of most of our embarrassments and perplexities. I suggested to R.K. that perhaps it might do good if two or three of us, say he and Inge and I, sent a letter to *The Times* setting out his Bolshevist business clearly and trying to arouse the country to a sense of all its horrors. He is going to think the matter over but is rather afraid that if we did so it would be set down as a 'Northcliffe Stunt'. As a matter of fact neither he nor I nor Inge (if the last would bear a hand) has anything to do with Northcliffe and I think that the world knows this. Kipling believes also that the worst thing that is happening to us as an Empire is what he calls 'the handing over of India'. This is a matter which he understands and I do not, therefore I shall not discuss it, but from what I have read I have little doubt but that there is mischief afoot.

24th December, 1919

Eight ladies have now been put upon the Commission of the Peace. I am a very old Chairman of Magistrates and I say advisedly that is not the place for them. To begin with many of the cases are unfit for their ears. But I speak as a fool, nothing now-a-days is unfit for a woman's ears. We must revise all our ideas about their sex.

25th December, 1919

Another Xmas Day — a green Yule — damp and dreary. The country is making a great feast of it, money is being spent like water; people in London are paying huge prices for dinners at the fashionable restaurants (where perhaps they will find no one to wait upon them) and buying all manner of costly things. Yet really it is a sad Xmas for England which, except when her fate trembled on the hazard of the war, was never more beset with dangers and anxieties that I need not set out anew. Please God that we win through them somehow, though it is hard to see our road.

There are no papers today and therefore no news reaches us. I feel that I am becoming more and more a mere spectator of events. There seems little left for me to do. Well, at my age that is a common experience, so I must not complain. And yet I think I could still do some good work for the country — if I had the chance.

31st December, 1919

This is the last day of an unhappy and disappointing year. I hope that the next may be better and more prosperous, but I cannot see any reason to suppose that it will.
Vale 1919!

1920

Increasingly Rider Haggard felt out of tune with his times and irritated by the successes of more popular writers (especially if they were female). At the beginning of the year he became involved in an anti-Bolshevist movement he called the Liberty League. It was a fiasco, the subscriptions being purloined by an official. Having with difficult extricated himself from the resulting mess, Rider Haggard returned with relief to Ditchingham. He was busy there, but much time was spent sorting out his affairs, including ordering the destruction of the last of his valuable orchid collection.

As one who had in the past often been accused of plagiarism, it must have been strange for Rider Haggard to be involved in two cases where others were accused of copying his work. One of these provided an unexpected but very welcome financial windfall — a film company paid a substantial sum for the 'shameless plagiarism' of his novel Cleopatra.

Before going to St Leonards for the winter, Rider Haggard visited Belgium to see the war cemeteries and the battlefields. The trip, however, did nothing to cheer him. At the end of the year he could but conclude that it had been a wretched year and that things would not get any better.

1st January, 1920

I amused myself as the Old Year passed last night in reading the last paragraph of *A Farmer's Year*[1] which I wrote at the same moment on 31st December, 1898 — 21 years ago! It is a passage that has been much praised and quoted, but I do not find it quite as good as it might be[2]; one never does with anything!

8th January, 1920

I have just paid my first instalment of income tax for this year. It is terribly heavy, so heavy that one wonders whether it is worth while to work so hard when one begins to need rest. Nearly half of what one has is taken in cold cash. Also the assessment is run up by the inclusion of all the wife's income, which if it were assessed separately would, of course, pay much less.

12th January, 1920

I have received a curious souvenir of old Umslopogaas, my Zulu hero (or more properly 'Umhlopezazi'), sent to me by Mr S. B. Samuelson, the son of the late Under Secretary of Native Affairs in Natal. It is the Victoria Medal given to certain Zulu Chiefs on the occasion of her late Majesty's completing her sixtieth year of queenship, and to Umslopogaas among them. He handed it back to the late Mr Samuelson a few days before his death many years ago. Evidently he always wore it as I know by the scent. I never thought that I should live to smell old Umslopogaas again!

14th January, 1920

Today I have received a letter from the Foreign Editor of *The Times*, Mr Steed, asking me to see him in connection with the Bolshevist peril. What he wants me to do I am unable to say.

22nd January, 1920

Yesterday I went to town to attend the Pilgrims' dinner to the Prince of Wales. In

[1]In this book, which was published on 2nd October, 1899, Rider Haggard records his farming experiences on his Ditchingham estate throughout 1898.
[2]'Now, above every time and season, in this moment of midnight while the world beneath us leaps to the pathway of another year, to Him who, with an equal hand, makes the Star, the Child, and the Corn to grow, and, their use fulfilled, calls back the energy of life He lent them; to the Lord of birth and death; of spring, of summer, and of harvest, let us make the offering of a thankful spirit for all that we have been spared of ill and all that we have won of good, before we rise up in quietness and confidence to meet the fortune of the days to be' (p. 458).

the afternoon, by appointment, I went to see Mr Steed, the Editor of *The Times*, and there met Colonel Maitland Edwards[1], who was also bidden. Mr Steed unfolded to me a mighty plan for fighting Bolshevism in this country by means of elaborate propaganda. The idea is that a council is to be formed, which he thinks would have the blessing of the Government, with representatives of the various churches on it and I know not who besides — that remains to be decided. By a process of elimination he had arrived at the conclusion that I should be the best man to be President of the Council as being well-known, trusted by the people and honest. The objection to me, in his opinion, was that I had a title. I told him I did not agree with him: for instance the fact that I was a writer, which he thought was more in my favour than against me, also that I was getting on in life, and — as I would take no money — must consider my own business. Ultimately after nearly an hour's talk, I suggested that John Ward, who chances to be a friend of mine, should be the President if he would accept it, while I as a Vice-President should play the part of 'ghost' under him. To this idea he agreed. There is to be a further meeting of those who are likely to be interested, probably at a luncheon. I told him straight out that my fear was lest the business be looked on as a 'Northcliffe stunt'. He answered that it was nothing of the sort, but that it was perfectly true that there was the gravest uneasiness among capitalists about the advance of these doctrines and that any amount of money would be forthcoming to fight them. He said £100,000 to begin with. I told him that I thought a million would be wanted before the end. The object is, of course, to split the Labour Party in two and to separate the Constitutional sheep from the Bolshevist goats, one that in my opinion is perfectly legitimate and proper. To sum up — naturally I was much gratified at this testimony to myself coming from those whose business it is to weigh men in very accurate scales, but at the same time I feel that I was right to decline the honour. I am sure, under all the circumstances, that Ward is the better man, and I hope that he will accept the office. It is no use writing more about the business at present.

The dinner for the Prince of Wales was a great success. I was seated exactly opposite H.R.H. and studied him carefully. I must say that I formed a most favourable opinion of him. He is just a young English gentleman of the best class, rather modest I should say but with all the characteristics of his blood. In speaking, his delivery and voice are not particularly good and of course some of his speech was written for him. However, he has capacities of his own in that line as was shown by a little incident. The Chairman talked of him as being domiciled in England. In his reply the Prince remarked that he should have said that he was domiciled in the British Empire, which in view of his position and everything else, was distinctly acute of him. Two others I studied also, neither of whom I had ever seen before, namely Lord Reading[2], Rufus Isaacs that was, and Lord Birken-

[1]He had been part of the British Headquarters Staff attached to the Russian Army immediately after the Revolution.
[2]He was then Lord Chief Justice of England. In 1921 he became Viceroy and Governor-General of India.

head[1], late F. E. Smith. Lord Reading's struck me as an extremely unhappy face — I should say that that man suffers a great deal about something or other, notwithstanding his enormous success in life. Also he doth protest too much. It was rather absurd to listen to this member of an ancient Semitic race declaiming with a somewhat forced enthusiasm about the glories of being an Englishman. As for Lord Birkenhead, I thought his cast of countenance not very refined and I did not stay to listen to his speech. It was curious to look at the young Prince of Wales and to reflect upon what things he may see if he lives to the limit of our days. I hope that they will be fortunate things for his country and himself, but I am not sure. God's blessing be with him!

I went to the British Museum today and, I think, for the third or fourth time within the last year or so found the Egyptian room which I wished to visit in possession of an army of 'official flappers'. Really the thing is monstrous.[2]

30th January, 1920

Today I went to town and saw the representatives of the Anti-Bolshevik and Freedom Defence League at present in embryo, namely Colonel Maitland Edwards and Mr Bower, the Secretary. This I did in response to a renewed invitation to me to become President of the League. We went into the whole matter somewhat exhaustively and in the end I consented, subject to certain minor conditions which I recorded on a piece of paper and to which, as I understood, a formal acceptance is to be sent tomorrow. First, however, I suggested that it would be as well to ring up Wickham Steed, the Editor of *The Times*, and ask whether he was still of the same opinion as to the desirability of my assuming the high office of President of this great movement and whether I should have the unqualified support of *The Times* if I did so. The poor man was aroused from his bed to answer these questions and replied emphatically in the affirmative both to Colonel Edwards and myself. So there the matter stands for the present. Apparently all the money required will be forthcoming and the impression left upon my mind is that the real backer of the business is Lord Northcliffe. Needless to say I take no pay beyond my railway fares; what I do, I do in the hope that it may help the country, which has always been my lot in life, not too successful as I fear, though perhaps directly or indirectly I have done something in sundry directions.

3rd February, 1920

Last night I dined with my brother Will at the dinner of the Royal Geographical

[1]Frederick Edwin Smith, 1st Earl of Birkenhead, was a lawyer, businessman and politician. He was Lord High Chancellor of Great Britain.
[2]The matter so upset Rider Haggard that he wrote to *The Times* about it that day calling it 'an absolute scandal'.

Club. Amongst a number of distinguished people, the Prince of Wales was there, looking as pleasant as usual. After dinner he spoke to Will and myself. He remembered having served with my nephew Hal, and said something to me about my books, which he said he had read with pleasure.

4th February, 1920

I have spent the whole day in consultation over the affairs of what is at present called the Anti-Bolshevik League.

6th February, 1920

Today I received a telegram from *The Times* begging me to write something about their Cairo to the Cape Air Flight. As I do not like to be disobliging I have done so, setting down such thoughts as came into my head. I must admit, however, that all these demands for gratis copy (I think I have received three today) are becoming somewhat overwhelming. What between my private work, an ever-growing miscellaneous correspondence, my humble efforts for the public weal, and all the ordinary social call of life, I have no time left to myself and there will come a time, I fear, when the burden must prove too heavy to be borne by one now growing old. This diary alone, together with the reading that is necessary for its composition, takes me at least an hour a day, often more. Soon it will have to end.

10th February, 1920

I contemplated making certain small repairs to this house (lifting the roof-passage etc.) which before the war would have cost, I believe, about £250. I have just received the estimate for them. It turns out at well over £1000, and no guarantee is given that this price will not be raised in accordance with the possible increase in the cost of labour and materials. Needless to say those alterations will remain undone.

12th February, 1920

I have been to town to attend a Council meeting of the Royal Colonial Institute as to the proposed amalgamation between it and the Overseas Club. It will, I think, go through and be a good thing. In every department of public life there are too many bodies duplicating the same work. Of course this amalgamation will add enormously to the numbers of the Royal Colonial Institute.[1]

[1]Although the amalgamation continued to be discussed over the next fifteen years, it never did take place.

I have been to town today. The Anti-Bolshevist League, or the Liberty League as I have renamed it, seems to be taking shape. I have just heard that *The Times* will start a fund and back the movement for all it is worth.

19th February, 1920

I rejoice to read that the British Museum is in all probability to be 'freed by Easter from the intrusion of Government Departments'. I am glad I wrote that letter to *The Times* a little while ago; it may have helped.

I forgot to say that a week or so back Ambrose Williams, my old carpenter at Ditchingham, died. He was a most peculiar man and I really believe that I was the only person who could get on with him, since with everyone else he quarrelled violently. But in his way he was a great artist. He had had no education beyond that of a journeyman carpenter, and he could not make a plan except in the form of meaningless marks upon a board, yet like the old monks who built the cathedrals he did beautiful things, as some of his panelling and other work at Ditchingham House will show. Few such craftsmen are left in these days of machines and fixed hours and strikes and clamouring for higher wages, few who live their work for its own sake as Williams did who, when he was not quarrelling, thought of it and nothing else. Now there is one less of them in the world.

3rd March, 1920

Today there appears in *The Times* the letter (more or less as I wrote it) announcing the foundation of the Liberty League[1], also a strong commendatory article in that paper. So that bolt is shot, whether with or without effect we shall know in due course!

4th March, 1920

There is lots more about the Liberty League in *The Times*, also an interesting letter from Mr Edward Price Bell, who suggested that it should link up with a similar body in the States known as the American Legion. My doubt about the whole business is as to whether the necessary funds to run it will be forthcoming. However, I and others have done what we can and now the matter must rest in the hands of the public.

[1]The letter is signed by H. Rider Haggard, Rudyard Kipling, Sydenham, H. Bax-Ironside, John Hanbury Williams, Algernon Maudslay, and G. Maitland Edwards. It asks for donations to be sent to Lieutenant-Colonel Maitland Edwards at 17 Bruton Street, Mayfair, London W.

12th March, 1920

Today I have been much employed on the affairs of the Liberty League, which I hope will take on with the loyal and law-abiding sections of the community.

18th March, 1920

Yesterday morning I sent a letter to *The Times* under the heading of 'The Daughter Left Behind' in which I tried to expose some of the horrors of Bolshevism and dwelt on the utter indifference of the attitude of this country towards them. For various reasons, however, I was doubtful of the wisdom of publishing this letter and told Mr Steed so in a covering note, asking him to exercise his own judgement upon the matter. Today I have received from him a letter in which he expresses agreement with this view. He says: 'Thank you for your letter. In the circumstances, I think it is more expedient not to publish it. It would, no doubt, make a passing impression, but at this moment, and with the public mind in its present state, it is not sufficient as a text to preach from.'

23rd March, 1920

Today at the offices of the Liberty League I was shown most terrible photographs of murdered people in Russia, some of whom had evidently been tortured to death. They are too hideous to describe. Surely many of these Russians can be scarcely human. I have been engaged all day discussing a proposed amalgamation with another Anti-Bolshevist Society which has done a great deal of good work. Personally I hope it may come about, as united effort achieves more than separated effort. If it does, they wish to take the name of 'Liberty League', and apparently that I should remain Chairman of both the affiliated societies. They have already spent a hundred thousand pounds upon their propaganda. I now await a formal letter from them.

25th March, 1920

Mrs Humphrey Ward[1] is dead. She was a most able and active woman and will be a great loss. Once I used to know her a little, but we have not met for a long time. Personally her books did not appeal to me any more probably than mine would appeal to her, but then I never did care for these long and rather ponderous semi-religious discussions in the form of fiction. For one of her works, *David Greive*, it is said that she received £20,000, which I can scarcely believe, at least I never knew a novel, however dull, to bring in so much. I cannot resist repeating a story which Charles Longman told me of my late friend, Andrew Lang. They were going out of town to fish somewhere together, and at the book-stall Andrew bought one of

---

[1]Mary Augusta Arnold (as she was called before her marriage) was the grand-daughter of Dr Arnold of Rugby. Her many books were extremely popular.

Mrs Ward's novels. I think it was this very *David Greive*. For a while he read it, then suddenly opened the carriage window and threw it out on to the line, remarking immediately afterwards, 'I should not have done that!' 'Why not?' asked Charles, thinking that perhaps he referred to the waste of an expensive book. 'Because it is so heavy that it will probably upset the next train!' replied Andrew.

1st April, 1920

Lilias has been given the M.B.E. for her war work as a nurse and as a volunteer motor-driver.

6th April, 1920

Yesterday was Bank Holiday and as usual at Easter the weather was wretched. I was driven to town in a motor-car to open 'The South African Week' at the Albert Hall. It astonished me to see the determination of the British people to enjoy themselves. There they were by the thousands on the road, many of them on bicycles without coats and still upon pleasure bent notwithstanding the cold and gusty showers. The entertainment at the Albert Hall was interesting. First there was the lunch at which I was the Guest of Honour, where I made a speech. In the course of my remarks I touched upon the great responsibilities of the producers of films which have such an enormous influence upon the young. Many of these films, especially those that come from America, I am convinced do much harm. Leaving other matters aside, the glorification of crime, which is frequent, must be most mischievous. After I had formally opened the exhibition and spoken a few words urging the necessity for more English population in South Africa, we attended the performance of *King Solomon's Mines*. It was well given and the audience was great; so far as I could see the Albert.Hall must have been about two-thirds full, and after it was over the people poured out by the thousand. As the film has already been screened in various parts of London, this is remarkable and suggests that it must have considerable popularity.

8th April, 1920

Mr Kenneth Mackenzie, the well-known Cambridge agricultural expert, has been lunching here. He has been a friend of the Ashford family for very many years and was telling us about Miss Daisy Ashford and the tale she wrote when she was nine years old, which has been published under the name of *The Young Visiters*. The success of this little story in America has been astonishing; I think he said that the author's receipts from the sale of it there up to November last and therefore before the Christmas sales amounted to quite fifteen thousand pounds, to which must be added the English receipts which are about one-third as much. There is no doubt as to these figures as Mackenzie's brother is the author's solicitor and he has them from him. The boom must have been much the same as that of my early books in the States, with this difference, that I had no copyright and therefore was robbed of every farthing. Had I received what was due to me, I should have been a very rich man, but as a matter of fact this tremendous success actually has done me great injury in America, since as my first books are obtainable there for a few pence, few will pay 6/- for the copyrighted works that follow. Such is the fortune of war! Mackenzie says that Miss Ashford could not now write a line to save her life, also that she is now charming whereas she used to be a most odious and priggish child. She has married a 'Tommy' whom she nursed in hospital. He is now being taught farming under Mackenzie's supervision and the pair are to set up on the land upon the proceeds of *The Young Visiters*. However romantic, he considers it a deplorable alliance — but such again is the fortune of war.

14th April, 1920

I spent last night in London and took the Chair at the Royal Colonial Institute meeting at the Central Hall on the occasion of the reading of the paper by Mr Christopher Turnor on 'The Organisation of Migration and Settlement within the Empire'. I introduced the lecturer with a speech in which I insisted upon the necessity of a redistribution of Empire population and pointed out the danger in which Australasia and South Africa stand today.

I had a long talk this morning with Mr Seeley, the Manager of Barclay's bank, or Gosling's branch of it, with which I deal. The Stock Exchange is in a bad way but I have made a small speculation in the bonds of the last French Loan which stands at a heavy discount. The French have never yet repudiated their obligations and I hope that they will justify my faith in them now. It is difficult to know whether to invest money or to leave it on deposit.

20th April, 1920

Today I go to town after spending the winter at St Leonards.

National Club, London   *21st April, 1920*

I have had a hard time since I reached town over the affairs of the Liberty League. I cannot set down the details even here, but — all men are not honest![1] However, I

[1] Rider Haggard never described exactly what had happened, but on 14th October, 1924 he wrote this in his diary: 'While in London I attended a Council meeting of the Royal Colonial Institute and there heard the Council decide unanimously to strike the name of Colonel Maitland Edwards off the list of Fellows. It seems that this gentleman has involved the Institute in a settlement scheme which has come to an end under circumstances strangely resembling those that marked the decease of the Liberty League, with which I was so painfully concerned. On this occasion, however, he was assisted, not by Captain Bowen, but by two other persons whom he succeeded in persuading the Council to elect as Fellows of the Institute — with horrid results. The loss on this occasion, however, was heavier. Indeed I understand that £6,000 or £8,000 have vanished.'

hope that not much harm has been done as luckily the business was discovered in time. Yesterday I had to see Mr Wickham Steed, the Editor of *The Times*, and most of the day I have spent in the company of Mr Algernon Maudslay, one of my co-signatories of the letter to *The Times* and the head of the Russian Red Cross, and of his solicitor.

22nd April, 1920

Another long day over all the Liberty League business, beginning with an exhaustive interview with Lord Sydenham in the company of Mr Algernon Maudslay. I am glad to say that Lord Sydenham throughly agrees with Maudslay and myself upon all points and endorses our proposed course of procedure. It looks to me as though we have become involved in a veritable romance of fraud, if fraud can be romantic. If so, none of us are to blame; the foolishness is in another quarter. Some day I hope to be able to set out the story. One's natural impulse would be to return the subscriptions and wash one's hands of the whole affair, but that would be almost a national catastrophe and cause Bolshevists everywhere to rejoice. So I suppose the burden must be borne. This is the sort of thing that often happens to those who try to help their country, however pure their motives.

24th April, 1920

Yesterday I was hard at work all day. I attended at the Liberty League office morning and afternoon. I went to *The Times* luncheon to Lord Atholstan[1], and in the evening to the Festival Dinner of the Royal Society of St George, and finally only got back here about 12.30 a.m. (It was an interminable festival.) Kipling's address at the dinner was very learned, very profound and very analytical, but it took no hold of the large audience, much of which, I think, could not hear him. Evidently he had learned it by heart in his usual fashion and its acute and polished periods smelt of the lamp. However, it reads well in the papers to which, I imagine, it had been furnished beforehand. I do not know whether the possession of such a marvellous memory is a blessing or a curse.

During the dinner, which was enlivened by the presence of enormous Beef-eaters and Yeomen of the Guard dressed in the ancient uniforms and by a procession in which four white-robed chefs bore a huge baron of beef around the great hall of the Connaught Rooms that they nearly managed to upset on Kipling's head, I became a Life Member of the Society. When at length it was over, the Kiplings and I, after a furious hunt for a taxi, returned to their rooms at Brown's Hotel and there I set out all the melancholy facts concerning our Liberty League imbroglio, which, as he remarked, gave him 'something to think about'. He is coming to the meeting next Thursday. Then I walked home dog-tired. The

---

[1] He was a Canadian press-baron and enthusiastic supporter of Imperial projects.

Kiplings, who have just returned from France, say that opinion there against England is very bitter. Nor, after going through the devastated areas, do they wonder at it.

I have had plenty more Liberty League business today, including two hours at the lawyers, Messrs Rye and Eyre, with Miss Hector this morning. I am sick of it and it tires me very much, especially as I am not in the least responsible for anything; Wickham Steed, who as Editor of *The Times* introduced me to Colonel Maitland Edwards, is really responsible for the blunder and no one else. I only undertook the prospective presidency of the League and accepted its personnel on *The Times* introduction.

Louie has come to town and I lunched with her at the Empress Club.

26th April, 1920

Another long day at the Liberty League.

27th April, 1920

I have had another long day at the Liberty League.

29th April, 1920

This afternoon we have had our first meeting of the Committee of the Liberty League, at which I was in the Chair. Kipling, Wickham Steed, and all the other members were present, except Lord Sydenham. I set out all the circumstances of the disastrous conspiracy of which we have been the victims. Mr Algernon Maudslay and Sir H. Bax-Ironside were appointed a Finance Committee and the meeting was adjourned until Monday next to allow Mr Wickham Steed to see Lord Northcliffe and ascertain what he is prepared to do, bearing in mind that our troubles are rooted in the action of *The Times*. I do not know how the business will end, but I have done my best and on the whole feel easier in my mind.

Tonight I attended a dinner at the Langham Hotel given by Alderman Lea of Liverpool and proposed the toast of the Royal Academy and Kindred Institutions.

The weather continues to be most vile and bitterly cold.

30th April, 1920

Today I have been to the private view of the Royal Academy. The pictures seem much the same as they were five and thirty years ago when I used to look at them with Andrew Lang, trudging through the identical 'leagues of long Academy' as he called them. It seemed to consist mainly of a totally different set of people. The private view of old days used to be a very smart function. Now nobody could call it so. I bought another little bronze by F. J. Halnon, called 'The Spirit of Renaissance', a beautiful thing as I think. It is a companion bust to the 'Crown of Victory' which I purchased last year and I believe done from the same model, but now there are wings upon the head instead of a laurel wreath and the work is made to breathe of hope and rebirth in place of grief tinged with triumph. Louie and I had a long talk with Gosse who seems wonderfully well.

1st May, 1920

Today near Trafalgar Square, Louie and I were nearly held up by an endless procession of Labour Agitators and their supporters marching to Hyde Park. I was struck by the sight of a number of brakes filled with children, most of whom waved red flags. One party of them was labelled 'Socialist Sunday Schools'. I wonder into what kind of citizens children thus educated will develop.

Garland's Hotel   *3rd May, 1920*

There has been another meeting of the Liberty League Committee. We shall all of us have to pay up money as a result of the defalcations — goodness knows how much. Wickham Steed told me lots that was interesting about the Jewish danger.

4th May, 1920

Today Greiffenhagen began to paint his second portrait of me, or rather he did a trial sketch in chalks. I think that when it is finished it ought to be called 'Wrinkles'. To my mind, his portrait of the late William Beattie is the finest in this year's Academy.

More Liberty League bothers. The black-mailing is beginning now! or rather, it is being attempted.

5th May, 1920

Tonight I dined with the Benchers of the Inner Temple. It was a distinguished and an interesting gathering. I was 'taken in' arm in arm by Justice Sir Sydney Rowlatt, a charming and simple man — a very quaint custom. After dinner in the library I had conversation with Mr Justice Darling, the Lord Chancellor (Birkenhead), H. G. Wells and others and was driven back to the Athenaeum by Parsons[1], the inventor of the famous Turbine. We discussed all sorts of things, including the status of illegitimate children with Wells. Lord Birkenhead seemed to be very familiar with my books. It is odd to see so young a man Lord Chancellor of England. He looked quite a youth in the Company. I enjoyed the evening and the old customs. In the body of the hall a number of barristers and students were dining. Among the latter I noticed a coal-black negro and one nice-looking young lady qualifying for the Bar. I wonder what this Portia will do when she gets there!

[1]Hon. Sir Charles Algernon Parsons was Chairman of the steam turbine, electrical, optical and engineering works, C. A. Parsons & Co., at Heaton, Newcastle-on-Tyne.

7th May, 1920

The Liberty League worries are overpowering. I spend most of my days trying to deal with them but without much result. We seem plunged in an atmosphere of deception or worse. Today I have been talking to Mr Wickham Steed on the telephone and told him straight out that if Lord Northcliffe makes up his mind that he will not help we must wind up the League. He said that *The Times* acted in good faith. I answered that so did we all, but that would not prevent attack and scandal. He agreed. Now I have suggested by letter that Mr Maudslay and I should see Lord Northcliffe. I think the best thing would be to wind up.

8th May, 1920

Today I have had an interview at the Athenaeum with Mr Alexander Thompson, the *Daily Mail* Labour expert (who is much in the confidence of Lord Northcliffe), about the Liberty League and its affairs. He is going to try to arrange a meeting between Lord Northcliffe and Maudslay and myself so that we may explain the situation. On the whole he seems to think that the best thing to do would be to shut down the League and I am inclined to agree with him.

10th May, 1920

I have received a letter from Lord Northcliffe in which he utterly repudiates all that *The Times* has done about the Liberty League and declares his belief that no Bolshevism exists in England. This is pleasant for Wickham Steed.

11th May, 1920

Plenty of Liberty League again today, concerning Lord Northcliffe's letter to me which we all think disgraceful.

12th May, 1920

I presided this afternoon at the last meeting of the Empire Land Settlement Committee of the Royal Colonial Institute. At the conclusion of the meeting Sir Godfrey Lagden moved a vote of thanks to me for all my work in connection with Empire Land Settlement work of the Royal Colonial Institute.

14th May, 1920

Today there was a meeting of the Liberty League at which it was agreed that we should combine with National Propaganda and all our unhappy complications were ventilated. I am sick to death of this business and especially of *The Times* and Lord Northcliffe, whose behaviour has, in our opinion, been despicable. Everyone says, however, that he is practically mad with vanity and bemused with the idea that he is a reincarnation of Napoleon. Poor pinch-beck Napoleon! Rudyard Kipling and Mr Maudslay are going to draft the reply to his letter addressed to myself as it is thought better that it should be answered by the Committee as a whole, so my rough draft is to be adapted.

Tomorrow I go to Ditchingham, thank God! This day, so far as I am concerned, I hope, Greiffenhagen finished painting his portrait of me. Lord! what a wearisome business is that 'sitting' day after day. I think it is a fine picture and he told me triumphantly that he considered it the greatest work he had ever done. It is extraordinarily like my father!

Ditchingham   *17th May, 1920*

I came here on Saturday after six months or more of absence and found the place looking charming as it always does at this time of year. The house is upside down and pervaded with men who are putting in the electric light (as inexpensively as possible). It is not easy to wire a solid brick house that is full of panelling and parquet floors though I think a good job is being made of it in a modest way. Notwithstanding the rise in prices, I am getting the business done for less than half what I was asked before the war — thanks to Tom who understands such matters. We could no longer stand the darkness in this house, especially now that there is no one to do the oil lamps, of which we had such numbers in the old days. I hate gloom! it depresses me.

The weather here is chilly, but there was a good and much-wanted thunder rain here this morning.

21st May, 1920

I hear today that there is a good prospect of the amalgamation of National Propaganda with the Liberty League, under the name of the latter Association. If so, this will be a way out of many of our difficulties which have resulted from the frauds that have been practised on us as a result of the introductions and assurances given by the Editor of *The Times* to myself.

I have been to Norwich today; some of the tradesmen there anticipate a slump.

22nd May, 1920

I have been to Kessingland today. It is in a better state than when last I saw it but it will take years to bring it back to what it was before the soldiers wrecked it. The garden is still a melancholy waste.

29th May, 1920

After the sudden departure of one of the maids to nurse her mother, Mrs Mason, the gardener's wife who cooks and has served us for very many years, tells Louie that a complete change has taken place in the habits of the labouring classes. Formerly for some small consideration they would help each other in minor sickness whereby the sending for daughters in service was obviated. Now, for the most part, they will not do so, owing principally to their having more money. So the girls must go and do go continually. It is part of the great change — not one for the better — that is taking place in rural England.

I have at last received the French translation of *She*, about which book there has been so much excitement in France in connection with Benoit's *L'Atlantide*.[1] It is a mere soulless bald précis of my work, much abbreviated without advertisement thereof, and I am so disgusted that I cannot go on reading it.

22nd June, 1920

My birthday! How the years go by and how quickly the world slips past us. However, I think we live long enough. I can imagine no fate more awful than that of 'She' left alone like a hard, everlasting rock on a water-scoured plain. Already I begin to be left alone. Shakespeare talks of 'troops of friends' as an accompaniment of age, but mine are nearly all gone and, if we live again, as I hope and indeed believe, how know we that those friends will still care for us yonder? They may have forgotten or new interests may have intervened! It was one of my mistakes in life to make friends with men older than myself, and now time has taken nearly all of them. Ella writes me a birthday letter giving details of my arrival in this world which, as she says, she alone remembers of any living, and with startling clearness as generally we do recall events that happened in our youth. As I was the eighth (to say nothing of a brother born dead) my appearance can scarcely have been welcomed. I should never have been missed. Why do we come, I wonder?

I often wonder about that when I am sitting on the Birth Rate Commission. I presume that *my* chief function is to amuse people, especially the young (I have just received a charming letter or scrawling from a child which suggests the thought) and perhaps now and again to try to do some little kindness. If so, one has some use: it is better to amuse than to bore, though the office of the tale-teller is but humble. But all such reflections are useless. We were not, we are, we shall not be — that is the sum of what we are allowed to know.

23rd June, 1920

Today, I have received through Watt an ultimatum from two publishers so identical that I think it must have been arrived at by agreement. It is to the effect that the royalties on the 2/- editions of my books must be cut down to a penny half-

---

[1] An article in the *French Quarterly*, written by Henry Magden, accused Benoit of having plagiarised *She* in *L'Atlantide*. The accusation was reprinted in the Paris *Matin* and a great controversy ensued in France.

penny which in future is to be my share of the 2/-. They say that this will not leave them any larger profit than before; to share the loss does not seem to have occurred to them — that, according to the common fate of the primary producer, is to be the author's burden. They give, however, excellent reason for this reduction, namely the fearful and continuous increase in the cost of labour. Unless the public will consent to pay more for books that already have risen from 7d. to 2/- for a more poorly produced article, it begins to look as though the trade of writers must come to an end. My humble works command a very large sale indeed in these cheap editions, in fact all the copies that are printed are sold. Yet the publishers say that unless I will consent to these reductions they must give up supplying the market.

25th June, 1920

I have been to town to attend a deputation of the National Birth Rate Commission on the occasion of its presenting its report to Dr Addison[1], the Minister of Health. I was to move the vote of thanks to the Minister and to take the opportunity of dwelling upon the Empire side of this population business. Unfortunately, however, the speakers who went before me and Dr Addison in his reply took so long that, as he had to be in the House by midday to attend to some business that could not be postponed, there was no time left for me in which to speak.

At the Athenaeum I saw Oliver Lodge who has just returned from his American tour and was full of information about the properties of the ether which he intends to spend the rest of his life in investigating.[2] Also he told me a lot about wireless telegraphy which with Hirsch he discovered, though out of it, after the way of great inventors, he has got little, in fact nothing to speak of, while the adaptors, Marconi and others, have made millions.

I saw Watt also about the letters from publishers which I have mentioned. I think that if he is right, I did them an injustice in supposing they bear no share of the loss owing to the rise in price. He believes that they also suffer, although they do not say so explicitly. The position is very serious indeed and none of us know how it is to end.

2nd July, 1920

Today Mr Leney, the Curator of the Castle Museum [Norwich], has been here to take away certain antiques which I have presented to the Corporation, of which the principal are a very beautiful, large and perfect bowl and platter of Roman or Tyrian glass, taken in past years from a tomb in Tyre; a fine and graceful Etruscan vase representing, among other things, the struggle of Hercules with the lion; and the bust of a lady of the late Roman period in white marble much over life size. I

---

[1]Christopher Addison was made Britain's first Minister of Health in 1919. He became 1st Viscount Addison in 1937.
[2]*Ether and Reality*, the report of his investigations, was published in 1925.

part with some regret with these noble objects of ancient art, but on the whole I think that they are better in the museum where all the world can enjoy their beauty, rather than in a private house, where they must be either hidden away or subject to the risks of spring cleanings and, should they survive, in the end go I know not whither.

4th August, 1920

Today is the sixth anniversary of the declaration of war — for six long years have I kept this diary. It is strange to look back and to reflect upon the difference of the world of the 4th August, 1914, and that of the 4th August, 1920. Can we say that it is happier or better? I think not.

10th August, 1920

Nearly a fortnight ago I returned a proof of the catalogue of my MSS. in the Castle Museum, asking for a revise of the few corrections I have made. Now I am informed by the museum authorities that the matter is hung up 'as the printing works are closed for 9 days' holiday'. It is strange to think of the printing works in a great city like Norwich being utterly closed for nine days — and this when thousands are out of employment, nearly 154,000 ex-service men alone being unprovided with work. Another sign of the times!

11th August, 1920

Yesterday I attended the funeral of my old friend and neighbour, Mr Sancroft Holmes, late Chairman of the Norfolk County Council, whose death leaves me one of the few survivors of this neighbourhood as it was when first I knew it. With the exception of John Scudamore and Robert Mann, all the rest have gone. In truth time flies and bears all its sons away. It was a largely attended and impressive ceremony.

This is the fortieth anniversary of my wedding day. Still I should be thankful that after so many years we are both alive and that I am still able to do some work.

25th August, 1920

Today there was a very successful show of poultry, rabbits and vegetables on the lawn of this house, organised by Lilias. It was a small affair got up at short notice, but this success, as I said in a few remarks I made on giving away the prizes, does suggest to me how much could be done by the organisation of efforts in similar directions. With a little encouragement, an enormous amount of food could thus be produced, which at present is imported from Denmark and other places.

There is a most interesting debate going on in the columns of the *Morning Post* on the subject of the manners of our modern youth especially with reference to their treatment of parents and elders. Today a young gentleman, Mr Beverley Nichols[1], the President of the Oxford Union Society, takes a hand in the game. Apparently he attributes the war and our losses in it, a catastrophe in which I do not gather that he was called upon to take a share, to the mismanagement, if not the actual wickedness, of the aged and finds it very wonderful that the young should have fought in this war. One wonders what he, and other writers of this sort, would have had them do, or if it occurs to them that these much despised old men also bore a hand in their country's cause of youth, according to their opportunities, and, as I can testify from personal experience, did not hesitate — many of them — to risk their person in the recent struggle. He sneers at those 'elderly poets' who wrote sonnets about 'the happy warrior' and adds: 'They have had their day, and a long day and a bloody day it has been. If you wish to see what young men think of war today you will not find their opinion in any of the Romantics of the Victorians. You will not find it in the flamboyant insolence of Rudyard Kipling, you will not even find it in the poems of Rupert Brooke. You will find it in the verse of Siegfried Sassoon. It is white-hot bitterness, it is challenge flung with passionate hatred into the faces of Age.' I am not fortunate enough to be acquainted with the works of Siegfried Sassoon[2], who, from his name, I presume is a Jew of the advanced school. But I do wonder whether the Beverley Nichols and the Siegfried Sassoons and the Sitwells with the rest will lead their country. Well — if they are spared to shed their wisdom upon the world, a time will come when they also will belong to the despicable multitude of the Aged. I should like to see a letter written by Mr Beverley Nichols on the same subject on this day fifty years and check it by the opinions under consideration.

Today I was at the cottage, called Naboth's, where I am doing some repairs. A young man was engaged in painting the windows at about 5 minutes to twelve. There came past some other young men who are painting the greenhouses in the garden. They called to him — 'Come out of that, Jim, it is Saturday.' Now these young men must have left work at the house at least 10 or 15 minutes before their time, thereby defrauding their master to that extent. I thought the incident a remarkable example of the spirit of the age and of its youth whom Mr Beverley Nichols admires.

7th September, 1920

The sailing of the *Mayflower* is being commemorated at Plymouth, where many

[1] His public school novel *Prelude*, the first of his many books, was published that year.
[2] Since I wrote this I have read these verses. They are feeble and depressing rubbish. H.R.H.

speeches have been made of an appropriate sort. In other times these ceremonies would have excited more interest than they do today. My own connection with them has been unfortunate, inasmuch as Miss Hector and I spent a great deal of time and labour in writing the scenario of a Film play dealing with the Pilgrim Fathers, by special request, for which, in the end, I was never paid. I understand that the producer went bankrupt, a common event where British films are concerned.

I see that all the refreshment places between Lowestoft and London have put up notices saying, 'No brake, char-a-banc or omnibus party served here.' They have been driven to this by the scandalous conduct of these parties including 'the wholesale pilfering or breaking of glasses and jugs, unpaid bills, insults to women members of the staffs, smashed windows, and rowdiness and violence of behaviour generally'. Here is a strange development of our advanced civilisation. The average European, especially if he be English, looks down upon Easterns and natives of all sorts whom he names 'niggers'. But would savages behave in such a way as this? So far as my rather extended experience of them goes, I should say 'No!' At any rate they have culture of a sort, they have manners — often quite distinguished manners — they have breeding and they have traditions. Lastly they are not vulgar. Can we say as much of our 'charrybangers', excursionists, sea-side crowds and others?

18th September, 1920

Egerton Castle[1] is dead. I think that with the exception of Edmund Gosse, who is an evergreen that the frosts of time never seem to touch, and myself, Castle is the last, or practically so, of the group of us who used to lunch together on Saturdays at the Savile Club between 1886 and 1890. Now from Besant[2] and Lang down, all, or nearly all, have gone, a fact that saddens me.

Lord Faber[3] also died yesterday. When he was Mr Beckett Faber I stayed with him at his charming house at Harrogate while I was carrying out my *Rural England* investigations in Yorkshire. I was extremely unwell at the time and he was most kind to me, helping me in every way possible. It was in his house that, to my astonishment, I discovered a picture of the late Pettie called, I think, 'The Duel'. This picture Pettie was working on at the time when he painted my portrait many years before. So as I was handy he made use of me to serve as a model for one of the combatants, the man with the fair hair.

[1]He wrote, often jointly with his wife, many books and plays. An accomplished swordsman, he captained the British fencing team at the 1908 Olympics.
[2]I am not sure but I have some recollection that it was at the Savile that Besant declared that *She* was 'the greatest work of pure imagination in the English language'. It may be, however, that he wrote it to someone. I remember being much flattered when I was told of this pronouncement of his. H.R.H.
[3]Edmund Beckett Faber, 1st Baron Faber of Butterwick, was a banker who lived at 'Belvedere', Harrogate. Rider Haggard's visit is recorded in *Rural England,* Vol. 2, p. 303.

1920

Today I have given orders for the cremation of all that remain of my collection of orchids which took me 20 years to gather together. These plants were worth some hundreds of pounds before the war, but now they must go to the funeral pyre, for I can no longer afford the fuel necessary to keep them in health through the winter. It is sad, but what can be done, especially as no one else wants them? The houses must in future be devoted to growing stuff that has a sale value in order to help to pay the expenses of the garden.

28th September, 1920

Last night the monument to the fallen of this parish was unveiled in the church before a crowded congregation. It is a very fine thing of its sort — a recumbent effigy of a dead infantry soldier by Derwent Wood, R.A., beautifully and faithfully executed in every detail in bronze. Personally I should have preferred something that gave some idea of hope and life rather than that of doom and death — say a living soldier standing on guard over the tablet on which are graven the names of the fallen. This, however, is a matter of individual opinion and of the dignity of this memorial there can be no doubt. Of its cost, which was considerable, Willie Carr has generously borne much the greater part.

In returning from the service by the narrow Church Lane, some of us had a great escape. A huge motor vehicle that was conveying the military band back to Norwich overtook us in the darkness of the lane. We retreated on the grass at one side, whither for some unknown reason the motor followed us. It struck Miss Hector and knocked her down as though she were shot. In her fall she overthrew my sister, Mary d'Anethen, who is not so active as she was, throwing her on her back. She in her turn, or I suppose that it was she, upset me into the fence. Mercifully, except for some bruises, that was the end of it, as the bus, of which the wheels can only have missed us by inches, proceeded on its way (until its driver realised that an accident had happened). My daughters, Angie and Dolly, who were just ahead, escaped it by scrambling up the bank. It is wonderful how suddenly these things happen. Until I found myself in a bed of nettles and heard Mary calling out 'Ida is killed', I never realised the position, although I had been watching the approach of the motor and calling to the others to stand back as far as possible. I expect that the brilliant head-lights dazzled us all; we saw them and nothing else. These great char-a-bancs and motor busses should not be allowed in lanes of less than a certain width. They are a terrible danger, especially at night.

29th September, 1920

I have just returned from the funeral of Louie's cousin, Lucy Hartcup[1], a most

---

[1]She was the daughter of Louie's father's eldest sister, Louisa Jane. She was born in 1850 (the third of five children).

kind-hearted maiden lady of the old style who for the last half-century has been a part and parcel of this neighbourhood and concerned in every useful and social work hereabouts. She was one of the few local residents who remained of those who lived here in 1879 when first I knew this district. Now very nearly all of them are dead. She will be much missed.

Grosvenor Hotel, London   *7th October, 1920*

I came to town this morning to attend a meeting of the Empire Settlement Committee of the Royal Colonial Society before we proceed to Bruges on Saturday for a holiday. The business about passports is most troublesome and unnecessary. It is quite hot here, warmer than it has been all this so-called summer.

8th October, 1920

I went with Louie to the Passport Office in Lake Dwellings, St James' Park, to get our passport. It is a strange place with miles upon miles of passages up and down where flit endless 'flappers' and Boy Scouts conveying bewildered passport-seekers from department to department. Presently these young folk found out who I was with the result that I was called upon to write autographs for them using the back of a Boy Scout for a desk as there was none other available. It must have been an amusing sight in that passage. Then to Bedford Square to get the said passport visa at the Belgian Office, which is in a kitchen, the officers sitting between the store and the dresser. This cost £1. 2. 0. each although it was only 1/3 last week.

Most of the afternoon I spent at the British Museum talking to my old friend Sir E. Budge and looking at Egyptian things, the rooms having at last been reopened. They will be very nice when finally arranged. Budge took me into two that are not yet finished. There is nothing that I enjoy more than a talk with Budge and a solitary walk in the museum.

Hotel de Flandre, Bruges, Belgium   *9th October, 1920*

Louie, I and Jessie Hartcup came here today from London. A crowded train and steamer and many formalities. Ostend still shows many signs of war — station unroofed, bridges blown up, much glass shattered etc. On the whole, however, it is wonderful how the place has recovered itself. Bruges, having been in the occupation of the Germans, is practically unharmed. I am informed that they behaved very well here and governed the place excellently. As they looked upon it as their future property naturally they were careful to work it no injury.

11th October, 1920

Have just returned from motoring around the battle area in this neighbourhood. First we went to Passchendaele and found the new British Cemetery there, which I was told contained 4000 graves: at any rate there are a vast number. The sight is sad and impressive: row upon row of little wooden crosses and on each, stamped upon a tin label, the name and regiment of the dead soldiers. Or rather this is so where these are known, but on the vast majority, so far as I could see, was inscribed 'An unknown British soldier' generally with the regiment added, since often this was quite ascertainable from the remains of the uniform. In Plot 8, Row A, Grave No. 19 lie the remains of my nephew and godson Lance. On his grave lay two pieces of rusted shell. I took one of these and Joan took the other. Afterwards it occurred to me that these might be the missiles which caused his death. I wish to see no more battlefields.

13th October, 1920

I am suffering from a chill caught in this rather old hotel but this afternoon I have been buying a few pieces of old oak furniture which is still obtainable here at about a third of the price it would command in England. Indeed one can still obtain excellent and beautiful articles dating from the 16th century for a smaller sum than common modern stuff would command at home.

14th October, 1920

My chill prevented me from going with Louie and Jessie to see Zeebrugge today, but as they brought back some excellent photos of the broken mole etc. I feel as though I had seen as much of it as they did. I only went out to see about some of the pieces of old furniture that I have bought. This hotel is icy!

18th October, 1920

Yesterday (Sunday) I could not go to church because of my cold, the weather having turned very sharp. I went out, however, and in the afternoon Jessie and I found a curiosity shop where I bought the most beautiful Gothic wall-cabinet that ever I saw.

G.E.R. Hotel, Harwich   *20th October, 1920*

Dawn: The formalities and inconveniences of getting into England are now many. A number of different papers to fill up. Strict searching of baggage, the bustling of passengers off the boat at 5.30 a.m. to wait for hours for their train because of something to do with 'immigration regulations', and I know not what beside.

Ditchingham

Evening: We reached home after a dawdling journey and find things as usual; also,

I am glad to say, that a good supply of wood has been sawn. The weather is very fine but cold when the sun sets.

21st October, 1920

No business of importance at the Bench today, but I observed that all the magistrates, some of them businessmen, were very depressed about the outlook for this country. They declare that nobody will work (a few old men excepted). It is impossible to get things done, even at great prices.

I am thankful to say that after about a year and a half of effort I have at last recovered £2,000 of the amount due to me, or rather the amount on which we compromised from the American pirates, the Fox Company, for their purloining and exhibition of *Cleopatra*.[1] Whether I shall get the rest I do not know but this sum will enable me to pay my debts for all the various repairs of property into which I have been forced at a great price on various buildings after the long neglect and maltreatment from the war.

25th October, 1920

My friend, Doctor Bright[2], who has spent his last years at Holly Lodge in this parish in order to be near his daughter, Mrs Carr, died on Friday, although I never knew it till the Sunday when I was contemplating a call upon him. He told me that he was 'vanishing away' and now he has vanished. He was a quarter of a century older than myself, but of later years there has grown up a curious intimacy between us and therefore, though naturally it pleased me to be remembered at such a time, it does not altogether surprise me to hear that among his last mutterings that could be distinguished were these words, 'Give my love to Rider Haggard.'

27th October, 1920

I have just returned from the little memorial service to my old friend Dr Bright at Ditchingham Church. Scudmore wanted me to read the lessons, but on such an occasion I declined. For some mysterious reason a kind of jangling peal was rung as we entered the church instead of the usual tolling and the altar did not seem to be properly draped.[3]

North Lodge, St Leonards   *5th November, 1920*

I arrived here tonight after a long day, having started early with the servants and

---

[1] The film, starring Theda Bara, was directed by J. Gordon Edwards.
[2] Dr James Frank Bright was from 1881 to 1906 Master of University College, Cambridge.
[3] This was presumably in response to Dr Bright's wishes. He rejected the divinity of Christ while remaining a regular communicant.

Jeekie, our spaniel, whom a heartless guard sent into the van; coming from London here, however, he was more fortunate, being allowed to travel with the servants. The journey was very uncomfortable, about ten people being crowded into a first-class carriage and the whole train packed, as a result of the coal strike, the fogs and the blocking of the Charing Cross line by fire. However, we arrived at last. This house, at which my wife has been working like a horse for the last few days, is still in some disorder after the repairs necessitated by the falling in of the front passage roof.

6th November, 1920

Thank heaven, I have at last recovered my damages for the shameless plagiarism, to use a mild word, of my film rights of *Cleopatra* by the Fox Film Co. Of course I cannot touch them in America, but of what they have taken here I have, after a struggle lasting for the best part of two years, recovered not all indeed but still a substantial part. I hope this may be a warning to these people and others. If the adaptation had been in any way accidental, I might have felt some sympathy for them but this was not the case. They took my plot, including incidents in it that were mine alone, but altered the names and in other ways tried to cover their tracks. In the end, however, they did not dare to face an action, although they did everything in their power to delay the issue and to wear me down. I owe the discovery of the proceedings of these people entirely to my friend, Major Cyril Davenport, an earnest student of my books and especially of *Cleopatra*[1], who chanced to see the film here in St Leonards and to talk to me of it as my own. Although I never had an opportunity of seeing it myself, I followed the matter up with energy and by the help of the Society of Authors and an expert ran the purloiners to earth. The business is a singular example of the results of casting one's bread upon the waters. Major Davenport in past years had studied and admired my romance *Cleopatra*. Shortly before the pirated film came to this town I obtained and gave to him a first edition of the book which thereon he reread. A week or two later he saw this film with every incident of the tale fresh in his mind. Thus came about the discovery which, in the end, has put a large sum of money into my pocket. If only I had all from America that is due to me I should be a rich man!

10th November, 1920

Today all the talk is of the burial in Westminster Abbey tomorrow (Armistice Day) of the 'Unknown Warrior'. I think that this is a fine idea, but wish that it had been originated by us and not by the French. How many of such 'Unknowns' have I seen recently in Flanders.

[1]This book, which was first published on 24th June, 1889, was one of Rider Haggard's better money-earners. For the British serial rights alone the *Illustrated London News* paid £1,500.

I have received a letter from Mrs Bainbrigge who tells me that my late dear friend Bainbrigge appeared to the Rev. Mr May, a curate at St Thomas, 'very vividly' coming out of the little chapel where the Reserved Sacrament was and, it seems, still is kept. The suggestion is that the spirit of Bainbrigge was agitated by an intention of the present vicar to remove this Reserved Sacrament and took this method of remonstrance. I know not, but I do know that Bainbrigge talked to me a good deal about this same Reserved Sacrament which he obtained the permission of the Bishop of London to place in a jewelled pyx in the chapel. He said that it gave great comfort to many, especially, I think, to those who had served or lost friends in the war.

11th November, 1920 (Armistice Day)

Two minutes silence, coincident with the committal of the bones of the Unknown Warrior in the Abbey, was observed here as elsewhere this morning at eleven — all the trams and traffic stopping. So far as I could see from the club windows the people about, however, were not so much impressed as on the first celebration. I only saw one remove his hat, and some old ladies walked past in the midst of it chattering gaily. Of those gathered in the club also but one or two stood up at attention. The English are not by nature demonstrative, unless gathered in great crowds in a city like London.

America, more modest than this country, has declined to allow Dr Marie Stopes' book *Married Love* to be circulated. Someone interested, pecuniarily or otherwise, in the extension of its sales has asked me to sign a statement that such circulation should be sanctioned *pro bono publico*. I have replied that I do not consider it right that we in England should lecture America as to what its people should or should not read!

12th November, 1920

I have been to London today on business. First I went to the bank to see about the investment of some money and, after consultation with Seeley, determined to put it into Victory Loan for the benefit of those who come after me that they may use it in the payment of the enormous death duties which are now demanded from those who have been criminal enough to save anything. I confess, however, that I grow weary of all these preparations for decease, though such I suppose are necessary and perhaps someone may thank me for them one day — if they consider the matter at all.

This afternoon I stood at the top of Parliament Street on my way to Charing Cross Station and watched the crowd flowing down it past the Cenotaph. It was a remarkable sight — touching too. What I can never understand on all these great occasions, of which I have now witnessed many, is how so many tens — or hundreds — of thousands of people in London can find the time to attend them unfailingly in the course of working days.

When I was a boy of nine, now some 55 years ago, I was sent to a private tutor, the Rev. Mr Graham, at Garsington, near Oxford, who died, an old man, within the last five years. Mr Graham wore a thick gold ring engraved in a curious, but rather conventional, frieze pattern with symbols in it that may have been meant to represent the sun. He told me that an old friend of his who had business in Peru or Central America had opened some burial place and in it found a chamber wherein, round a stone table, sat a dead and mummified man at the head and about a dozen other persons ranged round the table — whether male or female or both, I do not remember, if indeed Mr Graham knew. All that I can recollect of the rest of the story is that the man at the head of the table wore this ring upon his hand and that the discoverer of the tomb took it thence and gave it to Mr Graham in after years. (I seem, however, to recall that he said that after the tomb was opened all its inmates crumbled into dust, but of this I am not sure.)

The tale made a deep impression on my youthful mind and, in fact, first turned it towards Romance. I used it in *King Solomon's Mines* when I depicted the White Dead sitting round the stone board under the presidency of the White Death. Oddly enough also, with variations, I have used it and this very ring in another unpublished romance of Peru which I wrote last year under the title of *The Virgin of the Sun*.[1] A month or so ago I received a letter from Sister Margaret Osyth, C.S.P., of St Peter's Grange, just above this house, who told me she was a daughter of the late Mr Graham, born long after I left Garsington, though now a middle-aged woman, and asking my advice about certain matters. In answering the letter I enquired if she knew anything of this ring and of what had become of it. She replied that it had descended to her sole surviving brother, Douglas, that her father had always talked of it as 'the Inca's Ring', but that she believed that Douglas had sold it. Today when I saw her she produced the ring, which he had *not* sold, and after over half a century of time I recognised it at once. What is more I purchased it as her brother does not seem to value it particularly, and being, poor fellow, hard up, like so many ex-officers, is quite ready to sell. It is a strange history. Indirectly I owe much to that ring concerning which I seem to recollect more than do any of the Graham family.[2]

I have been in London all day attending to some complicated cinema business with the help of Miss Hector, also a council meeting of the Colonial Institute.

[1]The book was published on 26th January, 1922.
[2]In January, 1921, Rider Haggard presented the ring and a brief history of it to the Trustees of the British Museum.

1st December, 1920

Sir Alfred Bateman, who is down here, tells me that Edmund Gosse arranged for the publication of Mrs Asquith's memoirs in the *Sunday Times* and in book form in this country, for which she received a sum of £13,000. She was so delighted at this result that she came to see Gosse and kissed him on both cheeks. Now, however, Bateman says that she is abusing Gosse because of what people say about her dreadful book. As Bateman is very intimate with him, no doubt he had these details from Gosse himself. The *Memoirs* appear to have been published solely to obtain money.

9th December, 1920

Angie and Lilias (whose birthday it is) have just returned from their trip to London. Lilias is a member of the best known and oldest established mixed club in London. Her umbrella, a very handsome one with a tortoiseshell handle, after what looks like a deliberate attempt by another member which was frustrated by the hall-porter, was stolen from the cloakroom where she had placed it for safety. Angie, who was her guest there, in one of the sitting rooms placed her handbag on a chair which she left for a moment. When she returned it was gone with her money, a cheque book that has her husband's name on every cheque, some theatre tickets and other miscellaneous property. Complaints to the Secretary only elicited the information that nothing is safe in the club; the very toilet articles are continually taken, down to the hand glasses and soap. This is a pretty state of affairs. It is shocking to think that there are so many common thieves among persons who belong to clubs and ought to know better.

13th December, 1920

Olive Schreiner[1] is dead. She wrote one fine book *The Story of an African Farm* and no more that was of any account. I think that it came out just before *Jess*. I admired it very much and had some correspondence with her; also I went to see her. My recollection is that she was a small dark young lady, clever and agreeable, but not particularly striking in any way. In her views she was strongly 'feminist', which perhaps accounted for her retaining her own name when she married. Also she was very anti-English, which is not wonderful, seeing that she was the daughter of a German missionary. Particularly did she hate the Chartered Company and all its works, which of course were not invariably admirable, and I think that her sympathies were with the Boers during the war. She spent many years in writing a book about women for which the Missionary Society was banned during the war, so that only a fragment of it was ever published. It is curious that an author whose first work of fiction, written in her early youth, was so full of

[1]Olive Emilie Albertina Schreiner wrote *The Story of an African Farm* under the pseudonym Ralph Iron. It was published in 1883. Her *Woman and Labour* appeared in 1911.

promise, should never have written anything more of value. It would seem as though in that tale she emptied herself of all she had to say. I never met her again after 1885 or 6.

25th December, 1920

Again Xmas Day finds the world drowned in miseries and flaming with every sort of wickedness; again our hopes that the year which is dying would bring a humble and a contrite heart to the nations have been disappointed. 'Good will towards men' there doubtless is above, but here below there is no 'peace on earth'.

30th December, 1920

Today I have been to London to attend a Council meeting of the Royal Colonial Institute. Also I have been to St Thomas and seen the Rev. Clarence May and Louisa, who for many years has looked after the church, as to the alleged spiritual appearance of my old friend Bainbrigge.[1] There seems to be little doubt that he *did* appear.

31st December, 1920

I leave the year 1920, to my mind one of the most wretched in our history, more full of doubts and fears than any of those of the war. Our country and the whole world boils with unrest and half-developed evil. I pray that these shadows of worse trouble to come may be dissipated in the course of the dawning year, though that this was so I can find little reason to hope. On the contrary it looks to me as though our political and social sky is banking up for a great storm.

[1]Both claimed to have seen Bainbrigge after his death in the church. Rider Haggard took down statements from both of them.

1921

Throughout the year Rider Haggard was concerned about the effects on the country of strikes, growing unemployment, diminishing trade, and rises in the rates of income tax. Although he had ceased to be actively involved in public affairs, he was often publicly fêted, being invited to a select party at Buckingham Palace, a Royal garden party, and, as guest of honour, to several dinners. His portrait, painted by Greiffenhagen, was one of the attractions at the Royal Academy Exhibition.

With Ronald Ross, the only close friend he had made for years, he went on two fishing trips. At last, after over forty-five years of phrenetic activity, he began to find a measure of contentment. But his health was a cause of concern. After returning to St Leonards for the winter, he again suffered from an attack of gout, but this time with 'unpleasant complications'.

1st January, 1921

All the papers seem to recognise that 1921 begins with poor prospects for this country, which financially is in a bad case indeed and also finds itself face to face with many political troubles. One can only hope for the best, but if I were a young man I should get out of England; also I should rid myself of any property I had here of which the cost of the upkeep has become enormous; indeed I am crippled with bills for repairs and little enough is done for the money.

4th January, 1921

In an interview I had yesterday with the representative of a firm of film-producers, he informed me that they had not been able to sell a single one of their productions in Australia, although some of these, such as that of *King Solomon's Mines*, have been highly praised in this country. The Australians, he says, will not look at any work which is not American in its origin. When I was in Australia I noted much the same thing where books were concerned. With the exception of cheap British fiction of a loose character, whereof there were piles on the bookstalls, mostly the work of lady novelists, I saw few save American novels in the shops.

6th January, 1921

I attended a meeting of the Empire Migration Committee at the Royal Colonial Institute. Lord Sydenham was in the chair and we discussed the matter in its wider aspects. Commissioner Lamb asked formally if I would be willing to go out again to try to resecure the offers made to me by the Dominions Governments in 1916. To this I gave a non-committal answer. The truth is, however, that such a mission would be useless unless it were carried out under Government authority, in which case an official would be sent not a person like myself. Nor indeed am I anxious to undertake it at my present time of life.

11th January, 1921

Today I lunched with Sir William Bull M.P.[1] at the Constitutional Club. His other guest was ex-King Manuel of Portugal. My experience of Royalties is limited, but if they are all as clever as King Manuel there is much to be said for them. Indeed I thought him a very able as well as a most agreeable man and capital company. He is much interested in the *She* and *L'Atlantide* controversy, of which he had heard a great deal in France. We discussed all sorts of things, including the quality of imagination and what it is and the inability of man to fight against his destiny, which as Shakespeare has pointed out leads him whither he must go. Poor King Manuel said with a sigh that very evidently this was the case, doubtless thinking of whither his destiny had led him. What led to this conversation was

[1] He was a solicitor and M.P. for Hammersmith South.

some remark about my having been obliged to leave the Bar owing to the success of *King Solomon's Mines* and Sir W. Bull asking whether I regretted that development.

When giving me a cigarette King Manuel showed me a gold and jewelled cigarette case, which he told me was the one always used by King Edward. Queen Alexandra presented it to him as a souvenir after Edward's death. Of him he said emphatically, 'Ah, Sir Rider, had he lived there would have been no war!' I wonder whether any turn of the wheel of fate will ever bring King Manuel back to his throne. Personally I am inclined to doubt it, and if this happened I fear that he would find the crown of Portugal to be one of thorns.

26th January, 1921

I have been to town today and spent a very pleasant morning with Mr H.R.H. Hall, the assistant keeper of the Egyptian department, who examined certain Egyptian antiquities which I took up with me, and for two hours conducted some friends of his and myself round the Egyptian collection, explaining many things. What treasures are here! Thank heaven the German bombs missed the museum.

I also visited the New English Art Club, thereby completely wasting 1/9. It may be that I am a Philistine, or an old fossil who does not move with the times; at least I saw in that place hardly a picture that I should have cared to take the trouble to carry away. I remember the New English Art Club when it started over 39 years ago and that in it then were works that I thought beautiful. I cannot say as much today, but perhaps the fault is mine and not that of the artists.

3rd February, 1921

Last night I dined with the Bishop of Oxford at the annual dinner of the Norwegian Society at the Hotel Cecil. In a speech I had to make I told the company of my excavations at the house of Njal, at Bergthorsknoll in Iceland, many years ago and how I came to the hard floor of the hall in which seemed to be the sand that the Saga of Burnt Njal says Bergthora sprinkled there in the day of the burning, also on many other evidences of the conflagration. Lord Bryce, a student of the Sagas, was deeply interested and said he hoped I had kept some written record. I have an idea that I did write something about it, but cannot remember where.[1]

Sir Ronald Ross was also present. To my mind he is one of the foremost men of the day, though few seem to recognise the fact. Mosquitoes do not interest the general public — until they get fever!

14th February, 1921

Sir W. B. Richmond R.A. is dead. Strangely enough I was thinking of him only

[1] I find it was in *A Farmer's Year*, p. 211. H.R.H.

216

yesterday or the day before. I have known him for a generation and it is well over 30 years ago since Lang and I dedicated *The World's Desire* to him and I gave him a very beautiful large Cyprian vase of which the fellow is now in the Norwich Museum. Of late I have not seen much of him; and indeed I think our last conversation was a couple of years ago at the Athenaeum, when he wanted me to join him in some rather violent campaign against the evils that afflict the country. He was a fine painter in his day; witness his splendid portrait of Andrew Lang of which Andrew gave me a photograph that I have at Ditchingham. He was a picturesque figure with his long hair parted in the middle and a large and floppy necktie fastened in a bow; indeed about him was a belated air of the aestheticism of my early youth; not that he was in any way an aesthete in character, rather the reverse in fact.

It is strange how few are left today of those I knew when first I began to write. Indeed as Arthur Cochrane, who has been staying here on his return from one of his periodical visits to South Africa, and I were saying yesterday, hardly any whom we knew in our youth remain; we have almost no surviving friends.

16th February, 1921

There is no doubt that times are now very hard throughout the country, for the reason that excessive taxation takes most of its spare cash. I find an instance of this in the account of the sales of a number of my cheap editions which I have just received. The public is buying fewer of them, without doubt for the reason that the great reading class as a whole can no longer afford to pay 2/- for a badly printed and badly bound sevenpenny book. Indeed I hear that the publishers report that the book trade generally is in a very bad way indeed.

3rd March, 1921

Today with Louie, whom I met in London, I have attended a function. Their Majesties, or someone connected with them, I know not why, since we do not move in those exalted circles, were pleased to ask us to a small and select afternoon party at Buckingham Palace. Thither we went as in duty bound in the best clothes that we could muster, to find ourselves in a line of 300 or 400 people, also in their best clothes, who were one by one marched past the King, the Queen and the Princess Mary, who shook us by the hand in a kindly fashion and to whom we made our regulation obeisances. I do not think that Buckingham Palace on a dull afternoon before the lights are turned up is a particularly cheerful place for a party especially if you know but a few of the other guests. After you have stared at the Archbishop of Canterbury and the Lord Mayor and a few other celebrities, there is nothing to do but to stare at the pictures, for which the light is not good, although historically many of them are interesting enough, as are those of the Dutch school. All of them strike me as having been overdone up and varnished. Through the kindly help of one of the officers of the Household whom we chanced to know, we managed to get away in time to catch our train back to St Leonards.

21st March, 1921

Charles Longman, who has been stopping here, tells me that owing to the enormous cost of printing in this country at the present moment he is having books set up in Holland, Germany and India. Either wages must come down or Britain will lose both her overseas trade and her internal prosperity.

29th March, 1921

I have just heard by wire of the sudden death from heart failure of my dearest sister, Ella Maddison Green. The news came immediately after the receipt of a post-card written by herself announcing that she was recovering from an attack of pleurisy and expected to be up in a few days. She was the eldest of all of us (75), having been born in Rome in the year following my mother's marriage, and perhaps the best beloved. I remember with gratitude that to the best of my recollection we never had a cross word or even a difference of opinion; indeed we loved each other very dearly. She led a full, useful and active life in mind and body to the last. She was fond of reading my stories and of romance generally, for which reason I dedicated *The Brethren* to her years ago.

Haddon Chambers is also dead suddenly. I knew him in bygone years when with Stanley Little he dramatised *Dawn*, under the name of *Devil Caresfoot*.[1]

Garland's Hotel   *6th April, 1921*

I came to London yesterday with Louie for Phyllis's wedding to Captain Wickham R.E. which went off very successfully today at Brompton Church. Everything is much upset; there is trouble in the air.

North Lodge, St Leonards   *8th April, 1921*

Louie and I got back today and were glad to do so, as one never knows when a strike may develop. Already the railway has a curiously deserted appearance. However it may not occur — no one knows. At present affairs look fairly desperate.

A while ago[2] I wrote to General Smuts, the Prime Minister of the Union of South Africa, and offered to come out (in an honorary capacity) and report on the suitability of the Union as a place of settlement for upper class inhabitants of the

[1]It was first produced at the Vaudeville Theatre on 12th July, 1887, being transferred to the Strand Theatre a month later. Janet Achurch played Angela, and Charles Charrington was Devil Caresfoot.
[2]The letter was written on 16th February, 1921.

United Kingdom, thousands of whom (as in 1820) are seeking some quieter, more profitable and less highly-taxed abode and at present drifting elsewhere. I explained to him that my object was to ensure that South Africa should be made safe for the British Empire. Now I have a private letter from him that concludes, 'I shall turn over the matter in my mind and communicate with you again later on.' There the matter stands for the present. I do not know whether anything will or will not come of it, but at least I have made my offer and my effort, which evidently Smuts is considering very seriously.

Garland's Hotel, London   *18th April, 1921*

I have arrived here from St Leonards to spend a fortnight or 3 weeks in town on our way home to Ditchingham. Fireless London seems very cold. In a review of the film of *Stella Fregelius*[1] *The Times* talks of the 'terrible anti-climax' due to the alteration of the end by the adaptors to make the picture-play finish happily.

20th April, 1921

I have spent the last two days in seeing (privately) the Italian made film of *Beatrice*.[2] It has good points (especially those of the heroine's eyes!), but for an author the experience as usual is somewhat heart-breaking. Why in the name of goodness, for instance, when a poverty-stricken Welsh clergyman is described in the book as living in a vicarage of the meanest sort, almost a cottage indeed, should he be represented as inhabiting a costly palace from the upkeep of which an archbishop would blench? Or why should the hero, Geoffrey, a man getting on for forty with a powerful legal stamp of face, be impersonated by an oily-haired young person of about 22? Only a film producer can answer these questions. Meanwhile the critic comes along and descants learnedly on the unsuitability of novels for film purposes. The novels are right enough; it is their ignorant careless adaptors who are to blame.

1st May, 1921

I went to the private view at the Royal Academy yesterday. My portrait by Greiffenhagen is hung in one of the most prominent positions in Room III, but I did not venture near enough to examine it closely. All the Academicians rave about it, as I see does the art critic of the *Observer* who calls it 'superb', but D'Abernon does not like it and it horrified Lilias. Certainly it is an imposing work of art,

[1]The film, called *Stella*, was directed by Edwin J. Collins for Master Films. It starred Molly Adair and Manning Haynes.
[2]Marie Doro played the part of Beatrice and S. Salvini that of Geoffrey Bingham. The film was produced by Herbert Brenon for the Unione Cinematografica Italiana.

though melancholy and certainly too Greiffenhagen has made the most of my wrinkles which indeed are exaggerated as is the kind of varicose vein he has painted on my face. I never set up for a beauty, but this picture with its harshness and accentuated realism will give posterity a queer side of my appearance at my present age. There was a crowd round it all day.

I had a talk with Mrs Lloyd George in the Academy, also with Lord Ernle, who is very despondent about the agricultural outlook.

3rd May, 1921

Yesterday I was taken to lunch at Claridges and emerged feeling almost socialistic. Such displays of wanton wealth as I saw there must do much harm in these times. London is fuller than ever. Wherever one goes are enormous, baffling crowds. Moreover these crowds to me seem to be possessed by a curious restlessness; they want something of everything and not much of anything, because, I think, their minds have lost the power of concentration and continuity of thought. Like the Athenians continually they seek some new thing — in snippets. Also they are bent on amusement of the vapid order and follow eagerly after all those things that do not matter.

Last night I saw a tragic play called *The Wandering Jew* which ends in the burning of that legendary personage at an Auto-da-Fe. After two Acts I heard one empty head behind me say to another empty head, 'I say, I haven't seen anything *funny* here yet.' He had come to find jokes in the story of *The Wandering Jew*.

Today I attended the trade view of the film of my book *Beatrice* at the Alhambra. On the whole it was not inadequate and Miss Marie Doro made a beautiful and pathetic Beatrice. Still one could pick holes as doubtless the critics will do in due season.

Ditchingham

5th May, 1921 (9.30 p.m.)

I have returned here after six months or more of absence. So far as I can judge in the failing light, the place looks charming. Notwithstanding the cold weather (which is playing havoc with the fruit-blossom) all the trees grow green though the may is not yet out.

7th May, 1921

I have not been feeling very strong of late. I suspected an attack of influenza of the non-feverish kind, when I was working so hard at the conclusion of *Child of Wisdom*.[1] Today I have been thoroughly overhauled by the doctor. So far he finds

---

[1] *Wisdom's Daughter*, as it was then called, was published on 9th March, 1923. The contract for the book was signed on 18th March, 1921, at which time Rider Haggard had not completed the book.

nothing organically wrong with me but says that I am slack and run down in every way, and must take things quietly without hammering about. I suppose the truth is that age has got a grip of me; we all wear out at last and therefore I must not complain. I continue to receive rapturous notices of Greiffenhagen's portrait of me, but no one thinks it flattering: nor do I.

9th May, 1921

There is much unemployment down here. This morning at Bungay I saw a considerable group of men standing idle in the Market Place, looking very sullen, most of them. Sundry residents too are giving up the houses they hire because they can no longer afford to keep them up.

11th May, 1921

I went over to Kessingland today. Reggie's hard work has improved the place greatly since last I saw it six or eight months ago but it is an uphill job.

21st May, 1921

Trade is in a very bad way indeed. Last year the Junior Army and Navy Stores in which I had a few shares amalgamated with the Haymarket Stores. I have just received a balance sheet of the joint affair; it shows a loss of £58,000!

The drought continues with brilliant weather. There can be little hay this year. The price of all agricultural produce is falling.

8th June, 1921

Yesterday we had a small party here to which several guests, one of them a peer, came in motor-cars. All these cars were driven by their owners, because now none of those owners can employ a chauffeur at the new rates. In the old times there would have been several men having tea in the servants' hall; now there are none.

Garland's Hotel   *15th June, 1921*

I came up to town today on my way to go to Blagdon Lake fishing with Ronald Ross. As there is now practically but one train (and that from Beccles) I had to start early. It was not full, however. People seem to have given up travelling owing to the coal trouble. The line had a very deserted appearance. I do not think we met any train coming down. I noticed stacks of wood at the stations, also on the engine tenders, with some coke. All the fuel in the country is nearly exhausted. The factories we passed seemed to be doing little or nothing; few chimneys smoking and few men at work.

16th June, 1921

This morning I went to see General Smuts and Sir Thomas Smartt to talk over the proposition of my going to South Africa this winter of which I have written earlier in this diary. Smuts is, I noticed again, a very peculiar looking man, with his cold, far-away blue eyes and his impassive face. At first I rather gathered that he had forgotten all about the business, so much so that I remarked that I was sorry I had not brought a copy of the correspondence. Thereon I found out from his answer that he was fully seized of its every detail. The upshot was that he appears to wish that I should go but is postponing decision till the whole matter of Empire Migration has been discussed by the Imperial Conference. Smartt I missed, but he caught me in the Savoy courtyard and I went back into the hotel where we thrashed out the business. He also seemed to wish very much that I should undertake this mission with the idea of which he was acquainted. There the matter stands for the present. I was glad to see him again.

I lunched with Ronald Ross as did Lady Ross and Lilias, and in the afternoon visited the Egyptian Loan Exhibition at the Fine Arts Society, a truly delightful show — also the dentist. Tonight I attended the meeting of the Society of Antiquaries where I exhibited and explained the history of the 'Inca's Ring' which I have given to the Nation, which was brought from the British Museum for that purpose. My account of this curiosity and of my connection with it seemed to interest the audience very much indeed. Sir Martin Conway was in the Chair.

Last night with Lilias I attended the Soiree of the Royal Society, of which the present President, Professor Charles Sherrington[1], was, as he reminded me, a school-fellow of mine at Ipswich.[2] There was a great crowd but the exhibits were not so interesting as usual. In the old days these functions were described at length in the Press, but now all the space the papers have to spare is occupied with accounts of racing and other sporting events or with reports of divorce cases.

The streets this morning were blocked with motors and char-a-bancs going to Ascot. The display of all this wealth by profiteers and other rich folk is doing vast mischief at the present time. I observe a most bitter article about it in the *Daily Herald* today, contrasting it with the cutting down of the unemployment allowance etc. It is nothing short of a public misfortune that the extravagance of the few should be so much in evidence just now.

Butcombe Farm, Blagdon, near Bristol   *17th June, 1921*

I have come to this quaint farm house for a week's fishing with Ronald Ross, though in this breathless drought of fishing, or rather of fish, there is little chance. I write this out fishing on Blagdon Lake, having once again realised the admirable

[1]Sir Charles Scott Sherrington (1857-1952) was Professor of Physiology at Oxford. In 1932 he won the Nobel Prize for medicine.
[2]For two or three years Rider Haggard was a pupil at Ipswich School.

patience of the angler. For two and a half days Ross, Lilias and I have toiled from 11 a.m. till 11 p.m. and so far we have bagged but four trout.

By the lake side, Blagdon   *22nd June, 1921*

Again my birthday. I am now 65! Alas how swiftly the years go by and I sink into old age. Disguise the truth as one will, it remains a melancholy truth that for me middle age has followed youth into the limbo of the past leaving at best but a few short years of life to be travelled before the last eclipse. Every year my friends grow fewer. Of the small number who still write to me upon my birthday my sister Ella was always one. And Ella has gone whither soon all of my generation must follow her.

Garland's Hotel   *27th June, 1921*

I returned to town from Blagdon yesterday (Sunday), having enjoyed my holiday with Sir Ronald Ross and Mr Shelling, though for fishing purposes the weather was so impossible that we only caught six trout between us. The journey was very hot and crowded as everybody rushed for the few available trains.

28th June, 1921

Last night I was the 'Guest of Honour', as the term goes, at the Lyceum Club Authors' Dinner. There was a great gathering and the sound of some hundreds — there seemed to be hundreds — of ladies all talking at once was really deafening. I made a speech on the subject of 'Romance', which seemed to please the audience. I sat between the Chairwoman, Mrs de Crespigny, and Lady Aberdeen[1], ex Vice-reine of Ireland. The talk turned upon that country and I remarked that if De Valera came to England in answer to Lloyd George's invitation he ought to be accompanied by an escort of the widows that he and his company had made! It loosed the floodgates. Lady A. held forth about the wickedness of the Government that, as she said, had butchered countless innocent Sinn Feiners, also of Ulster which stood in the way of the fulfilment of their aspirations. For the loyal murdered she had no word of regret or sympathy. It exasperated me to listen to such talk and I was glad to escape from the conversation without saying something strong that I might afterwards have regretted.

29th June, 1921

Lady Randoph Churchill is dead. I knew her in past years when we used to lunch

[1]Ishbel-Maria Marjoribanks, as she had been before her marriage, was the youngest daughter of 1st Lord Tweedmouth. She was very interested in questions concerned with both women and the Irish peasantry.

with her, but have not seen her for a long time.[1] She was then a sprightly and beautiful American woman, with lots of brains. She has been twice married since those days, once to Mr Cornwallis-West whom she divorced, and again recently to whom I forget, a young man, I believe.

30th June, 1921

Last night I attended the League of Nations dinner with Ronald Ross for my guest. It was absolutely the worst managed affair at which I ever assisted. Fortunately Ross and I went together or we should never have found each other. A long passage leads to the cloak room at the Hyde Park Hotel which it took us about ten minutes to negotiate owing to the tangled *queue*. The people were not received by anyone — the list of the guests and of where they had to sit had not arrived, and everybody was told to sit where they could. There followed the spectacle of 700 people trying to find places at hazard. At last Ross and I found two vacant chairs and sat down at a table with a portly Roman Catholic Monsignor, a pleasant ecclesiastic to whom we introduced ourselves, and two quite young gentlemen. When we had eaten our first course Lord Grey of Falloden, the Chairman of the Union, wandered up with the Princess Alice[2], being unable to find seats anywhere. The two young gentlemen (of the modern school) sat tight as wax, so of course Ross and I had to go, being elderly persons of another upbringing and generation. At length we found a haven in a corner between a young lady who told Ross she was a Sinn Feiner and had been learning to smoke a pipe and who called me 'a literary person', and a young American married woman who had nothing to say for herself. Ross replied to the Sinn Feiner by suggesting that she had better murder the Secretary of the League of Nations Union. The feast went on, the waiters demanded tips, the wine-steward tried to overcharge me, etc. Speech time came; a heated mob burst in upon us from another room, our tables were dragged away to make room for them leaving us to put our wineglasses on the floor. So we sat stifling and listened. The addresses of Lord Grey, General Smuts and Lord Roberts were quite good. They urged the cause of the League of Nations (with which I sympathise heartily enough in theory) with force and even passion, but one and all of them omitted to touch upon the real rock in its path, namely that it had no force behind it with which to enforce any decrees it may promulgate.

After Lord Roberts disappeared behind the crowd of heads, we followed his example without waiting for Mr Balfour and the others and left that gay perspiring throng. In the cloak room was more confusion as a result of which I got somebody

---

[1]Lady Randolph Spencer Churchill (Jennie) was the mother of Sir Winston Churchill. Her third husband was Montagu Porch.
[2]Princess Alice, the Countess of Athlone, grand-daughter of Queen Victoria, had in 1904 married Major-General the 1st Earl of Athlone (Queen Mary's brother).

else's old umbrella in place of my own. Still, it was all amusing in a fashion — except the incident of the umbrella. Sir Henry Lambert tells me that he had an equally agitated time and finally had to leave with his wife without hearing the speeches at all. I do not think that I want to attend another League of Nations dinner.

Ditchingham   *1st July, 1921*

Last night I attended the dinner of the Royal Colonial Institute, which was presided over by the President, the Duke of Connaught, and attended by the Prince of Wales. It was a most successful and well managed function, which afforded a strange contrast to that League of Nations Union feast of the night before. The attendance was very large — 500 people or more — and the speeches were very good, especially that of Sir Thomas Smartt who has a fine voice and a sense of oratory. The Prince too spoke well, but being near to him I noticed that although he keeps his face very still he is really of a nervous temperament, for his hand trembled much, also that all he had to say was carefully prepared, except a few interpolations dealing with current matters. I had to do some of the receiving for the Institute, when Sir Godfrey Lagden and Sir Harry Wilson went to meet the Royalties.

I heard at the Athenaeum this morning that the unfortunate Princess Alice had an unhappy time in the seat which Sir Ronald Ross and I gave up to her at the League of Nations dinner. It seems, or so Lord Byng told a friend of mine, that every waiter who went by knocked her on the head as there was no proper space for them to pass. There is a great deal of talk in London about the scandalous management of this affair; indeed I have met several people myself who are loud in their complaints.

This morning I attended a conference of the Royal Colonial Institute at which members of the District Institutes expressed their· views — at some length.

The scene at Liverpool Street Station today was extraordinary. My taxi-driver deposited my luggage on the foot way and departed and there it lay for a quarter of an hour or more until I could get a porter; indeed I was fortunate to catch the train at all.

I find the drought here very severe indeed. Never before have I seen the country in such a state at the beginning of July. It is reported that June was the driest for a hundred years. Curiously enough the weather remains so cold that tonight a fire is very welcome.

4th July, 1921

Yesterday I went to Holly Lodge to deliver a note to the new tenants. It was strange to walk into Bright's room differently furnished, save for his library which remains there, and to look at the spot in it, now occupied by another chair, where on the last occasion I was in the place, when he signed my passport before our visit to Belgium, I bade him farewell, thinking to myself that I should never again look upon him alive. I do not think there is anything more pathetic in the world than a room long inhabited by the dead, when it is occupied by those who knew him not and its furniture has been changed.

7th July, 1921

We had a shower of rain here last night, but speaking generally the drought continues. The picture papers of late have been full of hideous photographs of young women doing violent and ungainly things, leaping into the air with their legs all over the place, and I know not what besides. I cannot say that the contemplation of these pictures enhances an ordinary man's admiration of the sex. Indeed to those of us who were accustomed to the gentle, graceful movement and attire of ladies 30 or 40 years ago, they are disgusting. Then it would not have been possible to see, as I did at a public function the other day, a stout but tall and handsome dark-complexioned woman of middle age wearing a kind of Eastern turban on her head and a garment that revealed the whole side of her naked body from beneath the arm to the point of the hip. Somehow I prefer the sweet simplicity of the savage in a row of beads. It is so much less indecent. I suppose that the object was to excite the admiration of men with the vision of the surging flesh and muscles. If so, in one instance at least it failed.

18th July, 1921

Suddenly, and quite contrary to all expectation, as we were bidden to Buckingham Palace in the spring, we have received an invitation to the Royal Garden Party on Thursday next, which, it has been announced, was to be reserved for those who were to have attended the abandoned Courts, which was not our case. This is a most inconvenient honour as Louie is due to attend her cousin Cecil's wedding at Reigate on that afternoon, and, to say nothing of the expense, I have no wish to go to town in this heat. However, there it is, since these 'invitations' are not of a nature that can be declined.

22nd July, 1921

I have just returned from London whither I went to attend the Royal Garden Party. It was an interesting function. Thousands of people more or less well-known, or the friends of the well-known who have obtained them invitations, including many of the most distinguished in the land, wandered about the great sun-scorched grounds of Buckingham Palace, talking to anybody they met whom they chanced to know, or squabbling over the possession of chairs. Also, if they were lucky, they had a chance of seeing the King and Queen in the distance with other royalties. Fortunately the weather was not too hot and very fine. So on the whole it was an agreeable entertainment.

The business reminded me of similar parties at Windsor many years ago when Edward was King. In those days I remember being impressed with the matchless way in which he received persons introduced to him — the bow, the lifting of the white hat, the few words of apt conversation, the renewed bow and second lifting of the white hat in dismissal. The same thing goes on in another generation. I saw it yesterday, but not I think with the same *chic*; such perfection is not easy to re-capture.

All the afternoon I searched for Louie who arrived later from Cecil Hilyard's wedding in a remote place, resembling, as some observer remarked to me at the Athenaeum today, Orpheus hunting Hades for Eurydice. It was quite useless. I never found her, and she too, abandoning the hunt, took refuge in coffee ices. I met a good many people whom I knew, among them the Kiplings. K. held forth about this diary, saying that he wished that I would make him my literary executor with discretion to publish such portions of it as he wished (I suppose that rightly he expects to live much longer than I shall). There is something in the idea. The work 'edited' by Kipling would be a formidable document!

I was thankful to get back to the Athenaeum and drink two large cups of tea.

The King has unveiled a statue of his father, King Edward, almost in front of the Athenaeum. Today I had a good look at it. It represents his late Majesty on a large and prancing entire horse, and I can only say that in my humble judgment it is a commonplace and indeed a somewhat fearsome work of art cast in raw coloured bronze and set on a base of disproportionate height — a view of it which I find very generally shared by others in this Club who are more competent to judge. As I think Lambert said to me at lunch, there should be a law passed making it penal to erect any more statues in London. However, those chiefly concerned seem to be satisfied and the sculptor was duly knighted, so nobody else need complain except the members of the Athenaeum Club who from generation to generation must contemplate that horse and the corpulent travesty of King Edward that sits upon it, waving what I suppose is the baton of a Field Marshal.

25th July, 1921

Mons. Pierre Benoit seems to have lost his case in the French courts, in which he claimed 40,000 francs against 'The French Quarterly Review' which accused him of having plagiarised *L'Atlantide* from *She* and *The Yellow God*.[1] At any rate he has been non-suited and ordered to pay the costs in the First Chamber of the Paris Tribunal. I daresay, however, that the business will not stop here. The drought still continues, though there has been some rain in different parts of the country.

[1]Rider Haggard took little part in the controversy. At first he was inclined to think that his works had not been plagiarised, but correspondence from the writer of the article made him change his mind.

29th July, 1921

Mr Burdett-Coutts[1], whom I used to meet in years past, is dead. He was an American by birth of the name of Ashmead-Bartlett, and at the age of 30 married Lady Burdett-Coutts at the age of 67. I believe that Queen Victoria herself remonstrated against this curious union, or so I have heard privately. It is also said that he was then engaged to another lady. I remembered the marriage well and the excitement which it caused. Since those days Mr Burdett-Coutts has for many years been Unionist member of Parliament and has done a good deal of useful and philanthropic work. Also he has a splendid stud of horses at Holly Lodge, Highgate. I recollect going to a garden party there to see them.

1st August, 1921

On Saturday we held our Fur, Feather and Vegetable Show on the front lawn here, a small local function that had been organised by Lilias. It was extremely successful. I think that gatherings of this sort are most beneficial in rural districts as I said in giving away the prizes, not only do they increase the growth of food by cottagers and others, they also bring all classes together in pleasant and interesting social intercourse. I wish that there were more of them in the Eastern counties, as distinguished from the larger and more important Shows.

Yesterday morning, in my sleep, I heard some early tea crockery slip outside my room and awoke with this nonsense verse in my mind.

> Patience Ladies! She who smashes
> Frees you from your earthly cares:
> Heaven *loves* the glorious crashes
> Of our china on the stairs.

I enter this sleepy rubbish here because it seems to me to be full of philosophy. In other words it means that property is an infernal nuisance and that there is some law which is eternally at work to try to rid mankind of it for its own ultimate benefit![2]

Three Cocks Hotel, Breconshire   *25th August, 1921*

I have travelled here (Dolly and Lilias having come by car) to fish for salmon in Mr Caird's water in the Wye. The salmon fishing is an utter failure because there is no water to bring up fresh fish and those in the river will take nothing. I must say that

[1] Rt Hon. William Lehman Ashmead-Bartlett (Burdett-Coutts) was M.P. for Woolwich from 1885 to his death.
[2] The lack of profitability for farmers convinced Rider Haggard that he had been right to sell his farms.

I marvel at the enthusiasts who spend thousands on salmon rivers, seeing that five times out of six the story is the same: the water is always wrong. It is very disappointing but in this case our party (which includes Sir Ronald Ross) is pleasant, the weather is fine and the inn comfortable, so things might be worse. With salmon as with other things, if one expects nothing one is not disappointed!

27th August, 1921

Today this inn has been full of colliers who arrive in motor-cars. One very grimy couple had a particularly smart car that must have cost several hundreds. I observed that while they were in the house the landlady locked up certain localities, giving their presence as the reason, also that on departing they helped themselves to the carefully guarded flowers. She says that they are dreadful people whom she will never serve unless she is obliged. Our fishing continues to be singularly unsuccessful. It is wonderful to me that people can be found to pay £10,000 or more for a piece of salmon fishing out of which it is so seldom possible to catch a fish, as in nine cases out of ten the water is wrong.

31st August, 1921

Today at midnight the war will be declared officially to be at an end.[1] I only wish that its consequences were also at an end.

Ditchingham   *3rd September, 1921*

Returning today from Wales to Norfolk I am struck by the cruel fashion in which Nature has treated the east of England during this unprecedented season. On the banks of the Severn all was green and in the gardens the vegetables were splendid. Here all is still an arid waste; and leaves are already falling, the root crops are shocking and the pastures are brown and withered. Practically no rain has fallen since I went away and at present none seems likely to fall. The weather is only good for the cleaning out of ponds.

5th September, 1921

The trade depression is great and the awful Income Tax is absorbing nearly all the savings of the country. Meanwhile the middlemen of one sort or another are taking the most of such profits as remain. Here is an example. I have just received a six months account of some books of mine which are published at 2/- out of which a royalty of 1½d. a copy is my share! Of these books about 68,000 were sold during the six months, but when publishers and other agents have had their cut, all I — the author — get for this great circulation is £302, of which again nearly half

[1]The Treaty of Versailles was actually signed on 28th June, 1921.

will be taken by the Income Tax. I believe that where I get 1½d. Smith alone takes 3d. or 4d. while the booksellers generally also take more than I do out of these books. Such is the amount that books for which the public has paid £7,000 in cold cash, bring to their creator. Everywhere it is the same story.

12th September, 1921

The Press of England seems literally to have gone mad over the cinema star, Charlie Chaplin[1], and so have other people. Thus the Mayor of Southampton received him publicly on his arrival from America. Hideous pictures are published too of this very undistinguished-looking person, surrounded by crowds with folly stamped on every face. It really is extraordinary and as the *Morning Post* points out a great testimony of the power of the Publicity Agent who is working up all this excitement underneath.

21st September, 1921

Prices are coming down. Here is a proof of it. This morning I received a circular from a very eminent firm of wine-merchants, offering what seems to be excellent champagne at about 8/- a bottle. A little while ago I suppose £1 a bottle would have been the figure. It does not affect me since we have scarcely drunk a glass of champagne in this house for years, but it does suggest that most of those who have been willing to pay large sums for this exhilarating beverage are no longer in a position to do so. The slump in the value of the various securities on the Stock Exchange is really alarming.

On 23rd September, 1921, Rider Haggard, accompanied by Lilias, went to Liverpool to stay with Alderman J. Lea, whom he had met in April of the previous year. The following day, Rider Haggard opened the Autumn Exhibition at the Walker Art Gallery. One of the works on show was Greiffenhagen's portrait of him.

27th September, 1921

All yesterday I spent in the train returning from Liverpool on the conclusion of our visit there. Some of the country through which I passed, especially in North Norfolk, is suffering most terribly from drought.

20th October, 1921

Income and Super tax are terrific. (I have received a demand for the latter this

[1]Charles Spencer Chaplin had in 1914, at the age of 25, gone to Hollywood from England as part of Fred Karno's troop of actors.

morning that though cooked-up and wickedly unjust, must in the end no doubt be paid, that in addition to the ordinary Income Tax, to say nothing of rates, will absorb nearly everything I have put aside as savings, and no doubt my case is not exceptional.) In short these taxes to a great extent have now to be paid out of capital.

21st October, 1921

Here I am tied by the leg by a bad attack of gout with unpleasing complications, which makes sleep difficult and walking an agony. It is now impossible that I should go to London next week.

Garland's Hotel   *1st November, 1921*

I came to town yesterday on our way to St Leonards where we expect to spend the winter as usual.

Yesterday I attended a meeting of the Empire Migration Committee of the Royal Colonial Institute as to the sending of a deputation to Mr Churchill on the matter of emigration. It was a very interesting meeting but the problem is most complicated. What amuses me is to hear new-comers to the consideration of this question talking as though it had never been considered and threshed out in the past by some of us still living, and to see how unaware they are of its many pitfalls with which we have an intimate acquaintance.

I went to see Sir Thomas Horder today about my health. I am glad to say that he does not seem to find much seriously wrong with me — nothing organic so far as he can discover.

5th November, 1921

I came down here yesterday for the winter with a heavy cold caught in the fog and slop of London, where it rained steadily for three days. I have received an appeal, signed by Robert Cecil[1], asking me to subscribe £1,000 a year for the purposes of League of Nations propaganda! He must be mad. How many could find such sums?

19th November, 1921

Yesterday I went to town to be the principal guest at the dinner of the Delphian Coterie, where the subject for consideration was 'Quo Vadis — or the Empire a century hence?' There was a large and enthusiastic audience of a very intelligent order, gathered to welcome my fellow guest, Dean Inge, and myself. Before I

[1]Robert, 1st Viscount Cecil of Chelwood, as under-secretary for foreign affairs in 1918 helped draft the League of Nations Covenant.

spoke the Secretary read the following remarkable and to my mind most mischievous letter from Mr H. G. Wells: 'I regret very much that I cannot attend your gathering tonight. I hope and believe that one hundred years hence there will be no British Empire. Either it will have played its part in the development of civilisation and have changed into and given place to a much larger union of free states, or it will have become a danger and a nuisance to mankind, and have followed German Imperialism and Roman Imperialism to the dust heap.'

21st November, 1921

I have just received my Income Tax notification and I cannot conceive how England is to bear up for long against such an impost, which in a vast majority of cases can only be met out of capital.

30th November, 1921

Yesterday I went to town to attend the marriage of my niece Margery to Mr Archibald Charlton, our Consul-General in Berlin. Mr Charlton is a Roman Catholic and the service took place in a church of his persuasion. I cannot say that it was a cheerful function — a priest and his attendant, words muttered for the most part in Latin, no music till after the ceremony, and a general air of disapproval were its most marked characteristics. Were I concerned in any way, I think I should prefer a Registry Office rather than submit to such a religious arrogance.

17th December, 1921

Yesterday I went to town on a wild goose chase to make one of a deputation to the Colonial Secretary on the matter of Empire Migration, only to find that the notification of the postponement of the deputation had not reached me, owing to its having been posted to Ditchingham.

31st December, 1921

Vale 1921! To my mind one of its most remarkable features has been the triumph of expediency over principle in high places.

1922

Feeling now that he was growing old and that his health was failing, Rider Haggard spent what for him was a quiet year. He had time to visit friends (including Longman and Kipling), go on another fishing trip with Ronald Ross, attend a variety of functions, and make a sad, nostalgic visit to Bradenham. He also kept on writing, in April finishing Queen of the Dawn, *a story of old Egypt.*

There is again a great list of New Year Honours. Sir James Barrie receives the Order of Merit, to which I should have thought Kipling was entitled far before him. I expect, however, that when it comes to a choice for this distinction political colour carries weight and I believe that Sir James's hue is more in tone with that of Mr Lloyd George than is Kipling's. Also in this as in most other matters, if there is a question between a Scotchman and an Englishman, the Scotchman will stand the better chance and find most friends.

7th January, 1922

I have been to town today and accompanied by Charles Graves, went to the Private View of the works of recently deceased R.A.s at the Royal Academy. It is an interesting show and there is a certain melancholy pleasure in once more meeting with pictures that one remembers in long past years whose painters now have all 'gone down'! Among the exhibits is Strang's portrait of myself, but the picture which it pleased me most to see again was that of Andrew Lang by Richmond. For years I knew it well at 1 Marloes Road, and at Ditchingham I have a photograph of it that Andrew gave to me.

I heard at the Athenaeum (and have just seen it stated in the *Saturday Review* with the name left out) that the recently bestowed O.M. was first offered of all people in the world, to Sir W. Robertson Nicoll, the Editor of the *British Weekly*. He declined it, which shows that he is a sensible man, but pressed the name of his fellow Scotchman Barrie, who used to be a protégé of his, so to Barrie it went. A queer tale, but anything in the Honours List is possible now-a-days. The weather is horrible, a cold slushy drizzle but no heavy rain which is so much needed.

13th January, 1922

Mr Gibson Bowles[1] is dead at the age of seventy-eight, whereby this country loses a most valuable citizen and a most outspoken critic of officialism. When I was a lad in 1873, at which time he had become Editor or owner of the old *Vanity Fair*, I used to meet him a good deal at the house of some friends and had many talks with him, but since then we have never met again, that is except once when he came to call on me at 69 Gunterstone Road after the appearance of *She*, riding a very fine horse as I remember.

25th January, 1922

The papers are full of accounts of the 'Inca's Ring' I have given to the British

---

[1] From 1892 to 1906 he was the M.P. for King's Lynn in Norfolk.

Museum, of which I have spoken before. The story of it appears to appeal to the public imagination and I was kept at the telephone a long while, being interviewed on the matter by the *Daily Express* and the *Daily Mail*. I have just returned from London, where the weather is horrible.

28th January, 1922

Kipling, who came over to see me on Thursday, takes a most gloomy view of the Indian situation. I asked him his opinion. He answered that if Phyllis[1] were his daughter, simply he would not allow her to go (as though he could prevent it when she is another man's wife). Indeed he says that in answer to requests for advice on this very point, he had to reply that, as he supposes the truth as he sees it is what is wanted from him, he thinks it right to say that he does not think that any white woman should visit or remain in India. Indeed he said that he heard from Indian correspondents that no white ladies and children are ever left alone, especially at outlying stations. If some of the officers go out on duty or pleasure, others remain to watch them. In short his opinion seems to be that there is grave risk of our being faced with another mutiny. As he knows India if any man does, his view impresses me.

30th January, 1922

I have just returned from spending a most interesting day with the Kiplings at Batemans. As usual K. and I talked till we were tired about everything in heaven above and earth beneath. Incidentally too we hammered out the skeleton plot for a romance I propose to write under some such title as *Allan and the Ice Gods*[2], which is to deal with the terrible advance of one of the Ice Ages upon a little handful of the primitive inhabitants of the earth. He has a marvellously fertile mind and I never knew anyone quite so quick at seizing and developing an idea. We spent a most amusing two hours over this plot and I have brought home the results in several sheets of MS. written by him and myself.

He takes the most despondent view of the position in Ireland, Egypt and India, and even went so far as to say that it looks as though the Empire were going to fall to pieces. The only hope he could see was in young men who may arise, but when I asked him where these young men were he replied that he did not know. He trusts, however, that they may arise under the pressure of circumstances. So do I, but at present I discern them not. His Majesty's present advisers would not be flattered if they heard Rudyard Kipling's opinion of them.

[1] On 5th April, 1921, she had married Captain Wickham of the Royal Engineers, who had just been posted to India. Kipling was concerned about the anti-British feeling then current in India.
[2] The outline, with sketches and character names, is on six pages. Rider Haggard and Kipling shared the writing. The book was published posthumously on 20th May, 1927.

Today I have been to town to attend a deputation to the Colonial Secretary about inter-Imperial migration. Mr Winston Churchill has grown much more stout and solid than when I saw him last, and has a very large bullet-shaped head. In his answer to the speeches virtually he promised all sorts of things in furtherance of the cause of Empire Migration but, as I sat listening to him, I could not help wondering whether these would in fact ever be translated into performance under the present circumstances of the Government and the state of our national finances. A new Bill dealing with the matter, however, is, he said, actually in draft. Somewhat to my astonishment, he knew me again and came to shake hands with me.

I am delighted to see that my old friend Maurice Greiffenhagen has been elected a full Royal Academician. I observe that the *Morning Post* in commenting remarks that 'the remarkable portrait of Sir H. Rider Haggard is the most important painting he has ever produced'.

1st March, 1922

The wedding of Princess Mary to Viscount Lascelles is over. Its réclame and success has been what the Germans call 'colossal'. I remember that of the present King very well indeed and witnessed the procession etc., but I do not think there was half so much public excitement about it as there is over the union of his daughter and Lord Lascelles. But then in those days we did things more quietly; there were not so many competing newspapers to stir up enthusiasm. Cinematographs and the multitude of camera men also were unknown. What will happen when the Prince of Wales's turn comes, I wonder! If these things are done in the green tree, what will be done in the dry?

15th March, 1922

This morning from the windows of the East Sussex Club, I have been watching a seaplane fall into the sea and — owing to a combination of fortunate circumstances — the rescue of its three occupants. Nothing will make me believe that these air craft are desirable vehicles of locomotion, at any rate at present.

18th March, 1922

Last night, I was again the guest of the Delphian Coterie, when we discussed the question of women in connection with civic life. Harold Cox followed after me and as usual we totally disagreed. It was very amusing, but I wished that I had followed after him! His great remedy for all our ills is that English women should cease to produce children. He said that he would much rather see them compete on commerce than in cradles! It was a large gathering at the Holborn Restaurant and ladies were invited for the first time. I took Lilias with me.

24th March, 1922

I have been judging a number of essays by elementary and secondary school children[1] upon the subject 'Why we should help disabled soldiers and sailors'. Allowing for the fact that those sent to me are picked out of hundreds or thousands sent in for competition in the hope of winning valuable prizes, the work is extraordinarily good, so much so indeed that to make any selection was a task of much difficulty. Certainly it was infinitely better than I should expect from children of our own class at the same ages, I suppose because the system of education is better in what used to be the Board Schools. As I am the final judge, I can only hope that I have hit upon the best essays, but of this I am by no means sure, because many of them are practically of equal merit.

31st March, 1922

An Italian sculptor, La Monaca[2], has produced a bust of me which most judges think a fine and vital work of art. I have suggested to Dean Inge that he should be sculpted, pointing out that in after years, the bust might be useful for his monument in St Paul's. This idea, I imagine, appeals to him and he is going to sit.

3rd April, 1922

Of late years artists and authors, even humble and unfashionable ones like myself, have been tormented increasingly from all quarters by newspapers and others desirous of gratis copy, not to mention the outside 'something for nothing' public, who post by post are with us always. Behind these polite requests often enough lies a covert threat of 'Give — or it will be the worse for you when next you publish a book' — or whatever it may be. Scarcely a week passes without my receiving some such request, frequently of an absurd or an inquisitive nature. In these latter days the practice has spread to more exalted quarters. Those in high positions write round, asking for contributions to schemes they have in hand upon which their names are to appear prominently. For months past I have been bombarded about a certain dolls house which is to be given to the Queen[3], though what Her Majesty can want with such a thing I cannot conceive. An eminent architect is to design

[1] The competition was organised by the Lord Roberts Memorial Fund for Disabled Soldiers and Sailors.
[2] He worked in Rome, London and Paris, specialising in busts of important people such as George Bernard Shaw.
[3] It was designed by Sir Edwin Lutyens.

this house (I hope he likes the job); eminent artists are to paint the pictures for its walls; eminent authors are to write in tiny books to adorn its library. Hitherto by various artifices I have escaped, but now comes a letter from a Princess[1] of a personal nature, although I do not suppose that this royal lady ever set eyes on me, or has read anything I have written, or cares twopence about me, enclosing one of the horrid little books, not much bigger than a postage stamp, and requesting that I will write in it. For most of the morning I have been engaged upon the awkward task, although as it happens I am extremely busy, with the result that my temper is now none of the best. I can only suppose that the exalted ones of the earth, some of whom neither toil nor spin, do not understand that time is valuable to its workers; also that certain of these busy folks object to being set tasks which they consider futile and foolish, that yet, without positive rudeness, cannot be refused. To help a great cause or charity most of us will do much, but to write in toy books for a dolls house is not an occupation that can appeal to many, however delighted they may be forced to appear.

Garland's Hotel   *11th April, 1922*

Yesterday we came to town for a while on our way home.

15th April, 1922

The weather yesterday at last turned warmer but today there is a tearing gale. I have been reading a work on Einstein and his theories but, try as I may, I *cannot* understand, even if rays of light do bend in passing the sun, why this newly discovered fact should utterly destroy all that has hitherto been accepted as to the conditions of Time, Space, the Ether and I know not what beside. However, no doubt this is due to my dense stupidity: only I notice that when I ask eminent scientific friends to lighten my darkness, they generally turn the conversation. Can it be that these also find the business difficult?

17th April, 1922

For mid-April the weather remains of an unparalleled awfulness. Yesterday a furious gale; today bitter, with hail and cold rain, or snow in many places ... yet the papers keep on writing about the joys of the Easter holiday and publishing photographs (evidently faked in studios) of buxom young women in tight, befrilled bathing-dresses!

[1]She was Princess Marie Louisa (1872-1956) who, after her marriage to Prince Aribert of Anhalt was dissolved in 1900, returned to England and dedicated herself to charitable work.

27th April, 1922

The Empire Settlement Bill has been read a second time in the Commons, and I think will become law, thus for the first time putting migration from this country upon a sound, continuous basis. Although my share in the business is now forgotten, I look upon this advance with some pride since surely I have had some part in bringing it about.

East Sussex Club, St Leonards   *2nd May, 1922*

I have come here with Louie, who is staying elsewhere, to see to the removal of the furniture of the flat (26 Ashley Gardens, which I have transferred to Mrs Bentley who has hired it for the last two years) to North Lodge and to Paygate, in which Andrew and his wife are now living. I hoped to find the climate better and the cold less than in London, but these are much the same, the fact being that this Arctic weather, which has resulted in the latest and most bitter spring that I can remember, extends all over Europe. I suppose, however, that it must change sometime; the trees can scarcely remain leafless and the crops stationary till midsummer — unless we are at the commencement of a new Ice Age!

5th May, 1922

I have been pressed during the last few days since I left St Leonards, running about London in the appalling weather, being inoculated by Cowan Guthrie for my bronchial ailments and leg trouble, attending the general meeting of the Royal Colonial Institute to second a resolution, and finally getting myself home, to say nothing of visits to Watt and the bank.

9th May, 1922

Yesterday for the first time for many years I heard from my old friend Major Burnham[1], the scout of fame. It is a long and most interesting letter about all his adventures in the Yukon Valley etc. I imagine that Burnham's letter is a feeler of some sort, but probably it will all end in nothing. I am too old and ailing for exploration work, if such is intended.

17th May, 1922

I have spent most of the day trying cases at Loddon as Chairman of the Bench (of which I am now the oldest magistrate, by a few minutes!).

[1] Major F. R. Burnham, D.S.O., was an American whom Rider Haggard had met in about 1895. Burnham was an explorer, hunter, scout and treasure-hunter.

The weather after the recent abnormal cold has turned extraordinarily hot. The unprecedented temperature of 90 degrees in the shade was registered at Greenwich yesterday, and the thermometer here registered about 85. Ours is a strange climate! Tomorrow we go to fish at Blagdon.

Blagdon   *24th May, 1922*

10 p.m. Arrived here with Dolly and Lilias after a very hot journey; indeed I have seldom felt anything more oppressive than Paddington Station was today. It is much cooler here than in Norfolk. The streets of London today were full of dressed-up students and lightly attired young ladies selling flags for hospitals. It is Empire Day, an occasion, I am glad to say, that is being increasingly observed.

31st May, 1922

Our fishing has come to an end, without a single fish! The lake seems absolutely dead and probably because of a lack of rain to give oxygen to the water and the effects of last year's awful drought the trout will not stir from the bottom. Also there is a singular scarcity of the usual rises of the fly. However, although hot, the weather has been beautiful, and Dolly and Lilias have enjoyed themselves.

Ditchingham   *22nd June, 1922*

Today is my sixty-sixth birthday which tells me that I am now quite an old man. Time goes so fast in our declining days that the rapidity of its passage reminds me of the American tale of a gentleman, a stranger to the country, who was taken for a twilight drive along a straight road by a friend who owned a famous trotting horse. After a while he asked what great cemetery they had been passing through for the last hour. 'Stranger,' replied the driver, 'I guess that what you see flashing by so slick ain't memorials to the departed; I guess they're the milestones!' After sixty, time is that famous trotter and the milestones are our birthdays.

30th June, 1922

This morning I received a property balance sheet for 1921. The total receipts were £670.18. 5. Here are just a few of the outgoings: tithe and rates — £206.15.9; property tax — £146. 4.10; land tax — £17. 2. 3; repairs — £53. 1. 8; fire insurance — £37. 8. 2; on account of estate work — £60. The nett result is that nothing whatsoever has been received. I have had to find £100 and to pay many of the repairs out of my own pocket and the agent's fee remains in arrear. Thank goodness we have sold most of our land, but such are the returns for what remains.

22nd July, 1922

Yesterday I went to town with Louie and Lilias to attend the Garden Party at Buckingham Palace. Happily the weather was fine, though not so hot and dry as it was the previous year. The scene was very brilliant — some 5000 people wandering about the Buckingham Palace grounds, all the women in their best. What struck me, however, rightly or wrongly was the general inferiority in the beauty of these women to that of those whom I remember thirty or forty years ago when you really did see many beautiful women. For this there may be sundry explanations — first, that the observer at the age of sixty-six looks at women with a different eye than that which he possessed, let us say, at twenty-six; secondly, that the present style of dress does not appeal to him; and thirdly, though again this may be fancy, that the ladies of today taken as a whole lack the chic and the style of those of the Victorian era. However all this may be, personally I did not see yesterday a single woman whom I should call beautiful, although I saw many fine dresses and many large jewels. There were a great number of Indians present whose many coloured garments gave variety to the scene. Altogether it was a most interesting function and at it I met a good many that I knew, Kipling and others.

At the Athenaeum some of us who were going to the Garden Party — old fellows all of us — had a quite interesting competition as to which of us could boast the most antique frock-coat worn for the occasion. Sir Edward Henry won, at least I think it was he, because he was able to prove that his was marked 1900, but I believe that the honour ought to have been mine, which I am sure is Victorian and except for a few trifling moth holes almost as good as the day it was made. The fame of the discussion spread to the party, for one of the first questions that Kipling asked me was who had won, adding that if he had been there with his coat none other would have had a chance!

I went into English's, the Opera Arcade hatters, to have my tall hat ironed up. The expert surveyed it doubtfully and remarked that he thought it would do, adding, 'Lord! Sir Rider. We have had some relics in here this morning!'

27th July, 1922

Yesterday in a little speech I made as President of the Ditchingham Fur and Feather Society, I said that I think that in this country we eat too much dead foreign meat. I have always had doubts about this imported meat, for nothing will make me believe that Nature intended us to devour creatures that died months or years before they come to table.

The Show was an enormous success and reflected the greatest credit on Lilias, its backbone. Everybody seems to have enjoyed it very much, as mercifully the rain held off until after six o'clock. A great number of people attended and there is no doubt that were it wished, this Show might expand indefinitely.

Sir Henry Rew has been visiting us here. He kindly came down to speak at the Waveney Valley Show, of which I was the President, yesterday. He told me that Lord Northcliffe is undoubtedly mad, very mad, and that he was so certified in Cologne. He says too that one of the biggest London mental specialists, I forget which, states that Lord Northcliffe's case is the first in all his experience in which he has known megalomania to result in actual and acute insanity. It seems, however, that his case is complicated by some kind of heart trouble, and it is thought that he cannot live very long.

Lord Northcliffe is dead. He 'let down' Kipling and myself and others very badly indeed over the Liberty League business, which makes me rather afraid to write about him, because a man's mind must always be prejudiced against one who has given him away, especially in circumstances like those connected with the Liberty League, when all our troubles arose from putting confidence in the man to whom *The Times* had introduced us. There is no doubt that, if not quite as great as some believe who are dazzled by his wealth and his success, Lord Northcliffe was a remarkable man, who would have been more remarkable still had he possessed the saving grace of modesty. But vanity was his bane. Who with the slightest sense of humour at an entertainment of his employees could have caused himself to be prayed for as 'Thy servant Alfred' as though he were the King?

Yesterday I motored to Bradenham with my brother Arthur to lunch with my old friend, Canon Edward Winter, who is now the rector of both East and West Bradenham. Later we went to West Bradenham church where I wished to see the Litany stool which my wife and I gave in memory of my three nephews who have been killed in war. I was glad to see this church again which I have known from infancy and to occupy the pew where I have often sat with my mother while Edward Winter took two christenings. Afterwards we went round the church which is so full of mementoes of the Haggard family and, outside, of the graves of some of them. Edward produced a register book and showed me the entry of my baptism, or rather of my reception into the church some months later than my birth. This was done because not long after I was born my life was despaired of so that I was christened privately in the china bowl which I have in this house. My mother has often told me how when the doctor, old Clouting, had gone away saying that there was no more hope for me and that he had exhausted his resources in the fight against inflammation of the lungs from which I suffered, she took the matter in hand herself, dosing me with brandy and wrapping me in boiling flannels, with the result that I did not die after all. I have written on the bottom of this bowl that my brother Arthur was also christened in it, which certainly I should not have done without good authority, probably that of my late sister, Ella, who, I believe, was his godmother. He, however, knows nothing of the story. Yet it appears from the register that he was not christened till some months after his birth, so I am sure it has foundation. Perhaps my father in a panic baptised him himself, which baptism subsequently was ignored.

The church is quite unchanged. The same bees hive in the roof, the same red carpets stamped with a kind of fleur de lys are on the chancel floor. My brother John's remains, removed from Spain, are now buried without by the tower, but I observe that the cross of Bradenham oak which my sister-in-law has put over them is already cracking in the weather. Except it be under cover, oak is of but little use for such a purpose. The churchyard is now full of the tombstones of those whom I knew in my youth, such as poor old Sam Adcock who is the original of 'George' in my tale of country life *Colonel Quaritch*. Afterwards, as Arthur wished to do so, though I did not, we went on to the hall. Although the gardens are kept up in a fashion by the timber-merchant who owns it, the place is a wilderness and a desolation. All the trees in the plantation have been felled; even the oak planted to commemorate my father's and mother's marriage has been hacked down, for I found its stump near to the garden gate. Indeed the spot might well be such a haunt of owls and doleful creatures where satyrs dance as that written of in Isaiah. I went over the empty rooms of the house where the places upon which well-remembered pictures hung are shown by marks upon the wall. It was a melancholy experience and those empty, echoing rooms offered a strange and indeed a terrible contrast to what they were as I remember them, filled with life and noise and young people, most of them now dead, and with my father's voice ringing through the house. If ever a place should be haunted, it is Bradenham Hall.

26th August, 1922

Today there is a little sun, a fact so unusual this year that it is worthy of permanent record. Indeed the seasons have been most remarkable; now in August the weather is that of late autumn and up to the present moment I have not seen a wasp since the queens appeared in the spring.

7th September, 1922

Yesterday I visited the Castle Museum at Norwich which is growing into a noble institution. Mr Leney, the Curator, showed me with pride the record of visitors for August, the highest they have known. He added, and this pleased me, that nearly all of these visitors were greatly interested in the case containing my MSS. etc. which, he says, have proved a very considerable asset and attraction to the museum.

Yesterday I went to town to have the first of my autumn anti-bronchitis inoculations.

There is a terrific row in America over an alleged interview which Kipling was said to have given to Mrs Clare Sheridan[1], who I believe is an American sculptor, in the course of which he was reported to have expressed himself with point and vigour about the conduct of the United States in connection with the war, and the conclusion of the Armistice, as to the former saying much what Roosevelt said to me and what many think. Rudyard Kipling has now explained in a telegram to *The Times* that he never gave an interview to Mrs Clare Sheridan or said the things he has seen attributed to him. What she will answer I don't know, but I imagine that what has happened is that this artistic lady had reported the gist of some private conversation she had with Kipling and called it an 'interview' in the pleasing American fashion. Anyhow the business is unfortunate as of course thousands will not read or believe the contradiction and evidently Kipling's alleged remarks about America having 'got the gold' while 'we. have kept our soul' etc. have touched that country on the raw.

Garland's Hotel   *21st September, 1922*

I came to town yesterday to have more inoculations from Cowan Guthrie and after that business spent the afternoon at the British Museum, calling on Mr Joyce about the Execution Club of King Cakobau of Fiji (with 103 murders recorded on it by means of notches!) which I have presented to the Trustees, and seeing many things. The Museum grows almost too big, one loses oneself in its vast recesses and grows bewildered with the countless exhibits.

By the way Watt told me this morning that, as I guessed, the Kipling 'interview' was a report of a private conversation which he had in the intimacy of his own house with Mrs Clare Sheridan, whom he has known from a child. She is a daughter of Moreton Frewen, with whom I had many talks at St Leonards last year and with whom the Kiplings have been friends for years. Frewen, who is very ill, must have been much upset. Her mother is the sister[2] of the late Randolph Churchill and I think that she is married to an American. All this makes the business peculiarly discreditable, but why English papers should go out of their way to allege that Kipling could ever have said such things I am sure I don't know, unless, as usual, it is due to fear of America. There was nothing improper in the opinions attributed to him, whatever may have been his exact words uttered in privacy to an old friend. Indeed everybody has heard them scores of times, not so

[1] Clare Consuelo Sheridan was the European correspondent of the *New York World*. Her husband had been killed in France in September, 1915.
[2] Actually the sister-in-law.

infrequently from the lips of Americans themselves. It is the person who sent a garbled account of them to the Press who should be reprimanded.

5th October, 1922

Yesterday I was in London being inoculated.

19th October, 1922

We are busy packing as we leave here tomorrow to stay over the week-end with the Longmans on our way to St Leonards.

East Sussex Club, St Leonards   *23rd October, 1922*

I left Upp Hall this morning, spent the day in town being treated by Guthrie and arrived here this evening to find it less cold than Hertfordshire. My attention having been called to it by Longman in a catalogue of Maggs Brothers, this afternoon I went to see the MS. of Lang's well known sonnet on *She*, which is dedicated to myself, that they were advertising for sale. Sure enough there it was in the unmistakable handwriting and my name on it, but with some of the lines altered. I bought this relic which has much personal interest for me and perhaps shall give it to the Norwich Museum to be attached to the MS. of *She*. But how on earth did it come upon the market? That is the mystery. Someone must have obtained possession of and sold it. Mr Maggs did not, or pretended not to know, but said that he would enquire and let me hear anything that he could learn. I wonder whether he will. I can scarcely think that Mrs Lang disposed of the MS., but who else would have had it? I cannot now remember whether Andrew ever sent me this fine sonnet before it was published; if so doubtless it is among my papers.

Another thing that I was tempted into buying was the original drawing of myself by Leslie Ward ('Spy') which appeared as a *Vanity Fair* cartoon about 1887. I think that this also should go to the museum. An assistant in the shop produced it while I was talking to Mr Maggs and after some bargaining it became my property. I remember that Ward would not allow me to look at it while I sat for him, so now after thirty-five years I see it for the first time.

1st November, 1922

Today I have been up to town in the most deplorable weather. After my inoculation I went to lunch with Louie at the Empress Club, which was crowded. Whilst waiting for a table I observed that many of the fine, bejewelled ladies there were drinking cocktails in the lounge, as men used to do in American bars; also smoking cigarettes held in golden pincers. A sign and a celebration of the recent 'emancipation' of the sex, I suppose! Lord! What will it all end in?

North Lodge, St Leonards   *7th November, 1922*

Today we have got into this house again.

11th November, 1922

This is Armistice Day. I attended part of a service at Christ Church here for 'the silence', but as I could not understand all the singing and elaborate ritual, I came out as did Louie and Lilias. A flag-draped coffin was placed before the altar. It seemed to me that there were about fifty women present to every man. I suppose that a requiem 'mass' was being celebrated.

15th November, 1922

I was in town yesterday for my inoculations, enjoying a black and bitter fog that has now endured for several days.

I grieve to see in a paper that Kipling has gone to a nursing home where he may have an operation, which may or may not be true. A year or two ago he complained to me of his stomach, but said the doctors told him it was nothing to worry about, and, I think, the last time I was at Batemans he told me it was all right again. I hope it has not reasserted itself.

20th November, 1922

I have heard from Mrs Kipling. She says that 'Rudyard is going on well up to the present, but it was a so called "serious operation" and the first week is anxious work, but it's worth much to know they have removed the cause of so much pain and know there is no reason for it to return.' This still leaves me in the dark as to what is or was the matter with him — stone perhaps. However, she adds that he will be delighted to see me after next Wednesday, so I am now trying to arrange date and time to visit him.

22nd November, 1922

I have been to Oxford to address the Plough Club, whose guest I was at their annual dinner and to stay with my old friend and colleague, Professor Somerville. The fog in London yesterday was the most remarkable that I have ever seen. A darkness as of midnight hung over the city, but below it was clear — with all the flaring lights a scene from Dante's Inferno or from the Greek Hades or the Jewish Gehenna. It was amazing — even terrible to see.

24th November, 1922

I went this morning to inquire after Kipling, and, as Mrs Kipling hàd gone to see him in his nursing home, I saw Elsie[1] and had a long talk with her, which however has not left me much the wiser as to his illness. She said it was not cancer, or so they declared, but what it was she did not seem to know. It appears that the ailment has been going on for seven years and is the same as that of which he spoke to me a long while ago, grown worse so that of late he has had much pain, especially after eating. I suspect some kind of growth which has necessitated some short-circuiting operation. The doctors, she added, are quite satisfied with his present condition, although he still suffers pain. But then, as he remarked to her, I think yesterday — 'Doctors are d ..... d easily pleased.' I gather generally that he will probably recover from this trouble, but can scarcely hope to be the same man again. He hates his nursing home and they hope to get him out of it into the hotel as soon as possible.

I found my doctor, Cowan Guthrie, very jubilant over the discovery in the Rockefeller Institute of America of what is believed to be the true bacillus of influenza, which has been isolated after long and patient research. Guthrie hopes that this discovery will give them the mastery of the disease. Some of the vaccine (?) has arrived at Bart's Hospital and he hopes to procure a supply and proceed to make experiments.

30th November, 1922

Mr Howard Carter, whom I know and who, I believe, now works on behalf of Lord Carnarvon, has made a marvellous discovery in the Valley of Kings at Thebes. There below the tomb of Rameses VI, he has found a sealed cache of several chambers full of all the funeral furniture, also the chariots and throne of Pharaoh Tutankhamen, who was one of the shadowy successors to Akenaten, the heretic Pharaoh. Whether his body is in one of the chambers that remains unopened is not yet known.

13th December, 1922

I saw Kipling whom, to my delight, I found infinitely better than I expected. His operation has nothing to do with cancer, but was simply due to some constriction inside. I gave him my receipt for Dr Paget's Jam[2], which I believe is at least 100

[1] Kipling's daughter. In 1924 she married Captain George Bambridge.
[2] Rider Haggard gives the receipt in one of his note-books: 'Dr Paget's Jam — 1 lb. prunes or French plums; 1 lb. Demarara sugar; 1 oz. best ground ginger; 1 ½ oz. powdered senna; 1 claret glass of brandy — Soak the fruit overnight in enough water to cover them. Put them in a pan in the water they have been soaked in and simmer gently till soft. Remove the stones while hot. Add all the other ingredients, mixing and stirring well with a wooden spoon. Add remains of juice. Keep in jar with loose paper cover. (Add 2 cloves or 2 drops of oil of cloves on blotting paper on top of each jar.)'

years old, and expect that it will be of great benefit to him. I gave it also to Cowan Guthrie, who has passed it on to the Mother Superior of a convent, whom he doctors. She in her turn administered it to all her nuns who, I am told, bless me day by day. After all, old things are often the best things.

25th December, 1922

Christmas, whose delights the papers outvie each other in proclaiming, is after all no joyous festival to the old. It brings too many memories, of some of which one cannot write. Thus the mind goes back some fifty or sixty years and shows the throng of merry youngsters — brothers and sisters, nine of them, most of whom are dead — twisting the holly garlands to decorate the oak of rooms that today are the home of the spider and the bat. Where are they now? A few remain, bent, scarred and weary from struggling with the world, while the rest are dust — like the holly wreaths they wove. And whither they have gone we follow apace.

1923

Though still very active, Rider Haggard continued to be plagued by ill health. His gout and bronchitis were not helped by the cold weather that continued well into the summer. Several events caused distress. In May, Andrew, his brother, died. In the December General Election the Conservatives under Stanley Baldwin lost so many seats that it was obvious that, although still the largest party, they could not retain office. Such was Rider Haggard's condition by the end of the year that it was decided that for the first time for many years it would not be wise for him to spend another complete winter in England, even in the milder climate of Sussex.

1st January, 1923

Another year has come — the 23rd (I think) since I wrote the prayer — if so it may be called — which appears on the final page of *A Farmer's Year*. I read it again last night as I always like to do on the 31st December. Its words are still applicable and still express my thought.

2nd February, 1923

Yesterday I went to town to sit on the Empire Migration Committee at the Royal Colonial Institute. While lunching with Sir Squire Bancroft[1] at the Athenaeum, I chanced to say that I thought actors must be very strong men, as he is to this day though now old, to stand the draughts and the late hours. He answered that this is so, and he attributes it largely to the fact that they have to speak so loud in theatres even when they seem to be speaking low, which expands and continually exercises their lungs, making them resistant to disease.

9th February, 1923

There is a tremendous row in Egypt over the Tutankhamen discoveries. All the rest of the world's press is furious with Lord Carnavon and *The Times* because of the bargain made between them for their mutual profit that *The Times* should have the copyright of information as regards the contents of the tomb, and also of the photographs taken of those contents. The Egyptian Government and the Egyptian Department of Antiquities are taking a hand in the game and the air in Egypt is thick with threats and insinuations. (I suggested to *The Times* that I should go out for them to write about this business, but found that they had already completed their arrangements, also that the duties of their correspondent would involve a most complicated system of news dissemination, for which of course I should have been quite unsuited. Thankful am I indeed that I was too late since I can imagine nothing that I should have hated more than to have been involved in this somewhat sordid quarrel, which may have many unforeseen results.) The Egyptian Government is now demanding that if *The Times* correspondent is admitted to the opening of the inner chamber of the tomb, all other correspondents must be admitted with him, and that equal opportunity and information must be given to every one of them.

21st February, 1923

Today at the Athenaeum, I was delighted to see Sir Frederick Maurice. He has been elected to the club of which I am very glad — as I told him. Maurice has been

[1]He was for many years actor-manager of the old Prince of Wales's and the Haymarket Theatres. After 1885 he spent much time giving readings for charity.

a much ill-treated man, one of whom Mr Lloyd George tried to destroy because he told the truth, and I rejoice that his reputation has not been lessened by all the political malice from which he has suffered. His hair has turned snow white; it is said owing to his anxieties during the war.

24th February, 1923

Yesterday I took the chair at Hastings at a meeting which I understood to be in support of Lady Muriel Paget's work among children in Eastern Europe, but which, to my astonishment, turned out to be principally on behalf of the local branch of the League of Nations Union. I was much struck by the pro-Russian tone of some of the speeches made. In these there was not a word of criticism of the Soviet Government. Indeed one of the orators talked of their ill-doings as being much exaggerated. How they can do this in face of the facts that have come to light, I am sure I do not know.

This afternoon we have been to see the film *L'Atlantide*, founded on the romance by M. Paul Benoit. If it is not also founded upon a romance called *The Yellow God* by myself, all I can say is that the coincidences are very remarkable, especially in the example of the mummified remains of the heroine's lovers arranged in a hall, as in *The Yellow God*. Also the general idea of the book is reminiscent of *She*. The result, so far as I am concerned, is that a film of *The Yellow God* would probably now be impossible. Also some film producers, who were contemplating the reproduction of *She* upon the cinema-stage, have written saying that they fear it would not pay to do this as the picture play would too closely resemble *L'Atlantide*. So it seems that M. Benoit is lucky and I am not.

Garland's Hotel *2nd March, 1923*

Today we have been driven away from St Leonards by the influenza. First the housemaid got it and now the cook is down with worse symptoms and I think the parlour maid looks queer. So I decided that we must flit as work in the house, also food, are impossible. So I have come here and Louie has gone to the Empress Club. It is a great nuisance and of course puts a stop to my book.[1]

8th March, 1923

I am laid by the heels in this hotel by a sharp attack of gout and the doctor tells me that henceforward practically I should become a teetotaller, which is not cheering.

10th March, 1923

I am still confined to the hotel by my attack of gout.

[1] At the time he was working on *Heu-Heu*, a book published in an abridged form on 29th January, 1924.

North Lodge, St Leonards   *12th March, 1923*

With the help of sticks, and cabmen and porters, I limped back here this afternoon
(the influenza having, it is hoped, departed from this house), thus finishing a
somewhat disastrous and expensive trip to London.

20th March, 1923

I have been spending the day at Batemans with the Kiplings. I found Rudyard
looking drawn and considerably aged. He has been and still is suffering from
sundry minor consequential troubles as the result of his operation. I hope that
these are not serious but they are a great worry and keep him continually thinking
of his inside. It struck me that we were a pretty pair of old crocks, I lying with my
leg up on the couch in his study and he bending over the fire. We read bits of
Wisdom's Daughter which he was kind enough to describe as '------- good prose'
(this he repeated several times, making me re-read passages that he might note the
fall of the sentences) with other complimentary remarks. He has not yet finished
the book but described it as 'a philosophy of life' and an epitome of all the deeper
part of my work. He says he will write to me about it later. We talked of many
things and as usual I found that our views were practically the same. He is, or
seemed to be, now convinced that the individual human being is not a mere flash
in the pan, seen for a moment and lost for ever, but an enduring entity that has
lived elsewhere and will continue to live after death, though for a while memory of
the past is blotted out. He does not, however, think this of all individuals, but
holds that for some there is no spiritual future elsewhere, because they have no
soul to inherit it and no desire to uplift their hearts and attain to it, exemplifying
this argument by the name of one brilliant and much-praised writer — '*He* won't
live again,' he said. These were his views on this point, if I understood them
rightly. As to the future of our country he was despondent, not being able to see a
way out of all our troubles, any more than I can. The advent of a Labour Government, or even the near approach of it, would he thought produce a terrible financial crash, and he asked whether all those that we lost in the war, his boy John and
the rest, died to bring about such a state of affairs as we see today. We agreed that
we were both of us out of touch with the times, but he added grimly that these
clever young men who are so loud in their self-praise and air their views so freely
would learn their lesson before all was done, when in due course they found
themselves face to face with forces that are banking up on every side. Altogether
our talk was most interesting, for in Kipling there is more light than in any living
man I know, the same sort of light that distinguished Lang when he dropped the
shield of persiflage with which he hid his heart. There are three men with whom,
above all others, I have found myself in complete sympathy during my
life — Rudyard is one of them and the other two were Andrew Lang and Theodore
Roosevelt. The outlook of all four of us was and is identical — that is so far as I can

judge. Rudyard's memory is really marvellous; he repeated to me two long unpublished satirical poems of his without a single error. (These are aimed at America's post-war conduct which infuriates him especially where the debt is concerned, and if ever they are read by the citizens of that 'communal country' I don't know what will happen.) I believe that if he were put to it he could do the same with most of what he has written. To be short, we enjoyed our talk very much — in the middle of it he broke in to say, 'I am *so* delighted to see you here, old man.' I hope to heaven that he will get quite strong again but I must say that I was not altogether pleased with his appearance — he looks so worn and thin. They are going to the south of France soon that he may get warmth and rest. Meanwhile he is writing some amusing stories; he says that is how it takes him just now, perhaps in mental reaction to his physical worries.

22nd March, 1923

Rudyard asked me on Tuesday if I had noticed how every sort of superstition was becoming rampant in this country, which, I think he said, always presaged the downfall of great civilisations. It is perfectly true, the papers are full of such things.

I have just received a wire sent on behalf of the *New York World* which asks me to give my opinion as to the 'efficacy of magical curses against despoilers placed around ancient mummies'. This is apropos of Lord Carnarvon's illness in which the telegram states 'America is greatly interested'. I am afraid that the Reply Paid will be wasted so far as the *New York World* is concerned. How a paper can expect a man like myself to make a public fool of himself by expressing opinions upon such a matter, passes my comprehension.

27th March, 1923

My nephew, Harry Haggard, with whose bringing up I had something to do, is today gazetted a Rear-Admiral, and *not* retired. I am sure that if he gets a chance he will distinguish himself, as he is a most able officer, though I hope that this will not be in the course of another war.

Hotel Regina, London, S.W.   *12th April, 1923*

We left St Leonards for the summer today.

19th April, 1923

Yesterday I was one of a Deputation from the Central Chamber of Agriculture to the Postmaster General, Sir William Joynson-Hicks, appointed to urge the extension of Parcel Post and Telephone facilities in the interest of the Rural Districts and Agriculture. In speaking, I pointed out I was the first to publicly advocate the adoption of an Agricultural Post.

Today I attended the final winding-up meeting of the Agricultural Relief of Allies Committee, formed by the Royal Agricultural Society of England in January, 1915, on which committee I have served from that day to this. Certainly it has a fine record seeing that we raised and distributed among our necessitous allies £253,913 at a cost (not included) of under £11,000.

24th April, 1923

The Duke of York's wedding, like all Royal ceremonies, is causing much excitement and the Press is working it for all it is worth. I passed Bruton Street today and saw a crowd gathered round the door of No. 17. I hope that this gloomy mansion will prove a house of better omen to the bride than it was to me, for it was there I went through all my unhappy experiences in connection with the Liberty League. The weather continues most bitter and unseasonable for the time of year.

27th April, 1923

Yesterday, going to the Athenaeum from the Piccadilly Tube Station, I met the sightseers coming by the ten thousand from the Mall and the steps below the Monument to an earlier Duke of York. The strange thing was that the women among them seemed to outnumber the men by about 20 to 1. I could not place most of the female multitude; they might have been the wives and daughters of suburban shopkeepers, most of them, to judge by their appearance. Some of them seem to have suffered much, for in the afternoon I heard one say to another in Regent Street — 'I have been up since day-light and I haven't seen a thing.' Indeed there does not seem to have been much to see, since owing to what the papers, following the poet, rapturously describe as 'the glories of an April day', the carriages were shut and the troops wore their great-coats. However, everything seems to have gone off very well, except perhaps for the enthusiasts who spent the night in the Mall in the rain!

4th May, 1923

I sold my Czecho-Slovakian shares yesterday as I could no longer stand the constant anxiety of their possession. I believe them to be good but who can say what is sound in the present state of Europe? Any day something might happen which would halve their value. Therefore it was better to lose a few pounds and be rid of them. I am putting the proceeds into South Africans as I am quite sure the Dutch would never stand a capital levy!

Last night I attended a dinner to my old colleague, Edgar Bowring, on his retirement from the High Commissionership of South Africa. I was glad to see him again just the same, though his hair has gone white, but I must say that the speeches were not exhilarating. I have heard Lord Morris tell one of his stories to which we listened, two, if not three times on other public occasions.

The weather is now beautifully warm. I wonder how long it will last. I have never seen such crowds in London. The arrival of summer has been taken advantage of by the authorities to pull up most of the great thoroughfares such as Oxford Street in the most leisurely fashion possible.

8th May, 1923

Yesterday I had to go to St Leonards to visit my brother Andrew, who, I fear, is dying. It is sad to see one who all his life till late years has been so full of vigour, reduced to such a state, literally coughing himself to death with chronic bronchitis to say nothing of other complaints. It was a depressing interview, but it is better that he should pass away than continue to suffer so much.

I went this morning to the Royal Academy which is, in my opinion, a very poor show.

10th May, 1923

We return to Ditchingham this afternoon. The weather is again bitter.

Ditchingham   *14th May, 1923*

Alas! my dear brother, Andrew, has gone. He died last night at St Leonards, worn out with years of bronchitis. On this day week I went there to see him and was sure that he could not live long. Now the end has come. He was two years my senior and in childhood we were much together, as we have been during these last years at St Leonards. When he arrived there, I think it was in 1919, from Canada, I thought he was a dying man but he recovered wonderfully, largely, I think, from the joy of getting home, and after that did some good literary work, notably his *Madame de Staël*, which he dedicated to me. He was a brave and brilliant soldier in his day, as his record and orders show, and with a little more fortune and perseverance might have risen to the very top. But somehow he just missed doing this and wearying of his profession left it. Afterwards he wrote many books on French history for which he had an extraordinary flair; indeed his knowledge of it was wonderful. Only a few weeks ago, he brought out one on Victor Hugo, and the first sign of his final breakdown was a disinclination to correct the proofs. I am much upset, but most glad that, although I was not well, I went back to St Leonards to see him. Very glad am I to have been able to free his last years from anxiety of a certain sort. He loved me much as I loved him. I have in my pocket a knife which he gave to me some fifty-six years ago when we were boys at Bradenham. There it has been for over half a century on all my wanderings, except once when it was lost for some months on the veldt. May he rest in peace! I know he was glad to go for he suffered much.

18th May, 1923

Andrew was buried at St Leonards yesterday. He had a more or less military funeral — Generals and Colonels being the pall-bearers — a member of the Veterans Club carrying his orders on a cushion — coffin covered with the Union Jack, etc. It was very appropriate and must have been impressive. I could not be there because I am not well enough.

The weather remains bitter and most unseasonable but an improvement is prophesied. It is certainly due!

24th May, 1923

Never do I remember it so cold at this time of year or more unfavourable to the growth of the crops. Last night again there was a sharp frost and I think that there will be another tonight. The cuckoo has deserted us. Everybody has noticed its complete silence. I suppose it has returned to Africa. Wise bird!.

This is Empire Day, a fact of which one would remain ignorant in Ditchingham!

29th May, 1923

A while ago an American firm, the International Story Company, which I believe has something to do with the notorious Mr Hearst, approached me as to films of certain of my books. I replied, referring them to my agents. They answered to me and I believe to others that they did not wish to deal through agents, but preferred to do so direct, their obvious hope being that thus they would overreach persons inexperienced in business or at least it may be so interpreted without lack of charity. The affair went off as these American offers nearly always do. Meanwhile, my agent, A. P. Watt, had written to the New York firm saying that he was instructed to say that I could not accept their suggestion to deal with them direct and quoting these words from my letter to Mr H. Watt — 'You might point out that no one except a fool does important legal business without a lawyer and that the same applies in this case' — words, I admit, that I did not mean to be quoted textually, although absolutely true and inoffensive. Now this estimable firm has posted *me* Watt's letter to them, without any comment whatsoever. I presume that their object is to make mischief, or it may be pure insolence, for without doubt many of the lower class Americans are very insolent.

16th June, 1923

No one whom I meet in this parish can remember so awful a spring and summer, if summer it can be called. The cold today, for instance, with its heavy skies and raging N.E. gale is absolutely appalling and even the working men are going about in heavy overcoats. This on June 16th! The birds have almost ceased to sing and a miserable blackbird sits on the wall before me with puffed-out feathers as though it were the dead of winter. The curious thing is that the flowers still bloom — more or less — I suppose from the force of habit. But the roses are very backward, indeed there are few to be seen.

23rd June, 1923

Yesterday was my sixty-seventh birthday. How quickly they come round.

5th July, 1923

Yesterday I went to Norwich on the invitation of the Mayor, Sir George Morse, to speak at the official celebration of the gift of the Ancient Strangers' Hall to that city to serve the purpose of a folk museum. It was a pleasant and successful function. This is our first real summer's day, or perhaps the honour should be accorded to yesterday. The drought, however, continues severe and is injuring the crops, although of course it makes hay sell easy.

17th July, 1923

Sir Henry Howarth[1] is dead. I used to know him in bygone years and have a most pleasant recollection of a luncheon at his house in London, when he amused me enormously with his stories and especially of how Dean Buckland[2], famous for his strange tastes, actually ate Louis XIV's heart, which was preserved by some friends of Howarth's in a case on a mantelpiece. The Dean according to the tale was shown this relic which had descended in the family from a distinguished member of it who had been an ambassador there after the Revolution, sniffed at it, said, 'I wonder what it tastes like,' licked it, popped it into his mouth (it had shrunk to the size of a large walnut), gulped — and there was an end of Louis XIV's heart! Imagine such a finale for the most vital organ of 'Le Roi Soleil'! Sir Henry Howarth was a very learned man, if eccentric, and one of a most charming personality.

20th July, 1923

My tale *Wisdom's Daughter* has just been published by Tauchnitz, who has sent

[1] He was a Trustee of the British Museum, President of the Royal Archaeological Institute and a member of the Athenaeum.
[2] William Buckland (1784-1856) was Dean of Westminster. He was also a well-known geologist, investigator and wit.

me copies. Whereas in England cheap editions of the sort are vilely printed upon vile paper, in this case both the print and the paper are excellent, though I observe that no price is printed on the back as was done in old days. Perhaps this is because there is no room to print the numerals representing 180,000 marks or so.

We had a most unfortunate day for the Fur and Feather Show which was first organised by Lilias some years since. The rain poured till late in the afternoon and of course ruined the 'gate'. This was very unlucky as the show itself was admirable. It is wonderful how it has grown and improved during the past four years. However, with marvellous courage enough people defied the torrents to prevent the loss from being as heavy as was expected. The only consolation is that rain was much wanted throughout the country.

I have just returned from attending the royal garden party at Buckingham Palace for which we went to London yesterday. The weather being fine, though windy, it was a brilliant function with lots of fine dresses and fine jewels worn by the wives of the most distinguished people in the kingdom. I cannot say, however, that I observed any remarkable beauty. What I did notice was that so many of the ladies looked washed out, thoroughly fagged. I suppose that the end of the season and generally the strenuous life that they lead now-a-days accounts for this appearance. Of course it may be one of the illusions which we develop in age, but certainly I think that the ladies of forty years ago were as a whole both better-looking and fresher in their air. Of course, also at this party few young people were present; the most of them were middle-aged or old and some even appeared in bath chairs. One of the guests I observed making herself up in public with materials out of a bag, which I thought amusing. We did not stop very late as I found the wind cold.

This morning I went to Pathé's to see the cinematograph film which their representative made of me here a week or two ago. It was very good, especially of my poor old spaniel, Jeekie, but as the bright sunlight seemed to turn my hair snow-white, it made me look even older than I am. These cinemas, however, go so fast that it is difficult to take in details. In future generations they will form interesting records of persons of our age, that is if they are kept as Pathé people told me they were. It seems that these photographic interviews go all over the world and are very popular with the masses.

I should have said that the Queen looked extraordinarily nice at the party yesterday, to my mind much better looking than she used to be years ago. The King too wears wonderfully well. Kipling and I lunched together at the Athenaeum today. He is much better than he was, and as bright and amusing as ever. We were discussing the woman's vote and the advent of woman with a big W generally, as to which he told me and others stories of remarks he alleges I made in his presence in argument with the other sex that I have totally forgotten. He reproached me for not having acknowledged a long letter he wrote to me from Cannes about *Wisdom's Daughter*[1], a work of which it seems he thinks highly and desires that I should enlarge and elaborate on certain lines. But as I never received the letter naturally I could not answer it. I have no doubt it was stolen for the autograph, probably in the French hotel. He says that he will write it again, in order to develop his argument[2], but this I doubt.

8th August, 1923

I have been to town to give away my niece Audrey on her marriage to Lieutenant Webb, R.N. The bride was pretty, the photographers were legion and the heat was great, which however did not prevent the function from going off very well. Thence I went on to visit my brother Will at Hartlip near Sittingbourne, where he now lives, whom I have not seen for more than a year, during which time he has been very ill abroad. I found him frail, though looking well and handsome. He suffers from hardening of the arteries and indigestion which affects his heart. I was glad to see him again for the reports of his illness in Italy were alarming. It was rather melancholy to look at many of the old Bradenham furnishings and pictures in their new home.

23rd August, 1923

Yesterday at Loddon I sat for the first time with a lady as a companion on the Bench, an unmarried friend of my own whom I have known for years. First I was consulted as to whether she ought to enter the Court immediately after my-self — the Chairman — in virtue of her sex. I replied I thought that as the junior magistrate she ought to enter last (which apparently is not the custom where ladies belong to the Bench). But what happened in the end I do not know as I walked first and did not see.

8th September, 1923

German marks are now worth 1,000,000 a penny! Today I have received a Tauchnitz account for royalties on certain books of mine in his hands to the 30th June last, calculated upon prices fixed according to the value of the mark and the

[1]The book had been published on 9th March, 1923.
[2]According to Lilias in *The Cloak that I Left*, the letter was sent and says, 'The more I went through it the more I was convinced that it represented the whole sum and substance of your convictions along certain lines. That being so, it occurred to me that you might, later on, take the whole book up again for your personal satisfaction — and go through it from that point of view ...'

corresponding cost of the books. The total due to me, which has been paid to some mystic account in a Berlin bank, is 661,990 marks! That is to say not quite ¾d!!! Could there be a more illuminating example of a present financial position of the German Empire and of the plight in which those to whom she owes money find themselves?

29th September, 1923

Yesterday I was shown over the Norwich Hospital by the Chairman, Mr Burton F.R.C.S., and the secretary, preparatory to my taking the chair at the forthcoming meeting of the governors. The place, with its ordered ritual, its perfect arrangements, its mass of suffering humanity handled without sentiment or ostentation upon a general plan evolved from the experience of generations, made a great impression upon me.

10th October, 1923

I have just returned from London whither I went to join in the welcome to my nephew Geoff Haggard, who has arrived from Australia with his bride, Tom Garnett's grand-daughter, whom I met there when she was a child of eleven or twelve.

East Sussex Club, St Leonards   *30th October, 1923*

I have arrived here tonight.

Today Louie and I were at the Royal afternoon party at Buckingham Palace, where the Dominion Premiers were the chief guests. Except Mr Massey with whom I had a talk, they are all changed since I mixed with them (Smuts I did not see if he was there). The King and Queen looked very well and were cordial in their greetings. We chatted with the Gosses — really he is a wondrous evergreen; I think he looks younger than he did ten years ago — the Aston Webbs and Lady Bathurst with whom I discussed briefly the Protection campaign which her paper, the *Morning Post*, is advocating so fiercely. If I understood her aright, she is as doubtful as I am as to the ultimate issue of this Crusade. I also spoke on the same subject with Lord Gladstone whom I had not seen since we met in South Africa in 1914. As head Whip of the Liberal Party he is jubilant at the introduction of the Protection Plank by the Conservatives. I suggested that it would give him a good election cry and he answered *of course* it would, and they meant to oppose tooth and nail. I told him that I hoped that between them they would not let in the Socialists!

I saw Mr Winston Churchill (whose book is out today and excites much comment, not all of it complimentary, indeed I see that the *Daily Herald* says outright that it makes his further employment as a Minister impossible) but did not speak to him. I thought that he was looking worn and much older. Mr Asquith too looked very old (and so did Mrs Asquith). So also did the Bishop of London, but the Archbishop of Canterbury appeared the same as ever. Living quietly as I do in the country and only attending functions from time to time, one notices the changes in these distinguished individuals more than do those who see them every day. It was an interesting ceremony and the Palace chambers are wondrous places, but I think that the historical pictures have been over-restored and varnished.

2nd November, 1923

This afternoon Louie and I walked to the Church in the Wood at Hollington to see Andrew's grave in its rather overcrowded cemetery. 'God bless you,' were the last words I said to him when in the spring I came from town to see him while he was dying. At the grave I said them again.

10th November, 1923

I hear from Sir William Bull that the Council of the Imperial Society of Knights Bachelor have or are about to elect me as one of them. He has to attend a meeting of the Council on Thursday, 15th November. The date of the election is not yet fixed.

11th November, 1923 (Armistice Day)

At St John's Church the two minutes 'silence' was much marred by the coughing and sneezing of the congregation in this time of chills and cold.

13th November, 1923

Today I have been giving directions to the bank to sell stock to find the money to pay my income tax.

16th November, 1923

Yesterday, having been asked to join the Council of the Imperial Society of Knights Bachelor, I attended my first meeting at the College of Arms and afterwards lunched with Sir William Bull at the Constitutional Club. It is very cold here and I see the trees on the lawn naked for the first time for a good many years.

6th December, 1923 (Election Day)

This is the day of decision and a very important decision for Great Britain and the

Empire. All the three parties express confidence, but no one really knows how the thing will go. I have just been talking over the telephone with the Conservative agent for East Norfolk at Norwich and his belief is that the Conservatives will get back with a tiny majority and that subsequently some of the Liberals will support them on terms, so as to enable them to carry on the Government.

7th December, 1923

It is stated that last night a sudden fog descended upon the thousands assembled in the London streets to read the returns thrown upon the screens. I think such a fog, if of another order, enshrouds this country today. Poor Captain Falcon, until yesterday our member, is out with a majority against him of over 3,000. I saw him at the club in Norwich, when with his wife he was going to hear the result of the poll, and they told me with much dejection that they were beaten by 1,000. A few hours later I saw them again in the club, waiting alone in the hall for their motor and from their lips I learned the real result. In that same club many years ago, I underwent a similar experience of the bitterness of defeat in an East Norfolk election and, remembering it, my heart bled for them.

26th December, 1923

Xmas is over and I am glad. It is a sad season for the old and at the accustomed festival celebrated with holly, food and wine, whatever their lips may say the toast they drink in their hearts is one to the dead to whom — or to whose habitations — they draw near! At such times indeed these gather thick about the board. We went to church, forming part of a small congregation, though the weather, unlike that of today, was frosty and beautiful and the walking good. Indeed it was largely composed of what are called 'the gentry'. I wonder what proportion of the inhabitants of this land continues to take any *genuine* interest in the Christian religion. I wonder who will go to church at Ditchingham on Xmas Day 2223 and to worship at what altars.

1924

In January Rider Haggard and Lilias, his daughter, sailed to Egypt. Despite a gale in the Bay of Biscay and hordes of tourists, it was a pleasant if reflective time. He was, however, glad to get back to Ditchingham. Better in health, he enjoyed his visits, official functions and speech-making. In June, just before his sixty-eighth birthday, he was asked to serve on the committee considering problems connected with East Africa. For years he had been waiting to be asked to serve on a Government body such as this. This request came, however, not when the Conservatives were in power, but when the Prime Minister was Ramsay MacDonald, whom Rider Haggard had for so long detested. It is not surprising then that Rudyard Kipling questioned him about his decision.

In November Rider Haggard was asked to be the guest of honour at a luncheon given to celebrate the bicentenary of the publishers Longmans, Green & Co. There he made a speech that deeply touched his friend, Charles Longman. Later, while hurrying to catch a taxi, he was taken ill; but after a couple of weeks in bed he once again went to London, this time to take part in a debate on 'The Good and Bad of the Imagination'. It was the last speech he made. Once the meeting was over he was again taken ill. As a result the idea of spending the winter in St Leonards was rejected and he went back with his family to Ditchingham. A nurse was installed, and his condition slowly but inevitably worsened.

Literally there has been nothing to record since the New Year. A kind of numbness seems to have fallen on England since the Election and is reflected in the Press. The country is paralysed by the blow that has been dealt to it, and I think somewhat hopeless, although everybody tries to look cheerful and wave away the trouble before us as naught.

9th January, 1924

I am starting for Egypt tomorrow and sail per P. & O. *Malina* on the following day.

When he reached Egypt, Rider Haggard, accompanied by Lilias, sailed up the Nile inspecting excavations as he had done in 1887, but to his regret things had changed.

On board Victoria *on the Nile, Egypt*　　　　　　　*9th February, 1924*

Egypt is much vulgarised: the tourists, often a dreadful crowd enough; the screaming struggling mob yelling for backshish upon the bank; and many such sights are vulgar, more so than they used to be a generation gone. And yet the other night I watched the infant crescent moon, bearing the disc of the old moon, and not far above her Venus blazing like a silver point, and in the background the Valley of Dead Kings austere and solemn in the rosy glow of sunset, and at my feet the broad Nile on which sailed a single white-winged boat. Looking at these the vulgarity was forgotten for they are beyond the reach of its raucous shouts and grasping hands.

Deciding not to stay in Cairo, Rider Haggard returned instead to Luxor, where at the hotel he spent a fortnight in the same room he had occupied thirty-seven years previously. But once again he was disappointed.

Luxor Hotel, Egypt　　　　　　　　　　　*27th February, 1924*

Luxor is not what it used to be. Floods of Americans touring in ship-loads invade the hotels and make them dreadful so that one must fly to one's bedroom. The costumes they wear are often strange and indeed in the case of stout elderly women sometimes, to my old-fashioned tastes, positively indecent.

East Sussex Club, St Leonards　　　　　　　　*30th March, 1924*

Yesterday morning at 8 the *Yorkshire* reached Tilbury, where the confusion over luggage was horrible and resulted in Lilias losing her dressing-case. Miss Hector met us at St Pancras but half recovered from the flu, and after lunch I went to see

Curzon. I found him in and gave him the ring with the cartouche of Amenophis III that once was worn by one of that monarch's 'sealers' some 3,500 years ago. It pleased him much.

Ditchingham   *8th April, 1924*

We arrived here yesterday to find the country more backward than in any spring that I can remember. The trees are as in midwinter, only a few of the spring flowers are out, while the fields and garden beds are bleak and bare. Also the drought has become serious and I hear that the winter has been one of the most severe and sickly for years. Still I am very glad to be home again, who no longer enjoy foreign travel as I did in years begone and hate continuous packing and movement from place to place, as is common among those who grow old even in this restless age.

22nd April, 1924

Marie Corelli[1] is dead, suddenly in her sleep after influenza — a merciful end. I never met her but once at a party in 1887, I think, or it may have been '86, some thirty-seven or thirty-eight years ago when she was still a young woman, not more than thirty I should say. But since then we have corresponded on various occasions, the last not more than a year or two ago when she kindly sent me a book of hers, called *Ziska*[2] or some such name, I think (it is at St Leonards so I cannot make sure), accompanied by a long letter which, at the moment, I am unable to find. Also once she asked me to stay with her, but for some reason or other I did not go — perhaps because she rather alarmed me with her enthusiasms. Nearly a generation ago there was a craze for making absurd couplets about well-known people. One of the best of these ran:

Why was Rider Haggard?
Because he must Marie Corelli.

23rd April, 1924

Today Louie and I went to the house of a neighbour who has installed a wireless broadcasting set[3] of the best, to hear the King's speech broadcasted from Wembley at the opening of the great Empire exhibition. There we sat all about the room with ear pieces on our heads. The results were not satisfactory. I heard the

[1]She was adopted in infancy by Charles Mackey, a well-known songwriter. Her many books enjoyed great popular success.
[2]*Ziska: the Problem of a Wicked Soul* was first published in 1897.
[3]The British Broadcasting Company had started making regular transmissions in November, 1922.

Prince of Wales fairly and several times caught the words 'your Empire' but the King's reply I could distinguish little, except an allusion to the 'unfavourable weather'. Still that is marvellous enough, or would have been held so when I was young. I should add that the strains of 'God Save the King' also reached us in a faint and fitful fashion.

20th May, 1924

I received this morning a newspaper cutting from a leading American paper, which leads me to reflect upon the quality of reviews. It is a notice of my tale *Heu-Heu*[1] and remarkable for the fact that its writer actually seems to see what one is driving at, which no, or at any rate very few, professional reviewers do in this country. At least if they do they keep it to themselves. It is strange that a writer should have to go to America to look for insight!

National Club, Queen Anne's Gate　　　　　　　　　*29th May, 1924*

I came to town on Monday to attend a concert on behalf of the Ditchingham House of Mercy at which I proposed a vote of thanks to some royal ladies and the artists. It was crowded and the sisters netted £312. Also I was anxious to be present at the Centenary Dinner of the Athenaeum which took place at night. It was a great function, though under 1,200 members could be accommodated in the Coffee Room, but I cannot say that the speeches, even that of Lord Balfour who presided, came up to expectation.

Yesterday too I went to Wembley. Certainly it is a wonderful place, though tiring and hard to get at. It is impossible to enter on a description of all I saw, but I think that the walled city representing Nigeria impressed me most. Our host was Mr Tatlow, head of the South African Publicity Service, which enabled us to get into the South African pavilion and examine it quietly when the public was shut out, because the King and Queen with the Italian Royal Party were to go over it a little later.

Ditchingham　　　　　　　　　　　　　　　　　*2nd June, 1924*

I have today returned home after spending a week-end with my brother Will at Hartlip, Sittingbourne. I found him still very feeble; he has to be carried up and down stairs and submit to many other precautions. Still he is better than he was a year ago and although his deafness has increased somewhat, his mind is as bright and active as ever.

On Friday I went to Wembley for the second time with Ronald Ross. We made a great mess of getting there — the difficulty of its approach is one of the drawbacks

---

[1] It had been published in the United States on 4th April, 1924.

of this exhibition and both of us found the trudge about the Show tiring. However we saw many interesting things and by sacrificing our return tickets got back to the Athenaeum in comparative comfort on another route. There Ross, Oliver Lodge and I dined together. It was a delightful meal, rarely do I remember one more so, owing of course to the extraordinarily interesting talk of Ross and Lodge on many matters, spiritual and other.

The weather is becoming serious as the downpours of May are continuing in June, resulting in great floods in many parts of England. Still I have never seen vegetation looking more lush and beautiful.

4th June, 1924

When I was in London the other day I found the congestion of the streets worse than ever and the danger of crossing those of them, where there was no policeman in charge, not inconsiderable. Indeed I narrowly escaped being run over by a van which dashed from behind an omnibus in a narrow thoroughfare without any warning given. Had it not been for the driver of the bus who motioned to me to stop, I should probably have been caught.

20th June, 1924

Yesterday I received a letter from the Colonial Office asking if I would serve on a Committee to consider problems connected with Eastern Africa.[1]

I have replied that I shall be honoured to serve in any capacity that may be desired. I suppose that it is not wished to send me abroad on the Commission on account of my age. What the exact scope of this inquiry will be as yet I do not know.

23rd June, 1924

I was sixty-eight yesterday, a fact that sundry papers thought it well to chronicle. Their interest in an individual always seems to increase as he grows older. It is, I think, of a sporting sort, because the public is supposed to be astonished that one is still alive. Certainly these anniversaries seem to recur with startling speed — like the arrival of income-tax papers.

Ditchingham   *28th June, 1924*

For the last three days I have been stopping at Garland's Hotel in order to attend a Royal garden party which was much as are others at Buckingham Palace (except that there were more people so that one met fewer friends), also the dinner of the

[1]Rider Haggard had written to Curzon on 11th April, 1924, stating that he would like to serve on this committee.

Imperial Society of Knights on the following day, and yesterday the Prime Minister's garden party at Hampton Court, which we found it rather difficult to reach. Indeed had not Louie looked out trains etc., I don't know how I should have got there. However, it was worth while, as no place could be more suitable for such an entertainment on a fine day. Also after tea we had time to walk through the palace which I had not visited for many years and found extraordinarily interesting. How, I wonder, did these royal people live in those vast apartments, as the beds show that they must have done sometimes, illumined only by a few candles in the winter season and with but one fireplace to warm them. Truly our ancestors were hardy folk!

Also I visited the Colonial Office and saw Lord Arnold and Sir Herbert Reeve, one of the Under-Secretaries, about the East African Committee, upon which it seems that I am to serve. The Terms of Reference are wide and in some ways nebulous as evidently they think I am too old.

3rd July, 1924

On Tuesday (1st) I attended the Yarmouth Carnival to judge the Dickens Pageant, which I did with the assistance of the Mayoress, Mrs Ferrier. These tableaux were really wonderfully executed, and it was no easy task to select the best of them. At the luncheon I was able to give the company some reminiscences of Yarmouth as it was sixty years ago.

I confess that I enjoyed my day, including pelting young women like a boy and being pelted in return. It was what is called — a thorough change.

24th July, 1924

Since my last entry I have been to town to attend the first meeting of the East Africa Committee. A great variety of subjects were opened up at the discussion under the Chairmanship of Ormsby-Gore[1] in the absence of Lord Southborough. But at present I can only say that the inquiry promises to be interesting and fruitful, also I fear long. Further, I saw Sir William Bull and others as to my joining the Board of the Empire Land Settlement Corporation Ltd., a matter which still remains undecided.

Yesterday we held at this house our fifth annual Fur and Feather Show, in weather which after many vacillations at last made up its mind to be fine.

30th July, 1924

I went to town on Monday morning and it poured all day. After attending my East

---

[1] Sir William George Arthur Ormsby-Gore (in 1950 the 4th Baron Harlech), a long-serving parliamentarian, had in January ceased to be the Under-Secretary of State for Colonial Affairs.

Africa Committee yesterday I left a thunderstorm as violent as that of last week. Really the weather this year is beyond a joke.

1st August, 1924

My grandson, Archibald Rider Cheyne, has passed into Dartmouth as a naval cadet. I am glad, but the announcement makes one feel very old.

9th August, 1924

We have had much trouble lately by the invasion of this house by rats, against which we have been conducting a campaign.

5th September, 1924

There is no hiding the fact that this is a disastrous harvest, at any rate in our part of England and, as I hear, elsewhere. A few farmers, like Longrigg, have got up most of their corn, but the majority who are slow movers have a great deal out in the fields where the heavens drip on it day by day, causing some of it to grow in the moist warm air.

9th September, 1924

I have returned from spending the weekend at Upp Hall with the Longmans. There is still a great deal of corn out in those parts, but so far as I could ascertain farming is more prosperous there than it is here.

15th September, 1924

On Saturday just by our gate a little boy was killed instantly by a passing motor: I saw his blood upon the road. The fault seems to have been that of the child, not of the poor lady who was driving her invalid husband in the car and went half crazy with grief. Why cannot children be instructed in the schools to look before they rush across the road? And why, by the way, cannot wild-eyed, bare-headed youths who tear along upon motor bicycles at anything up to fifty miles an hour, as frequently they do in front of this house, be restrained in their selfish folly?

3rd October, 1924

I am just back from town where I have been to attend various meetings, especially that of the East Africa Committee. The work on this committee seems to be more far-reaching and prolonged than I thought. Yesterday it was settled that we must sit every Monday at the peculiar hour of five in the evening, which, it appears, is convenient to members of Parliament. Yesterday I met Lord Southborough, the chairman, for the first time. He is a very agreeable, diplomatic ex-official of the highest class and having had much experience of this kind of work will doubtless make an excellent chairman.

7th October, 1924

Yesterday I went to town to take the chair at the Author's Club dinner to Sir Joseph Cook, the High Commissioner for Australia. Being the first of the season it was quite a function and very crowded. I met with a warm, and I might say, almost an affectionate reception, who am one of the original members of the club that is now entering on its thirty-fourth year.

There seems now to be no doubt that we are on the eve of another General Election.

14th October, 1924

I have been sitting upon my East Africa Committee which seems likely to be a long and intricate business. At the club, I lunched with Kipling who is in town preparing for Elsie's wedding, which I am sorry to say I shall not be able to attend. In his amusing and allusive fashion he pointed out to me that in the Book of Revelations it is prophesied that the Beast will only be allowed to dominate a third of the earth and that Bolshevist Russia already occupied a fifth of the third so that there would not be very much more left to go mad and bad, begging me to consult the Bible on which he was so good as to believe me an authority! I propose to do so tonight.

Afterwards on the steps of the Duke of York's column, I met H. G. Wells whom I had not met for some years, and asked him if he were pursuing his blessed Communism in this election also. He replied no, that he was tired of it and of everything and was going abroad to be quiet and 'find his soul', adding 'Have you found your soul?' I replied that I hoped so and thus we parted. Query — has anyone found his soul? To do so I think he must dig deep. Wells looked well, but much thinner — I daresay that the search for one's soul does waste the flesh!

16th October, 1924

At lunch at the Athenaeum on Monday last Rudyard Kipling, supported by Hercules Read[1], were reproaching me for continuing to do public work in the way of sitting on Government committees, such as that which is considering many questions connected with East Africa. Rudyard said that any sound and respectable Englishman could deal with such business and that it was not the place of a

[1](Sir Charles) Hercules Read was from 1896 to 1921 the Keeper of British and Medieval Antiquities at the British Museum.

man like myself to spend his time thereon. I do not agree with him. Whatever his abilities, imaginative or other (and certainly I take no exaggerated view of my own) I think that every citizen should give the best that is in him to the State as a matter of public duty. It is because these public duties are so often left in the hands of the commonplace, the idle and the self-seeking that frequently they are not so well performed as they might be. The glory of England is that many of her sons undertake these duties without reward, giving to them the best that they have to offer.

For my part I believe that public service is my true line — all the rest are side shows.

25th October, 1924

I have been working against time engaged in entirely re-casting the subtitles of the film version of my Egyptian romance, *Moon of Israel*[1], which is to be produced very shortly. These, as they stood, were impossible, the result apparently of a double translation, from English into German and from German back into a most banal rendering of our tongue, with results that could only be called ludicrous. The picture play itself is in parts very fine, except wherever it leaves my story, replacing it with introduced incidents or modifications. Then it comes utterly to grief. It must have cost an enormous sum but whether any one makes much out of it depends probably upon whether or not the Americans will allow it into the States.

I hear today that some official from the Censor's Office has raised objections (1) to soldiers being shown with arrows sticking in them, (2) to too much of the heroine's back being visible in some scene (which I never noticed) and (3) to the warmth of the embrace which in the moment of her death, the heroine gives to her husband, the Prince of Egypt. Evidently the Censor expects that even at such a solemn time ladies should be careful of the proprieties! What Pharisees and humbugs we are in England! No wonder the foreigners make a mock of us on this matter. The Censor allows much poisonous propaganda, vulgar crime and corrupting innuendo to pass to the picture Stage, but arrows sticking in Eastern murderers, or a poor dying woman clinging to her husband's breast, he finds corrupting. The fact is, as I believe, this Censorship is very badly managed. Such power should be given only to men of wide views and education, who look under the surface of things. At any rate I know that it causes intense irritation to many respectable firms engaged in the film trade.

29th October, 1924 (General Election Day)

There is great anxiety in the country as to the result of today's General Election. I

[1]This was an Austrian film (*Die Sklavenkönigin*) made by Sascha-Film and directed by Michael Courtice. The leading parts were taken by Arlette Marshall, Adelqui Milla and Maria Corda.

hope and pray that things may go as we wish, seeing that on the issue hangs the immediate, and possibly the ultimate fate of our country, but it is all in the hands of God. One thing is sure — everything that is evil in the land is at the back of these Socialists who love the Russian anarchists because they have reduced that great empire to a condition which they hope to see re-duplicated in Britain and her empire also.

We have had a sad shock today. My sister-in-law Nitie[1], the wife of my brother William, is suddenly dead of heart-failure. The strange thing is that this was nearly his own fate a few weeks ago, but now she has gone and he is left.

31st October, 1924

It has been a remarkable election, perhaps the most remarkable that I can remember.[2] I sincerely trust that it will be the last with which the country is troubled for some years to come.

(In bed) *East Sussex Club, St Leonards*   *6th November, 1924*

On November 1st in pouring rain I attended the funeral of my brother Will's wife at Hartlip in Kent. It was a sad business and I don't think that the expedition did me any good. Poor Will was in bed with the gout, indeed I don't think he had been able to see his wife since she was suddenly taken ill with her heart. He is much broken by this blow and no wonder.

I did not return to Ditchingham but stopped in town at the National Club as I had to attend my East Africa Committee on Monday. On Tuesday night I met Louie and Miss Hector and we went to see the film of my book *Moon of Israel* at the Pavilion where it is running for a month. Of course it might be improved in many ways — thus the actress who plays Merapi is too coquettish and self-conscious, the Death of the First-born is quite inadequate and so forth. But on the whole it is a really wonderful production and I cannot conceive how effects such as that of the crossing of the Red Sea are obtained. Everybody seems to like it very much so I hope that it will be successful.

Yesterday was the day of the great luncheon given by Longmans Green & Co., to celebrate their bicentenary. It was attended by all sorts of eminent people who crowded the Stationers' Hall, and I found myself placed on the right hand of Charles Longman, the Chairman. My speech was to propose 'The Publishing Trade' coupled with the name of Charles Longman. I think it came off all right, at any rate Charles informed me that I had very nearly made him 'weep'. For all his

[1]Emily Margaret (Hancox), William's second wife.
[2]In the election the Conservatives gained what Baldwin described as 'the greatest majority our party ever had'. The Liberals were all but annihilated and the Labour Party lost more than 40 seats. It brought to an end the first Labour Government.

gruff manner he has a very soft heart! Then followed catastrophe so far as I was concerned for while hurrying to find a taxi in order to catch a train at Charing Cross (which didn't exist) I was seized with a most fearful attack of indigestion that almost seemed to stop my heart from beating. How I managed to get down to St Leonards and into this room really I do not know, but it was a great struggle. Luckily Scarlyn Wilson, the doctor, was in the Club and came to help me to undress and send for remedies etc. Today I am better but still have wind etc. The immediate cause of this attack was, I believe, eating some oysters and then a sort of lobster stew, after which I drank a glass of champagne and a liqueur brandy. Also the heat of the room followed by the cold of the street and the excitement of speaking may have had something to do with it. The fact is however, that I am no longer at all robust and I do not know how long I shall be able to undertake London engagements in winter.

The Socialist Government has gone, having apparently been able to come to no decision (that they cared to publish) as to the authenticity of the famous Bolshevist letter[1], and the conservatives are in power.

11th November, 1924 (Armistice Day)

I have spent most of the time since my last entry in bed but went out yesterday and today. I hope I am recovering but have come to the conclusion that in the future I must be an even smaller eater than I have been in the past. It will not be a great deprivation as for a long while I have had little taste for meat which is now generally very bad especially in London. There, even in the Clubs, I believe it is nearly all foreign or treated with preservatives of one kind or another.

I still breakfast in bed but hurried through the doctor's visit and skipped my bath in order to be down before eleven to listen to the Cenotaph ceremony on the wireless in this club. Then of course the machine went wrong and by the time that it was righted all I heard was the last hymn and God save the King!

13th November, 1924

Today, as the President of the little local '1920 Literary Club', I took the Chair at a luncheon to the Sussex novelist, Mrs Dudeney.[2] I believe that she is a most excellent writer but I was only advised of her coming last night and I had never read one of her books. It was a predicament but I got out of it by making a general speech and passing on the business of adulating the work of Mrs Dudeney to the Vice-Chairman, Mr Frankfort Moore. He rose to the occasion nobly and said that she

---

[1]This was the Zinovieff letter, which was at least partially responsible for the electoral defeat of the Labour Party. Rider Haggard wrote a letter to *The Times* about the matter. It was published on 29th October.
[2]Mrs Henry Dudeney, who died in 1945, wrote many novels including *Brighton Beach, Petty Cash* and *Portrait of Ellen*.

was the greatest novelist now living in this country! It was really a very pleasant and cheerful little luncheon and I was delighted to meet my old colleague Tom Garnett there, more or less recovered from his recent illness.

Garland's Hotel   *28th November, 1924*

On the 25th I came up to town for one night to attend the Dinner of the Delphian Coterie, at which months ago I had promised to open a debate on 'The Good and the Bad of the Imagination', was seized with gout at the dinner with other delights, and have been confined to my room here ever since. However, the debate went off extremely well, Ronald Ross and many others taking part in it, and seemed to please everybody very much. I think that what one finds at these meetings of the Delphian Coterie is the most intelligent audience I have ever had the honour of addressing.

Ditchingham[1]   *27th December, 1924*

Another Xmas has come and gone, a mild open Xmas with the sun shining. (Today it is blowing a great gale from the S.W. with torrents of rain.) It has not been a pleasant Xmas for me. About a month ago after various preliminary illnesses and symptoms at St Leonards and indeed before I left Ditchingham (including an almost total loss of appetite) on the top of an attack of gout, I was seized with a disease which the doctors have diagnosed as infection of the bladder by germs. Certainly it is one from which I hope that my worst enemies (if I have any) may be spared. To let the details be, it has made an invalid of me and there are symptoms that I do not altogether like. I had to sit through a Xmas Day dinner at which my grandsons, as children do on these occasions, did justice to their creature cravings, and I shall not forget the experience. Well, we must suffer what it pleases God to send us with such patience as we may, but I begin to think that my active career is at an end and that I must resign from all public work. Nor indeed at present am I fit to do any of whatever kind. I wished to begin a new romance, but I cannot face it.[2] On Xmas Day I did manage to get to the second service in a motor-car, and to sit it out. I suppose it is the first time I have been able to enter a church for about six weeks!

[1]Rider Haggard had returned there on 4th December.
[2]Rider Haggard had just finished *Belshazzar*, his last novel. It was handed over to A. P. Watt on 1st January, 1925, although it was not published until 26th September, 1930.

1925

For the first time since he had started this diary, Rider Haggard was prevented by his illness from making regular entries. There was, in any case, less for him to record. He was no longer fit enough to continue with his public work and, as he fought his personal battle against pain, it was natural that he thought less about the problems of the country he had striven so devotedly to serve. He did find time and energy, however, to mourn the passing of four men who had been among those closest and dearest to him: Arthur Cochrane, his long-time friend and colleague; Arthur Haggard, his younger brother; William Carr, his neighbour; and Lord Curzon, his erstwhile protector. As he wrote about them, Rider Haggard was all too aware that their deaths presaged his own.

The year that is gone has been rather a bad one for our family. Two of my sisters-in-law have died and other members of it are sick. These include myself who after some weeks of illness have developed a horrible form of bladder poisoning which causes me much inconvenience and distress and prevents me from sleeping well. However, the doctors think that I progress so I hope to conquer it some day, though I expect it will force me to resign from my East Africa Committee.

16th January, 1925

My oldest remaining and nearest friend, with whom in my youth in Africa I lived as a brother, Arthur Henry Douglas Cochrane, is dead after some years of failing health, though not unexpectedly. The loss to me is great, for though of late decades his domestic circumstances tended to separate us to a certain extent, we always remained close in spirit, as his last brief letters to me testify and there are few whom I more earnestly hope to meet again in some future state. This, I know, was also his desire. Our association began, I think, in 1877 when he came to the Transvaal with Sir William Seargeaunt. Subsequently Arthur Cochrane and I, who were both in Government Service, built the little house at Pretoria which is now known as Jess's Cottage and lived in it. Then, leaving the Service, we bought Sir Melmoth Osborn's farm, Rooipoint, near Newcastle, in Natal. Here, after my marriage I joined Cochrane at Hilldrop and we started a rather wild agricultural venture. Whether it would have succeeded or failed in the end, I do not know, because it was finished by the first Boer War which was fought all round us, whereof the results were such that we shook the dust of South Africa off our feet and returned to England. Shortly afterwards Cochrane married, but after some years of separation we foregathered in various ventures; once for a while in business[1], then in my East Norfolk electioneering campaign and afterwards — most important of all — in my Rural England researches, which indeed I could never have carried through without his assistance, as the mass of note-books in his handwriting that are now in the Norwich Museum suffice to show. So much did I feel this — that it was to him, and not to any exalted person, I dedicated the result of those labours in the work called *Rural England*, hoping as I do still that it my take down our names together to future generations. He was not a brilliant man, but extraordinarily hard-working and conscientious, also of an affectionate nature — at any rate towards myself. (It was his native name, by the way — Macumazahn — that I took for that of Allan Quatermain.) These qualities never did more than suffice to earn him a livelihood, mostly as a director of small South African Companies and as an expert who visited that country on sundry occasions to make reports upon landed

[1]This was in 1896 when Rider Haggard was, for nine unhappy and uncertain months, co-director of *The African Review*.

properties, which were always full, valuable and accurate. It was after his last journey thither, only a few years ago, that his health began to fail; indeed I think it was too strenuous for one of his age. I grieve that I am not well enough to attend his funeral. God rest him — as I am sure He will.

3rd February, 1925

Since my last entry there has been practically nothing to record — except a tale of deaths. Following upon that of Arthur Cochrane came the sudden carrying off of my brother Arthur, the youngest of all of us, who thus immediately followed his wife, killed ostensibly by some virulent form of kidney disease, but really, as I believe, by his ceaseless labours for year upon year on behalf of the Veterans Club and Association which he founded. He was indeed a good fellow and one of my brothers of whom I was most fond and I mourn his loss deeply.

Next came the sudden removal of my old friend and neighbour, William Carr of Ditchingham Hall, who died of heart-stoppage a few days ago. His last earthly act was to arrange by help of the telephone that I should come to visit him that morning, which hitherto I have been unable to do because of my own condition. Before the hour arrived for me to start, however, behold! he was dead.

26th March, 1925

It is a long while since I made an entry in this diary, for the good reason that I have been laid up very ill with a horrible disease of the bladder that has been threatening me for some months, and am indeed still laid up and suffering many unpleasant things on which I will not dwell. I do so now, however, to record the death of Lord Curzon who is buried today and over whom a service was celebrated yesterday with much pomp in Westminster Abbey. He was taken ill at Cambridge, moved to London, operated on, suffered for a fortnight, and passed away. To my mind, magnificent as it was and in many ways successful, publicly speaking his career was still a failure. He could never catch the ear of the crowd; his cold and rather lofty manner was against him. In short he had not the art of popularity. May this great servant of his country forever rest in honour and in peace.

By mid-April Rider Haggard's condition had so deteriorated that he was taken to London for further examination. On 11th May an operation was performed which, according to the doctors, was entirely successful. Three days later, about mid-day, Rider Haggard died. In the chancel of Ditchingham Church his ashes were laid beneath a slab of black marble inscribed with the words of his choice:

Here lie the ashes of Henry Rider Haggard
Knight Bachelor
Knight of the British Empire
Who with a humble heart strove to serve his country

Appendix

Rider Haggard's Published Books

Published   Title and Publisher

22.6.1882   *Cetywayo and His White Neighbours*   Trubner & Co.
21.2.1884   *Dawn*   Hurst & Blackett
18.12.1884   *The Witch's Head*   Hurst & Blackett
30.9.1885   *King Solomon's Mines*   Cassell & Co.
1.1.1887   *She*   Longmans, Green & Co.
3.1887   *Jess*   Smith, Elder & Co.
1.7.1887   *Allan Quatermain*   Longmans, Green & Co.
3.8.1888   *Maiwa's Revenge*   Longmans, Green & Co.
10.1888   *Mr Meeson's Will*   Spencer Blackett
3.12.1888   *Colonel Quaritch, V.C.*   Longmans, Green & Co.
24.6.1889   *Cleopatra*   Longmans, Green & Co.
12.1889   *Allan's Wife*   Spencer Blackett
12.5.1890   *Beatrice*   Longmans, Green & Co.
5.11.1890   *The World's Desire* (with Andrew Lang)   Longmans, Green & Co.
13.5.1891   *Eric Brighteyes*   Longmans, Green & Co.
9.5.1892   *Nada the Lily*   Longmans, Green & Co.
13.10.1893   *Montezuma's Daughter*   Longmans, Green & Co.
15.10.1894   *The People of the Mist*   Longmans, Green & Co.
12.8.1895   *Joan Haste*   Longmans, Green & Co.
27.3.1896   *Heart of the World*   Longmans, Green & Co.
29.10.1896   *The Wizard*   J. W. Arrowsmith
28.11.1898   *Dr Therne*   Longmans, Green & Co.
1.3.1899   *Swallow*   Longmans, Green & Co.
2.10.1899   *A Farmer's Year*   Longmans, Green & Co.
20.10.1899   *The Last Boer War*   Kegan Paul, Trench, Trubner
29.5.1900   *Black Heart and White Heart*   Longmans, Green & Co.
11.4.1901   *Lysbeth*   Longmans, Green & Co.
7.10.1901   *A Winter Pilgrimage*   Longmans, Green & Co.

28.11.1902 *Rural England* Longmans, Green & Co.
 2.3.1903 *Pearl-Maiden* Longmans, Green & Co.
 3.2.1904 *Stella Fregelius* Longmans, Green & Co.
30.9.1904 *The Brethren* Cassell & Co.
13.1.1905 *A Gardener's Year* Longmans, Green & Co.
18.8.1905 *The Poor and the Land* Longmans, Green & Co.
 6.10.1905 *Ayesha* Ward, Lock & Co.
 3.1906 *The Way of the Spirit* Hutchinson & Co.
 7.9.1906 *Benita* Cassell & Co.
 9.9.1907 *Fair Margaret* Hutchinson & Co.
25.9.1908 *The Ghost Kings* Cassell & Co.
 5.3.1909 *The Yellow God* Cassell & Co.
15.12.1909 *The Lady of Blossholme* Hodder & Stoughton
11.3.1910 *Morning Star* Cassell & Co.
 9.1910 *Queen Sheba's Ring* Eveleigh Nash
16.12.1910 *Regeneration* Longmans, Green & Co.
 6.4.1911 *Rural Denmark* Longmans, Green & Co.
28.8.1911 *Red Eve* Hodder & Stoughton
16.10.1911 *The Mahatma and the Hare* Longmans, Green & Co.
25.1.1912 *Marie* Cassell & Co.
23.1.1913 *Child of Storm* Cassell & Co.
29.1.1914 *The Wanderer's Necklace* Cassell & Co.
31.3.1915 *The Holy Flower* Ward, Lock & Co.
 6.1.1916 *The Ivory Child* Cassell & Co.
10.8.1917 *Finished* Ward, Lock & Co.
 4.4.1918 *Love Eternal* Cassell & Co.
31.10.1918 *Moon of Israel* John Murray
20.3.1919 *When the World Shook* Cassell & Co.
12.2.1920 *The Ancient Allan* Cassell & Co.
 4.11.1920 *Smith and the Pharaohs* J. W. Arrowsmith Ltd.
17.2.1921 *She and Allan* Hutchinson & Co.
26.1.1922 *The Virgin of the Sun* Cassell & Co.
 9.3.1923 *Wisdom's Daughter* Hutchinson & Co.
29.1.1924 *Heu-Heu* Hutchinson & Co.
21.4.1925 *Queen of the Dawn* Hutchinson & Co.
 9.1926 *The Treasure of the Lake* Hutchinson & Co.
 7.10.1926 *The Days of My Life* Longmans, Green & Co.
20.5.1927 *Allan and the Ice-Gods* Hutchinson & Co.
 4.1.1929 *Mary of Marion Isle* Hutchinson & Co.
26.9.1930 *Belshazzar* Stanley Paul & Co.

Index

The index entry for Sir Henry Rider Haggard contains only those details which could not conveniently be entered elsewhere, thus his visits to Canada will be found under Canada and his views on income tax under income tax. Throughout the index Rider Haggard is referred to as HRH.

Rider Haggard's works are given as independent entries, works by other people are entered under the author's name.